Career Counselling

Constructivist approaches

Edited by
Mary McMahon and
Wendy Patton

Routledge
Taylor & Francis Group

LONDON AND NEW YORK

First published 2006
by Routledge
2 Park Square, Milton Park, Abingdon, Oxon OX14 4RN

Simultaneously published in the USA and Canada
by Routledge
270 Madison Ave, New York, NY 10016

Routledge is an imprint of the Taylor & Francis Group

© 2006 Selection and editorial matter, Mary McMahon and
Wendy Patton; individual chapters, the contributors

Typeset in Sabon by
HWA Text and Data Management Ltd, Tunbridge Wells
Printed and bound in Great Britain by
TJ International Ltd, Padstow, Cornwall

British Library Cataloguing in Publication Data
A catalogue record for this book is available from the
British Library

Library of Congress Cataloging in Publication Data
A catalog record for this book has been requested

ISBN10: 0-415-38562-8 (hbk)
ISBN10: 0-415-38563-6 (pbk)

ISBN13: 9-78-0-415-38562-6 (hbk)
ISBN13: 9-78-0-415-38563-3 (pbk)

Contents

List of figures and tables   vii
Contributors   viii
Preface   x
Chapter overview   xii
Acknowledgements   xiv

PART I
Constructivism – an overview   I

1   Constructivism: what does it mean for career
    counselling?   3
    WENDY PATTON AND MARY McMAHON

2   Working with storytellers: a metaphor for career
    counselling   16
    MARY McMAHON

3   Usefulness and truthfulness: outlining the limitations
    and upholding the benefits of constructivist
    approaches for career counselling   30
    HAZEL L. REID

PART II
Constructivism, culture and career counselling   43

4   Career counselling theory, culture and constructivism   45
    MARK B. WATSON

5   Infusing culture in constructivist approaches to career
    counselling   57
    NANCY ARTHUR

6   The use of narratives in cross-cultural career
    counselling   69
    KOBUS MAREE AND MAISHA MOLEPO

PART III
Constructivist approaches to career counselling   83

7   Active engagement and the influence of constructivism   85
    NORMAN AMUNDSON

8   The Systems Theory Framework: a conceptual and
    practical map for career counselling   94
    MARY McMAHON AND WENDY PATTON

9   Career narratives   110
    ELIZABETH M. GRANT AND JOSEPH A. JOHNSTON

10 Using a solution-building approach in career
    counselling   123
    JUDI MILLER

11 SocioDynamic career counselling: constructivist
    practice of wisdom   137
    TIMO SPANGAR

12 Creativity and career counselling: a story still to be
    narrated   150
    MARY McMAHON

PART IV
Constructivist career assessment   161

13 Qualitative career assessment   163
    MARY McMAHON AND WENDY PATTON

14 Card sorts: constructivist assessment tools   176
    POLLY PARKER

15 Constructivist career tools on the internet: challenge
    and potentials   187
    HEIDI VILJAMAA, WENDY PATTON AND MARY McMAHON

    Index   202

Figures and tables

Figures

1.1	Career counselling observation sheet	12
7.1	The Wheel	88
8.1	The System Theory Framework of career development	96
8.2	The therapeutic system	99
10.1	Parameters of a scale	130
10.2	Example of the way a client could use a systems framework to describe career-related influences	133
13.1	A new location for career assessment	170
13.2	Guidelines for including assessment into the career counselling process	172

Tables

1.1	Influence of the logical-positivist and constructivist worldviews on career counselling	11
5.1	Structure and prompts for conducting a cultural audit of counselling practices	64

Contributors

Dr Norman Amundson is a Professor in Counselling Psychology at the University of British Columbia, Canada. He has extensive international experience and has published a number of books and articles including *Active Engagement: Enhancing the Career Counselling Process*, winner of the Best Book award by the Canadian Counselling Association.

Dr Nancy Arthur is appointed as a Tri-Faculty Canada Research Chair in Professional Education across the faculties of Education, Social Work, and Nursing at the University of Calgary. Her research and teaching interests related to counsellor education for working in global contexts focus on multicultural counselling, career development, and cross-cultural transitions.

Elizabeth M. Grant recently completed her Master of Arts degree in Counselling Psychology, with an emphasis in Career Counselling and Development, at the University of Missouri – Columbia. Her interest in career narratives grew out of her experiences as a performing artist, as she believes that each of us is writing and "acting out" the story of our lives.

Joseph A. Johnston is Professor of Counseling Psychology in the Department of Education, School and Counseling Psychology at the University of Missouri-Columbia and Director of their campus Career Center. He is an advocate for helping college students and faculty members find their voice and career direction in a variety of ways.

Professor Kobus Maree is a triple doctorate, author or co-author of more than 35 books and 70 articles, renowned psychologist and internationally known scholar. He is editor of the journal *Perspectives in Education* and a C-rated researcher with the National Research Foundation. He was recently honoured with exceptional achiever status by the University of Pretoria.

Mary McMahon is a lecturer in the School of Education at The University of Queensland. She is the 2002 winner of the New Hobsons Press and the Australian Association of Career Counsellors Inc. Excellence award for outstanding contribution to the career industry. She publishes extensively in the field of career development and is particularly interested in constructivist approaches to career counselling and assessment.

Judi Miller, a New Zealander, has a background in Vocational Guidance. She is a senior lecturer in and co-ordinator of the M.Ed. counselling programme at the University of Canterbury, where she has held a position since 1988. For the past 10 years, she has been teaching solution-focused counselling.

Dr Maisha Molepo was recently honoured with the coveted Laureate Award for rendering exceptional services to the broader South African community. The encompassing aim of his research is poverty alleviation/upliftment of rural communities in South Africa, and increasing the number of black learners at tertiary institutions in South Africa.

Polly Parker is a lecturer in the Management Department, Griffith University, Australia. Her PhD, from The University of Auckland, was on Career Communities. Polly has a life-long interest in teaching and learning which she has applied in both academic and corporate settings. Her current interests are in the areas of Career Management and Leadership Development.

Professor Wendy Patton is a Head of School in the Faculty of Education at Queensland University of Technology. She developed postgraduate programs in Career Guidance at QUT and continues to coordinate them. She has published extensively in the area of career development and is currently on the editorial advisory boards of a number of national and international career development journals.

Dr Hazel L. Reid is a principal lecturer at Canterbury Christ Church University, teaching in the area of career theory and guidance skills. She has published widely and presents papers at national and international conferences. Her recent research was concerned with the meanings given to the function of supervision for guidance and youth support workers.

Timo Spangar has worked for more than twenty years as a counselling psychologist in the Finnish Employment Service. From the 1990s onwards he has developed new activity-based and metaphorical counselling methods. Today he is an active counsellor trainer, researcher in the field of counselling as well as an evaluator of developmental social programmes in Finland and within the European Union. Fostering dialogical spaces for communication is the core element throughout his work.

Heidi Viljamaa has done pioneering work in designing and implementing web-based career tools since 1996. Her work has touched individuals and organisations around the world. She is the founder and managing director of CareerStorm, which is headquartered in Finland and has partners in Australia, Singapore, Sweden and the U.S.A.

Mark B. Watson is a Professor of Psychology at the Nelson Mandela Metropolitan University. He specialises in career, school and adolescent psychology and researches lifespan career development, with a specific focus on assessment and cross-cultural issues. He publishes in international and national journals, is the author of book chapters and is co-editor of the book *Career psychology in the South African context*.

Preface

Since its beginning in the early 1900s, career counselling has been steeped in the traditions of the positivist world view. In essence, career counselling involved quantitative assessment and diagnosis and prediction, where the counsellor assumed the role of an expert and the client that of a passive responder.

With the influence of the constructivist worldview, irreversible changes in the world of work, and increasing demand for career counselling services, career counselling has been challenged to modernise its practice. Increasingly, the constructivist worldview has influenced approaches to career counselling. Indeed it has been suggested that the more widespread adoption of constructivist approaches holds a key to career counselling remaining relevant in the 21st century.

One of the criticisms of constructivism is that in keeping with its underpinning philosophy, there is little instructional material to inform and guide its practice. In essence, the implications for career counsellor educators and practitioners are that while espousing and supporting constructivist thinking, they struggle to know how to teach it and how to implement it in their day-to-day work.

Addressing the "but how do we do it" challenge that their struggles pose was a primary motivator for conceptualising this book. Our main purpose was to provide readers with easy to read theory and practical ideas. It does so by structuring each chapter with a theoretical overview of a topic and a practical application. In essence the book

- provides a theoretical background to constructivism;
- outlines a range of constructivist approaches to career counselling;
- provides examples of the practical application of the constructivist approaches presented in the book; and
- assists career counsellor educators, practitioners and students understand and implement constructivist approaches into their work.

The book is structured in four parts. Part 1, consisting of three chapters, focuses on theoretical understandings of constructivism including a critique of constructivist approaches. In addition, it suggests that a new metaphor is needed for career counselling in the 21st century. Part 2, consisting of three chapters, examines the application of constructivism from a cross-cultural perspective. Part 3, consisting of 6 chapters, presents a range of constructivist approaches to career counselling. Part four, consisting of three chapters considers constructivist approaches to assessment.

We are excited by the richness of this book in terms of its variety and its capacity to address the "but how do we do it" question. We would like to acknowledge the authors and their generosity in sharing their ideas and approaches.

Chapter overview

Part 1 – Constructivism – an overview

In Chapter 1 Wendy Patton and Mary McMahon provide readers with a theoretical overview of constructivism and its influence on psychology and career counselling. In particular, the nature of the counselling relationship and the counselling process, the role of emotion and language, and career assessment are briefly discussed. In Chapter 2 Mary McMahon suggests that as a result of the influence of constructivism in career counselling a new metaphor of career counselling is needed. *Working with storytellers* is proposed as a possible metaphor. Hazel Reid provides a critique of constructivism in Chapter 3. She suggests that despite its appeal, constructivism brings with it a set of issues that warrant particular consideration by practitioners and theorists.

Part 2 – Constructivism, culture and career counselling

In Chapter 4, Mark Watson examines the influence of constructivism on career theory and how the concept of culture has been accommodated in constructivist career theory. Further he suggests that a challenge for career counsellors is to deconstruct and reconstruct the theoretical and assessment frameworks that inform their work. In Chapter 5, Nancy Arthur explores theoretical tenets that guide career counselling practice and proposes that culture be infused into all career counselling. She challenges career counsellors to consider the adoption of social action and advocacy roles, and suggests that career counsellors incorporate cultural auditing into their practice. In Chapter 6, Kobus Maree and Maisha Molepo use characteristics of a South African setting to propose a range of strategies for facilitating a narrative approach to career counselling in diverse settings. They provide practical examples of strategies that combine narrative approaches with idiosyncratic cultural characteristics.

Part 3 – Constructivist approaches

In Chapter 7, Norman Amundson introduces readers to his active engagement approach to career counselling. He guides readers through the steps and stages of a counselling relationship, illustrating them with practical suggestions. Mary McMahon and Wendy Patton overview the Systems Theory Framework of career development in Chapter 8. They then illustrate how this theoretical formulation may be used as a conceptual and practical map for career counselling. In Chapter 9, Elizabeth M. Grant and Joseph A. Johnston provide a comprehensive overview of key ideas related to narrative counselling. They then describe a range of applications and interventions that may be used in practice and counsellor training programs. Judi Miller describes the key principles of solution focused counselling and provides practical examples of its application to career counselling in Chapter 10. In addition, she raises awareness of challenges that may face career counsellors who choose to work this way. In Chapter 11, Timo Spangar presents his interpretation of the essential ideas characterising SocioDynamic counselling. He describes the key strategies of dialogical listening and life-space mapping and illustrates them with examples of counsellors incorporating the strategies into their own work. In Chapter 12, Mary McMahon opens a discussion on the use of creativity in career counselling and encourages readers to examine their understandings of creativity. She suggests that while the term *creativity* is frequently mentioned, its meaning in career counselling may not be well understood.

Part 4 – Constructivist assessment

In Chapter 13, Mary McMahon and Wendy Patton present a brief history of career assessment and suggest that historically the story of qualitative career assessment may have been silenced or overshadowed. They examine advantages of qualitative career assessment and present considerations for its practical use. Polly Parker discusses the use of card sorts, the most popular form of constructivist career assessment in Chapter 14. She describes how card sorts may be used to create meaning and generate personal narratives in a manner that is consistent with constructivist principles. In Chapter 15, Heidi Viljamaa, Wendy Patton and Mary McMahon examine the challenges of the internet to career development specialists. They explore the contribution that can be made by a constructivist theoretical perspective. They provide a case study in the use of web-based career tools.

Acknowledgements

This book has truly been an international collaboration with 14 authors from seven countries contributing chapters. We have appreciated the authors' genuine interest in the book, their willingness to share their ideas and to respond to our questions and comments promptly. We also appreciate Routledge's faith in us by publishing the book, and the support we have received along the way from so many Routledge staff.

Thank you all for working with us to produce a book that we believe is unique in the field. We hope it will find a very firm place in the professional lives of many academics and practitioners in the field of career counselling.

Mary and Wendy

Part I

Constructivism –
an overview

Chapter 1

Constructivism

What does it mean for career counselling?

Wendy Patton and Mary McMahon

This chapter will discuss the complex worldview underpinning of construct-ivism, and describe some of the theoretical fields from which its core components have been derived. The constructs which are guiding construct-ivism in career counselling practice will be outlined.

Underpinning worldview

A worldview has been described by Lyddon (1989) as serving the role of organising day-to-day experiential data. Collin and Young (1986) noted that career theories have so far been largely developed within organismic and/or mechanistic worldviews. The mechanistic perspective which views the world as operating in much the same way as a machine, and which suggests that we think in linear routes from the general to the particular and that we explain phenomena in cause and effect terms, is derived from mechanism. The organismic worldview which sees human development as an orderly maturational unfolding process, is the basis of prominent stage-based models in developmental psychology, and in particular the work of Super (1990) and Gottfredson (2002) in vocational psychology. The individual is seen as responsible for movement toward the next stage and any problems in this process are viewed as related to the individual.

In a number of fields in the social sciences, for example Collin and Young (1986) and Vondracek *et al.* (1986) in career psychology, and Steenbarger (1991) in counselling psychology, a contextual worldview which focuses on the world simply as "events" in a unique historical context, is being advocated. The contextualist worldview does not conceive development as maturational and unfolding in stages; rather, development is viewed as an ongoing process of interaction between the individual and his/her environment. Within this process, random or chance events contribute to a continually open state of being.

The contextualist worldview is reflected in the constructivist epistemology as opposed to the traditional objectivist or positivist epistemology. To explain these two positions, positivists emphasise rationality based on an objective value free knowledge; objectivity over subjectivity, facts over feelings. Constructivists argue against the possibility of absolute truth. However, to say that the constructivist approach is the opposite would be to oversimplify. Constructivism is directly derived from the contextualist worldview in that the "reality" of world events is constructed "from the inside out" through the individual's own thinking and processing. These constructions are based on individual cognitions in interaction with perspectives formed from person-environment interactions. "They are both individual and interactional, creating order for the person and guiding interactions with the environment" (Steenbarger, 1991, p. 291). Constructivism therefore views the person as an open system, constantly interacting with the environment, seeking stability through ongoing change. The emphasis is on the process, not on an outcome; there is no completion of a stage and arrival at the next stage as in stage-based views of human development. Mahoney and Lyddon (1988) emphasised the change and stability notion as follows: "Embedded with self-change is self-stability – we are all changing all the time and simultaneously remaining the same" (p. 209).

Constructivism in psychology

Constructivism has been acknowledged as the third wave in cognitive science (Mahoney and Patterson, 1992), with cognitive science itself being viewed as one of the four forces in psychology (Mahoney and Patterson) following psychoanalytic theory, behaviourism and humanism. In contrast to realism which asserts a single, stable, external reality, one of the key principles of constructivism is its emphasis on the proactive nature of human knowing, acknowledging that individuals actively participate in the construction of their own reality. Whereas realism asserts an objective valid truth, constructivism emphasises the viability of an individual's construction (a conceptualised personal reality) on the basis of its coherence with related systems of personally or socially held beliefs. "From a constructivist viewpoint, human knowing is a process of 'meaning-making' by which personal experiences are ordered and organized" (Mahoney and Patterson, p. 671).

In the special issue of the *Journal of Vocational Behavior* published in 2004, Young and Collin acknowledged the difficulty in presenting clearly delineating definitions of the terms *constructivism* and *social constructionism* particularly as they relate to career development: "[Constructivism] focuses on meaning-making and the constructing of the social and psychological worlds through individual, cognitive processes while [social constructionism] emphasises that the social and psychological worlds are made real (constructed) through social processes and interaction "(p. 375). Young and Collin emphasised that this simple distinction, while useful, was nonetheless likely to diminish the variety and differences between and within both. However, for ease of discussion within the career development field, Young and Collin subsumed both *constructivism* and *social constructionism* under the term "constructivisms".

Part of the complexity of the constructivism literature is that constructivism draws its key components from related theories. For example, the notion of proactive cognition is derived from motor theory which asserts that the mind is an active system which has the capacity to produce its output in addition to the input it receives. The individual is always interacting with the environment while simultaneously internally construing and constructing meaning about it. Knowledge is an interactive process and motivated through feed-forward and feedback mechanisms. Hence rather than reacting to external stimuli the human mind actively constructs reality through internal sorting and processing of stimuli. In addition, constructivism asserts that deep cognitive structures function at tacit and unconscious levels and that these tacit ordering rules govern the individual's cognitive processes. Peavy (2000) comments that many of the self-organising processes which typically exist at tacit levels of awareness can be made explicit through use of cultural tools in the counselling process. Peavy talks about "circumferences of awareness" to indicate the aspects of an individual's field of attention that are taken into account (p. 21).

Systems theory has also contributed to the key components of constructivism, in particular in relation to the notion that individuals are self-organising and that all learning and knowing is comprised of complex dynamic processes through which the self organises and reorganises to achieve equilibrium. The human system is viewed as purposive, ever-evolving and self-perpetuating. The process is interactive, and the human system operates interdependently with other systems (e.g., family, workforce). "Life is an ongoing recursion of perturbation and adaptation, disorganisation and distress, and emerging complexity and differentiation" (Granvold, 1996, pp. 346–7). The following description by Ford and Ford (1987) illustrates the systems theory contribution to this aspect of constructivism:

> The Living Systems Framework (LSF) is designed to represent all aspects of being human, not merely a particular facet of behavior or personality ... It describes how the various "pieces" of the person – goals, emotions, thoughts, actions, and biological processes – function both semi-autonomously as a part of a larger unit (the person) in coherent "chunks" of context-specific, goal directed activity (behavior episodes). It also describes how these specific experiences "add up" to produce a unique, self-constructed history and personality (i.e., through the construction, differentiation, and elaboration of behavior episode schemata), and how various processes of change (self-organization, self-construction, and disorganization-reorganization) help maintain both stability and developmental flexibility in the organized patterns that result (steady states). Thus the LSF cannot be easily characterized in terms of traditional

theoretical categories. Rather, it is a way of trying to understand persons in all their complexly organized humanness (pp. 1–2).

Within this framework, knowledge is viewed in a qualitative way and rather than be part of a process of acquisition, new knowledge is incorporated into existing frameworks in a relational and associative way. Self-knowledge is also viewed as evolutionary and relational as "More complex and integrated levels of self-identity are achieved through the assimilation of perturbations produced by interactions with the world" (Granvold, p. 347).

Constructivism in career counselling

Savickas (1995) asserts that "vocational psychologists are being challenged to revise their core philosophy of science and to reform their field into an interpretive discipline" (p. 18). A number of authors have developed approaches which can be grouped under the postmodern or constructivist perspective, although each of these approaches may focus on different aspects, and indeed have different names (e.g., perspectivism, interpretivism, constructivism). These approaches include the work on hermeneutical perspectives in career theory (Collin and Young, 1988; Young and Collin, 1988) and in research (Young and Collin, 1992). Hermeneutical approaches focus on bringing together the meaning or underlying coherence of, in this case, an individual's career, or the career experiences of a group of individuals. Other examples of contextualist approaches include Young and Borgen's (1990) work on subjective method in the study of careers, and Peavy's (1998; 2000) sociodynamic counselling perspective. More recently, Chen (2003) has proposed a model of career theory integration in an attempt to bridge the gap between objectivist and constructivist approaches to career development.

As understandings of career development have evolved and the notion of lifespan career development has become more widely accepted, the appropriateness of the traditional approach to career counselling has been challenged. Savickas (1993) urged that career counselling "keep pace with our society's movement to a postmodern era" (p. 205) and that its practice needs to move from "seeking truth to participation in conversations; from objectivity to perspectivity" (p. 205). As constructivism represents an epistemologic position that emphasises self-organising and proactive knowing, it provides a perspective from which to conceptualise changing notions of career in postmodern society. These changing notions include the importance of individuals becoming more self-directed in making meaning of the place of work in their lives and in managing their careers (Richardson, 1993; 1996). The active role of the individual in the career counselling process is emphasised within a constructivist approach, as career counsellors aim to work collaboratively with individuals, focusing on holistic approaches to life-career, and encouraging individuals to actively reflect on, revise and reorient their life-career relationship. Krumboltz (1998) exhorts career counsellors to recon-struct the goal of career counselling "to help people create satisfying lives for themselves" (p. 560). Within this approach, "increased learning and life satisfaction should become the outcome measures of career counselling success" (p. 563), outcomes which emphasise the synergy between interrelated life roles.

Fundamental to the constructivist approach is the proactive, self-conceiving and evolving nature of human knowing. In career counselling individuals work to construct and reconstruct reality through the use of language and dialogue with the counsellor. Language is fundamental to the creation of meaning and knowledge. Knowledge is shaped through dialogue between the career counsellor and the client, a process which incorporates the construction and coconstruction of an individual's reality. As such, key elements of career counselling have been influenced by constructivism. These include the counselling relationship, the nature of the counselling process, the use of language and the role of assessment.

The nature of the counselling relationship

"The development of a quality therapeutic relationship with such charact-eristics as acceptance, understanding, trust, and caring is a prime objective of constructivists" (Granvold, 1996, p. 350). Traditional career counselling approaches have seen the counsellor take on what may be described as an expert role whose task it is to solve the client's problems, to explain through assessment, or to provide advice. Rather than be the "expert" in the counsell-ing process, with the goal of drawing conclusions from information and advising, the counsellor operating from a constructivist perspective works with the client to facilitate an effective therapeutic relationship. The qualities of the relationship therefore become crucial to the career counselling process.

The nature of the counselling process and the role of emotion and language

Traditional positivist approaches to counselling have seen the counsellor in a central position, often as a provider of information or in a directive role to "fix" a problem. However, constructivists are less directive and aim to facilitate a process of exploration and restructuring, where the counsellor and client join to construct and reconstruct meanings considered important in the client's life. Within this process, possible new meanings are constructed and renewed life goals and outcomes are outlined. Peavy (1992) advocates the term "fruitfulness" to replace the term "outcomes", and suggests that the career counselling process should be fruitful, that is "it should provide a re-construing or changed outlook on some aspect of life" (p. 221).

Peavy (1992) advocated the dimensions of relationship, agency, meaning-making and negotiation for career counsellors working within the constructivist paradigm to keep in mind. He provided the following questions to assist in counsellor focus:

1 How can I form a cooperative alliance with this client? (Relationship factor)?
2 How can I encourage the self-helpfulness of this client (Agency factor)?
3 How can I help this client to elaborate and evaluate his or her constructions and meanings germane to their decisions (Meaning-making factor)?
4 How can I help this client to reconstruct and negotiate personally meaningful and socially supportable realities (Negotiation factor) (p. 221)?

Emotion is also important, and its inclusion in the counselling process responds to criticism that emotion and social meaning have been missing from career counselling (Young and Valach, 1996). Clients are encouraged to explore and express their emotions through a range of interventions including approaches from gestalt therapy and psychodrama such as empty chair technique, behaviour rehearsal, guided imagery and role play.

The precision of language and its power in constructing meaning is an important contribution of constructivist writers who argue that we construct reality through our shared and agreed meanings communicated via a common language; that is our ideas and beliefs are socially and culturally constructed. Savickas (1995) emphasised that "linguistic concepts and their definitions do not mirror reality: they inscribe meaning" (p. 22). Dewey and Bentley (1949) maintained that to name is to know, articulating the crucial relationship between language and our perception of reality. These authors noted the inextricable intertwine between language and our knowledge and under-standing of phenomena. Throughout the career counselling process, language and discourse is used to arrive at new meanings, which in turn lead to change. The coconstruction process demands that shared meanings between the counsellor and client can be developed within a shared context and using a shared language.

Our knowledge about ourselves is socially constructed. It is constructed not only through language but also by culture (Lynch, 1997). The emerging worldview, with its emphasis on the individual as part of an interconnected whole, has brought about challenges to objective universal truths, "grand narratives", and increased the importance of "local narratives", that is meaning from a particular context (Lynch, 1997). It is no longer possible, if it ever was, to "apply one grand narrative to everyone" (Savickas, 1993, p. 211). Thus the life narratives of individuals represent their own reality. Typically, a counselling relationship becomes a therapeutic conversation, where the counsellor and the client join as coconstructors of a new reality.

Within this context of language and shared meaning-making, Cochran (1997) has developed a narrative approach to career counselling that emphasises the focus on the subjective meaning with which clients imbue their work and career. Stories or narratives are a unique derivative of systems theory thinking and are key to constructivist approaches (Chen, 2002; White and Epston, 1990). Richardson's (1993, 1996) call for a focus on the individual and the place of work in people's lives, is useful as an example of the type of story that may be explored in career counselling. In addition, through story, the patterns and themes of an individual's life can be uncovered, and interconnections forged between previously unconnected events. "The power of stories to capture attention and convey meaning is reemerging as an important component in career counseling" (Krumboltz *et al.*, 1994, p. 60).

The role of assessment in constructivist career counselling

The use of assessment has traditionally been a major contributing factor in how the career counselling relationship has been defined. For example, the career counsellor, with answers based on the objective data provided through quantitative assessment instruments, could be seen as an expert to whom the client deferred. As career counsellors make increasing use of qualitative assessment with the postmodern shift from objectivity to subjectivity or from scores to stories (Savickas, 1993), the role of assessment will be defined differently. In line with Granvold's (1996) criticism of the "tyranny of technique" (p. 350), Savickas (1992) suggests that qualitative assessment "emphasizes the counselling relationship rather than the delivery of the service" (p. 337), such that the boundaries between assessment and counselling are less distinct. For example, the client becomes much more involved in the counselling process as the assessment is grounded in their lived experience of which they are the expert, and from which they have a story to tell. Thus the position of the client in the relationship is elevated from that of "passive responder" (Goldman, 1990, p. 205) to that of active participant. By contrast, the position of the career counsellor is changed from that of expert to one of interested inquirer, respectful listener and tentative coconstructor. Peavy (1998) asserts that career counsellors "have the privilege of hearing many stories and scripts and then joining the storytellers in the task of reauthoring them toward more preferred futures" (p. 30). As such, constructivist career counsellors who listen for life themes and stories act more as "biographers who interpret lives in progress rather than as actuaries who count interests and abilities" (Savickas, 1992, p. 338).

The most popular methods of qualitative assessment are genograms, autobiographies, early recollections, structured interviews, lifelines, lifespace map and card sorts (McMahon and Patton, 2002b). Goldman (1990, 1992) lists the characteristics of qualitative assessment as follows:

1   clients play an active role rather than that of a "passive responder" (1990, p. 205);
2   qualitative assessment is more integrative and holistic;
3   qualitative methods emphasize learning about oneself within a developmental framework;
4   qualitative assessment methods work well in groups;
5   qualitative assessment reduces the distinction between counselling and assessment;
6   qualitative assessment is valuable for relating to individuals of "different cultural and ethnic groups, socioeconomic levels, sexual identities, and to people with disabilities" (1990, p. 206).

To counsel using a practice framework steeped in constructivism does not imply that traditional objective assessment instruments should not be used. Rather, career counsellors working from a constructivist perspective will approach the incorporation of assessment into the counselling process differently. This will be described in more detail in Part Four of this book.

Applying constructivism in career counselling

One of the criticisms of constructivism is that it has failed to clearly articulate an approach that may be used by career counsellors; hence the question "but how do we do it?" is frequently asked. Rather constructivism presents as a way of thinking or a set of values that is illustrated throughout this book as a range of possible approaches and activities that are consistent with the constructivist worldview. A prescriptive approach such as a set of techniques or an interview sequence is not consistent with the constructivist worldview. Thus, practitioners are encouraged to internalise the values of the constructivist approach and to apply them as appropriate in their work. Such values have previously been articulated in this chapter and have far-ranging implications for the way career counsellors work as illustrated by McMahon, Adams and Lim (2002) (see Table 1.1). As mentioned earlier in this chapter, to assume that the logical positivist and constructivist approaches are oppositional would be an oversimplification. Rather, career counsellors are likely to operate on a continuum of practice between these positions (McMahon and Patton, 2002a).

In teaching constructivist approaches to career counselling, facilitating learning processes whereby beginning counsellors may internalise the way of thinking or values of constructivism represents an important goal. An application of Table 1.1 may serve as a useful learning tool (see Figure 1.1). Learners may be encouraged to watch experienced counsellors at work either in work observation or using videotapes or DVDs. As they do so they are encouraged to observe the process and record examples of the constructivist and logical positivist worldviews on the continuums presented in Figure 1.1.

Table 1.1 Influence of the logical-positivist and constructivist worldviews on career counselling

Elements of career counselling	Logical-positivist worldview	Constructivist worldview
The role of the client The role of the counsellor	• Passive responder • Expert	• Active participant • Interested, curious and tentative inquirer • Respectful listener • Tentative observer
The nature of the counselling relationship	• Counsellor dominated • Counsellor knows best • Test and tell • Problem solving approach	• Collaborative • Interactive • Mutual involvement
The place of career assessment	• Used as a starting point • Objective • Assessment scored and reported by 'expert' • Facts valued over feelings	• Story and meaning • Meaning is co-constructed • Subjectivity is valued • Feelings as well as facts are valuable
The use of career information	• Emphasis on facts • Provided by 'expert' counsellor	• Emphasis on information-seeking process • Client becomes information gatherer
The nature of change	• Sequential or linear • Emphasis on outcome or end point	• Recursive • Emphasis on process • Discontinuous
The nature of knowledge and learning	• Knowledge is imparted by experts	• Knowledge is created within individuals • Language is critical to understanding and the creation of knowledge
Wholes and parts	• Focus on traits such as personality, ability or interests • Little attention payed to context of client's life • Work and life viewed as separate	• Holistic approach – subjective experiences and feelings valued • Context is important • Work and life viewed as a whole
The counselling process	• Counsellor dominated • Sequential • Expectation of an objective outcome such as an occupational title	• Counsellors enter the client's life-space through dialogue • Expectation of client driven change

(*Source*: McMahon, Adams and Lim, 2002, p. 23, adapted from McMahon and Patton, 2001; Hale-Haniff and Pasztor, 1999;)

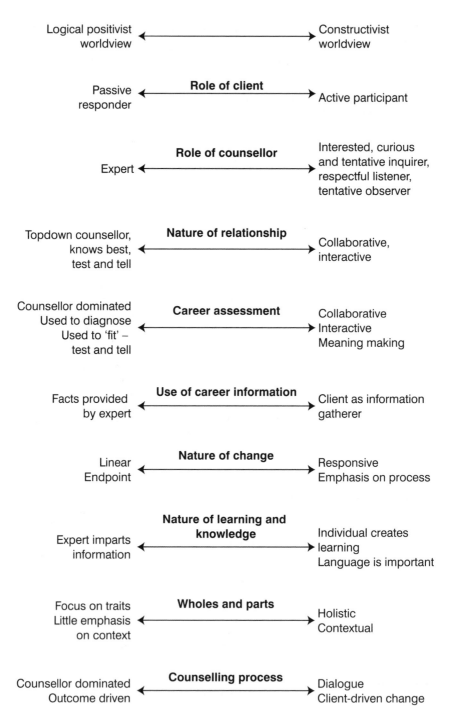

Logical positivist
worldview ←————————————→ Constructivist
worldview

Role of client
Passive ←————————————→ Active participant
responder

Role of counsellor
Expert ←————————————→ Interested, curious
and tentative inquirer,
respectful listener,
tentative observer

Topdown counsellor, **Nature of relationship**
knows best, ←————————————→ Collaborative,
test and tell interactive

Counsellor dominated **Career assessment**
Used to diagnose ←————————————→ Collaborative
Used to 'fit' – Interactive
test and tell Meaning making

Facts provided **Use of career information**
by expert ←————————————→ Client as information
gatherer

Linear **Nature of change**
Endpoint ←————————————→ Responsive
Emphasis on process

**Nature of learning and
knowledge**
Expert imparts ←————————————→ Individual creates
information learning
Language is important

Focus on traits **Wholes and parts**
Little emphasis ←————————————→ Holistic
on context Contextual

Counsellor dominated **Counselling process**
Outcome driven ←————————————→ Dialogue
Client-driven change

Figure 1.1 Career counselling observation sheet

Following this, they could engage in a discussion with the counsellor about their observations and the counsellor's practice framework. Alternatively, if a whole class has watched a video or DVD, they could engage in discussion about their observations. Discussion questions could include:

- How do each of the examples identified illustrate the values of the constructivist worldview?
- What may be the advantages of the two worldviews?
- What may be the disadvantages of the two worldviews?
- When may it be appropriate to operate more from one worldview than another?
- In what circumstances may it be important for counsellors to have a degree of flexibility in their approach?
- Consider cultural appropriateness from the position of the two worldviews.

A similar activity may be facilitated whereby learners watch a recording of their own work and analyse it according to Figure 1.1. Colleagues could also analyse the work. Peer group discussion about the similarities and differences of the observations could then be facilitated. Learners could be encouraged to identify their strengths and also goals that they would like to achieve.

Conclusion

The constructivist perspective emphasises the active nature of the individual as a self-building and self-renewing "self-organising system" as opposed to a passive organism at the whim of maturational and developmental stages and/or environmental forces. Career counselling work within this perspective focuses on individuals interacting with their social and environmental contexts and engaging in a shared process of life-career meaning-making with the counsellor.

References

Chen, C. P. (2002) 'Enhancing vocational psychology practice through narrative inquiry'. *Australian Journal of Career Development*, 11(1), 14–21.

Chen, C. P. (2003) 'Integrating perspectives in career development theory and practice'. *The Career Development Quarterly*, 51, 203–16.

Cochran, L. (1997) *Career Counseling: A Narrative Approach*. Thousand Oaks, CA: Sage.

Collin, A. and Young, R. A. (1986) 'New directions for theories of career'. *Human Relations*, 39, 837–53.

Collin, A. and Young, R. A. (1988) 'Career development and hermeneutical inquiry Part II: Undertaking hermeneutical research'. *Canadian Journal of Counselling*, 22, 191–201.

Dewey, J. and Bentley, A. (1949) *The Knowing and the Known*. Boston: Beacon.

Ford, M. and Ford, D. (eds) (1987) *Humans as Self-constructing Living Systems: Putting the Framework to Work*. Hillsdale, NJ: Lawrence Erlbaum.

Goldman, L. (1990) 'Qualitative assessment'. *Counseling Psychologist*, 18, 205–13.

Goldman, L. (1992) 'Qualitative assessment: an approach for counsellors'. *Journal of Counseling and Development*, 70, 616–21.

Gottfredson, L. S. (2002) 'Gottfredson's theory of circumscription, compromise and self-creation', in D. Brown (ed.) and Associates, *Career Choice and Development* (4th edn., pp. 85–148). San Francisco, CA: Jossey-Bass.

Granvold, D. K. (1996) 'Constructivist psychotherapy'. *Families in Society*, 77(6), 345–59.

Krumboltz, J. D. (1998) 'Counsellor actions needed for the new career perspective'. *British Journal of Guidance and Counselling*, 26(4), 559–64.

Krumboltz, J. D., Blando, J. A., Kim, H. and Reikowski, D. J. (1994) 'Embedding work values in stories'. *Journal of Counseling and Development*, 73, 57–62.

Lyddon, W. J. (1989) 'Root metaphor theory: a philosophical framework for counselling and psychotherapy'. *Journal of Counseling and Development*, 67, 442–8.

Lynch, G. (1997) 'Therapeutic theory and social context: a social constructionist perspective'. *British Journal of Guidance and Counselling*, 25, 5–15.

Mahoney, M. J. and Lyddon, W. J. (1988) 'Recent developments in cognitive approaches to counseling and psychotherapy'. *The Counseling Psychologist*, 16, 190–234.

Mahoney, M. J. and Patterson, K. M. (1992) 'Changing theories of change: recent developments in counseling', in S. D. Brown and R. W. Lent (eds), *Handbook of Counselling Psychology* (2nd edn., pp. 665–89). New York: John Wiley.

McMahon, M., Adams, A. and Lim, R. (2002) 'Transition in career counselling: what can solution oriented counselling offer?' *Australian Journal of Career Development*, 11(1), 22–6.

McMahon, M. and Patton, W. (2002a) 'Assessment: a continuum of practice and a new location in career counselling'. *International Careers Journal*, 3(4), (The Global Careers-Work Café). Available: http://www.careers-cafe.com.

McMahon, M. and Patton, W. (2002b) 'Using qualitative assessment in career counselling'. *International Journal for Educational and Vocational Guidance*, 2, 51–66.

Peavy, R. V. (1992) 'A constructivist model of training for career counselors'. *Journal of Career Development*, 18, 215–29.

Peavy, R. V. (1998) *Sociodynamic Counselling: A Constructivist Perspective*. Victoria, Canada: Trafford.

Peavy, R. V. (2000) 'A sociodynamic perspective for counselling'. *Australian Journal of Career Development*, 9(1), 17–24.

Richardson, M. S. (1993) 'Work in people's lives: a location for counseling psychologists'. *Journal of Counseling Psychology*, 40, 425–33.

Richardson, M. S. (1996) 'From career counseling to counseling/psychotherapy and work, jobs, and career', in M. L. Savickas and W. B. Walsh (eds), *Handbook of Career Counseling Theory and Practice* (pp. 347–60). Palo Alto, CA: Davies-Black.

Savickas, M. L. (1992) 'New directions in career assessment', in D. H. Montross and C. J. Shinkman (eds), *Career Development: Theory and Practice* (pp. 336–55). Springfield, IL: Charles C Thomas.

Savickas, M. L. (1993) 'Career counseling in the postmodern era'. *Journal of Cognitive Psychotherapy: An International Quarterly*, 7, 205–15.

Savickas, M. L. (1995) 'Current theoretical issues in vocational psychology: convergence, divergence, and schism', in W. B. Walsh and S. H. Osipow (eds), *Handbook of Vocational Psychology* (pp. 1–34) Mahwah, NJ: Erlbaum.

Steenbarger, B. (1991) 'All the world is not a stage: emerging contextualist themes in counseling and development'. *Journal of Counseling and Development*, 70, 268-96.

Super, D. E. (1990) 'A life-span, life-space approach to career development', in D. Brown and L. Brooks (eds), *Career Choice and Development* (2nd edn, pp. 197–261). San Francisco, CA: Jossey-Bass.

Vondracek, F. W., Lerner, R. M. and Schulenberg, J. E. (1986) *Career Development: A Life-span Developmental Approach*. Hillsdale, N.J.: Erlbaum.

White, M. and Epston, D. (1990) *Narrative Means to Therapeutic Ends*. NY: W. W. Norton.

Young, R. A. and Borgen, W. A. (eds) (1990) *Methodological Approaches to the Study of Career*. NY: Praeger.

Young, R. A. and Collin, A. (1988) 'Career development and hermeneutical inquiry Part I: the framework of a hermeneutical approach'. *Canadian Journal of Counselling*, 22, 153–61.

Young, R. A. and Collin, A. (eds) (1992) *Interpreting Career: Hermeneutical Studies of Lives in Context*. Westport, CT: Praeger.

Young, R. A. and Collin, A. (2004) 'Introduction: constructivism and social constructionism in the career field'. *Journal of Vocational Behaviour*, 64, 373–88.

Young, R. A. and Valach, L. (1996) 'Interpretation and action in career counseling', in M. L. Savickas and W. B. Walsh (eds), *Handbook of Career Counseling Theory and Practice* (pp. 361–75). Palo Alto, CA: Davies-Black.

Chapter 2

Working with storytellers
A metaphor for career counselling

Mary McMahon

Storytelling is healing. As we reveal ourselves in story, we become aware of the continuing core of our lives under the fragmented surface of our experience. We become aware of the multifaceted, multichaptered "I" who is the storyteller. We can trace out the paradoxical and even contradictory versions of ourselves that we create for different occasions, different audiences ... Most important, we become aware of ourselves as storytellers, we realize that what we understand and imagine about ourselves is a story. And when we know all this, we can use our stories to heal and make ourselves whole.

(Albert, n.d.)

Everyone has a story to tell. Indeed, our lives are composed of stories. Career counsellors are privileged to hear the stories of many clients and to work with them towards re-authoring more preferred futures (Peavy, 1998). One of the gifts career counsellors can offer clients is an opportunity to tell their stories and, in so doing, develop new stories of confidence, optimism and hope (Amundson, 2003). The notion of working with storytellers is a far-cry from the early days of career counselling where its logical positivist origins to a large extent dictated a linear expert driven process through which the client was largely a passive recipient (Patton and McMahon, 1999). Career counsellors informed by the constructivist worldview have the opportunity to create relationships with clients where the vehicles of story and metaphor may be guided in caring, creative and meaningful ways towards possibility filled futures.

Thus the stories that constructivist career counsellors tell about their work are very different from those told by career counsellors operating out of the logical positivist worldview. However, as suggested in Chapter One of this book, to present these worldviews as opposites is too simplistic. McMahon and Patton (2002) suggest that career counsellors are likely to operate on a continuum of practice that spans these worldviews. Therefore, it is likely that there are as many stories, if not more, about career counselling practice as there are career counsellors. Indeed, just as individuals construct their own life/career stories through which they make meaning of their lives, so too do career counsellors construct stories that enable them to make sense of their role and their work. This chapter will explore the use of story and metaphor. In particular, this chapter will focus on the use of story and metaphor as a means of conceptualising the role and work of career counsellors. Practical suggestions for working with story and metaphor in career counselling will be proposed.

A new metaphor emerges

There is increasing evidence of career counsellors being informed by the constructivist worldview (e.g., Amundson, 1998, 2003; Brott, 2001; Campbell and Ungar, 2004a, b; Cochran, 1997; Peavy, 1998, 2004; Savickas, 1997). Amundson (2003) suggests that "the starting point for many people in counselling is to be given the opportunity to tell their story" (p. 161). Story represents an attempt by individuals to make meaning of and to actively construct their lives (Patton and McMahon, 1999). Indeed our lives are multistoried as no story is capable of encompassing all of life (Morgan, 2000). Morgan further suggests that individuals are always negotiating and interpreting their experiences and mediating between dominant and alternative stories. The telling of stories and elaboration of meaning places a focus on the uniqueness of individuals who "come to understand who they are as part of a life narrative, or story, that brings cohesion and meaningful order to their experiences" (Campbell and Ungar, 2004a, p. 20).

The importance of story and meaning-making in people's lives is fundamental to the constructivist worldview, and necessarily suggests that career counsellors take a "self-as-narrative" view of clients rather than a "self-as-trait" view (Peavy, 1995, p. 2). Thus counsellors engage as co-authors with the storytellers in "negotiating stories that must take into account both the individual's life and the ecological context" (Bujold, 2004, p. 480). Importantly, as Bujold suggests, the use of story brings with it an holistic view of individuals as being contextually located. Stories may be located in a range of contexts and times in an individual's life.

From a constructivist standpoint, clients are viewed as experts in their lives. Peavy (2000) suggests that client and counsellor "enter an open communication interchange. What comes to be understood (shared meaning) is the result of negotiation. The two interpreters arrive at a fusion of understanding that takes the form of an agreement, understanding or shared knowledge" (p. 8). Indeed, Peavy (1998, 2001) refers to the nature of communication in counselling as dialogical, and explains that "dialogue refers to the flow of meaning reciprocally between communicators" (2001, p. 5). Further, he suggests that "dialogue is the pre-requisite for thinking together, or collective planning", and that it "makes possible the generation of new ideas, perspectives and frames of meaning" (2001b, p. 5). Career counsellors who work with story or narrative may capture the richness and subjectivity of people's careers and through co-constructing meaning, foster greater understanding of situations as well as the creation of future possibilities.

The notion that our lives are multi-storied warrants further consideration in relation to our work as career counsellors. For example, clients choose the stories they tell us, most usually their dominant story. However, there are also stories they don't tell us, stories that they don't know or realise, stories that they have forgotten and stories that have been silenced. In addition, while clients may be the main actors and characters in the stories they are living out (Christensen and Johnston, 2003), they may not always be the author of the story they are narrating. The counsellor and client dialogue facilitates clients connecting with new stories, new meaning, alternative stories or new endings to stories and with a future that prior to their involvement in career counselling they may not have envisioned as possible. This will now be illustrated through the examples and stories provided in Examples 2.1, 2.2 and 2.3 that are typical of those told to us in our work. Rita (see Example 2.1) provides us with the first example.

Example 2.1 Rita

The told story

"Now that the kids have left home I want to do something with my life. I haven't worked for years".

The untold story

"I stayed at home once I had my children and was actively involved in their education. As President of the P and C, I regularly met with school administration, local and state government officials. I prepared submissions for funding from local and state government authorities. As one of my children has a learning disability, I researched it to find out as much as I could and produced a booklet to help parents of children with a similar disability. I was invited to speak on the disability at two conferences run for teachers."

The unknown or unrealised story

"I didn't know that any of that would count."

The future story

"I think I'd like to study."

Rita's deceptively simple *told story*, brought with it meaning that devalued her unpaid life experiences as a parent, a volunteer, a community service worker, an advocate and an author. This meaning also limited her future stories. By encouraging a broader account of Rita's life story that drew on contexts and experiences other than paid employment, an *untold story* was revealed and the new set of meaning generated resulted in the telling of an *unknown or unrealised story*. The telling of Rita's untold story facilitated the co-construction of an unknown or unrealised story around personal qualities such as competence, ability, dedication and commitment, and skills such as organisation and communication. The information and meaning generated through the untold story and the unknown or unrealised stories provided a richness of possibility for the co-construction of a *future story* in which she thought she would like to undertake further study. In addition, uncovering Rita's *unknown or unrealised* story and elaborating its meaning enhanced her sense of personal agency.

Kathleen's (see Example 2.2) *told story* was one of frustration and what she saw as limited possibilities. She was so immersed in living the story of her day-to-day life, that she had forgotten a story from earlier in her life. Through the process of narrating her *forgotten story* she elicited meaning that enabled her to understand her dissatisfaction with her current paid employment and her ambition to "use her brain a bit more". The *forgotten story* put her in touch once more with a set of values that were important to her in deriving satisfaction from her paid employment.

Example 2.2 Kathleen

The told story

"I left school when I was fifteen. I do night-fill work and I hate it. I also worked in a laboratory and hated it because it was so repetitive. It's important to me to be available for my children but I'd like to use my brain a bit more."

The forgotten story

"When I left school I went to work as a secretary and before I knew it I was a personal assistant to the managing director. Even though I was very young I had lots of responsibility. Every day was a challenge and I loved it. I went to work overseas for the company and have worked in several countries."

Cameron's stories (see Example 2.3) will provide us with the third and final example.

The stories illustrate what Peavy (1995) describes as a "self-as-narrative" approach rather than a "self-as-traits" view (p. 2). However, as also illustrated by the above examples, clients may sometimes narrate brief and incomplete stories, or dominant stories that do not value or take account of other stories through which possible futures may be generated. In addition, they may tell the stories of others and in so doing lose their sense of agency. Morgan describes brief and incomplete stories as "thin descriptions" (Morgan, 2000, p. 12) and suggests that they produce "thin conclusions" (p. 12) which necessarily limit the possibilities for the future and frequently sustain problems. In this regard, Morgan (2000) suggests that counsellors consider the question "how can we assist people to break from thin conclusions and to re-author new and preferred stories for their lives and relationships?" (p. 15). Thus, as the case studies illustrate, career counsellors work with

---

Example 2.3 Cameron

The told story

Cameron was a young man who came to counselling wanting to study business. He had no enthusiasm in his voice or sparkle in his eyes and he had previously failed some business studies. He thought he would do better this time and was insistent about studying business.

The untold story

Cameron had saved up for a working holiday by doing labouring work on building sites. He enjoyed the team environment, being outdoors and using his hands. On his holiday, he had really enjoyed a type of "mr-fixit" job. In the telling of this story, Cameron was more "alive", his eyes sparkled and he sounded excited.

Narrator but not author

The story Cameron told and retold, where he had no passion was in fact the story of his parents, both successful business people.

The silenced story

Unable to tell his own story, Cameron had succumbed to the story told by his parents, and in so doing his own story, "I want to be a builder," had been silenced.

clients to explore alternative stories that might provide clues for constructing possible futures. As alternative stories are developed and "thickened" (Morgan, 2000, p. 15) through the telling of stories from other times and contexts, clients begin living their new stories and as a consequence develop "new self-images, new possibilities for relationships and new futures" (Freedman and Combs, 1996, p. 16). In the telling of their alternative stories, Rita, Kathleen and Cameron were freed to begin living their new stories.

New stories and metaphors for career counselling

As evidenced by the previous examples and the publication of this book, the influence of constructivism has become increasingly pervasive in career theory and practice. Thus a challenge for career counsellors is to reconceptualise or restory their roles and the nature of their work. This is reflected by claims of "too many lists, not enough stories" (Law, 2003, p. 25), the need to move to "stories rather than scores" (Savickas, 1993, p. 213) and away from the psychometric self to the narrated self (Peavy, 1998), and for career counsellors to act more as "biographers who interpret lives in progress rather than as actuaries who count interests and abilities" by listening for clients' life themes and stories (Savickas, 1992, p. 338). Further, Peavy (2004) suggests that the language and vocabulary of counselling that was developed in the positivist era may be becoming obsolete. For example, in his SocioDynamic approach he uses the metaphor of "help-seeker" rather than "client", and "bricoleur" to describe career counsellors' capacity to apply creative solutions to problems.

Each of these descriptions is in itself a metaphorical representation of career counselling that brings with it vivid images of what career counselling may be. In essence, the use of metaphor provides visual clues and a bridge towards deeper understanding of a situation (Hoskins and Leseho, 1996). For example, a common metaphor used to describe career counselling from the logical-positivist worldview is "test and tell" which provide clues to its emphasis on career assessment and the expert role of the career counsellor. The use of metaphor in the telling of stories is not uncommon for as Inkson and Amundson (2002) explain, the application of the special qualities of one concept or entity to another may provide clearer meaning or add colour to a story. The use of story and metaphor in career counselling may provide a vehicle for moving away from the conscious mind and prior meaning structures into uncharted territory where new meaning may be created (Lyddon, Clay and Sparks, 2001) and stories of possibility co-constructed.

Just as the use of story and metaphor may be used with clients to elaborate meaning and construct stories of possibility, so too may they be useful in constructing new meaning around the role and work of career counsellors. For example, in the following metaphor Monk (1997) paints a picture of the role of a narrative therapist.

With meticulous care and precision, the archaeologist brushes ever so gently over the landscape with an instrument as small as a pastry brush. With these careful movements, she exposes a remnant, and with further exploration, others soon appear. Disconnected fragments are identified and pieced together as the search continues. With a careful eye for the partially visible, the archaeologist begins to reassemble the pieces. An account of the events in the life of the remains is constructed, and meaning emerges from what was otherwise a mere undulation on the landscape (p. 3).

From this metaphoric description, Monk elaborates some of the qualities of narrative therapists as observational powers, persistence, care, deliberation and delicacy and suggests that "from a few small pieces of information, the beginning of a story located in a particular culture is constructed" (p. 3). While Monk's (1997) metaphor pertains to the work of narrative therapists, it also has relevance for career counsellors working from a constructivist perspective as they are both informed by the same worldview, constructivism.

As the archaeological metaphor suggests, in many ways, "entering the lifespace of a client" (McMahon and Patton, 2002, p. 8) is like being a visitor to a sacred site as the life of a client is also unique and special. The metaphor of a visit to a sacred site may give us some insight to our roles as career counsellors. For example, when we enter a sacred site we may approach in awe and in reverence. We may feel privileged and approach gently and cautiously with due respect for the customs and traditions of the place. We may also engage in periods of reflective silence where we try to get in touch with the meaning and spirit of the sacred site.

Similarly, career counsellors strive to get in touch with the meaning and spirit of their clients as they narrate their life/career stories. Their approach to clients is not unlike that of visitors to a sacred site as described above. To this end, increased importance is being placed on the nature of the counselling relationship. For example, Amundson (1998) describes Rogers' (1951) necessary conditions for counselling, genuineness, unconditional positive regard and empathic understanding, as "essential building blocks" (Amundson, 1998, p. 28) for career counselling relationships. In addition, Amundson suggests a fourth "building block", flexibility, which is counsellors' ability to be imaginative, creative and willing to be open to new situations.

As suggested by the metaphors presented earlier in this chapter, conceptualising the role and work of career counsellors under the constructivist worldview lends itself to the exploration of new and different metaphors. A further archaeological metaphor that may aid our understanding of the emerging constructivist stories of career counselling is offered by Aluna Joy Yaxk'in (2003), a sacred site guide who leads pilgrimages to Inca and Mayan sacred sites and describes herself as a spiritual archaeologist. In relation to her own work, she explains that:

Learning to hear the wisdom and history of a sacred site is as simple as getting out of our over active minds and get back to listening with open hearts. This is easier said than done, especially if we have studied a lot about a site. When we enter a sacred area thinking we KNOW things about the site or culture or have expectations about what we might learn there, we become closed to a multitude of messages. Also what we hear may directly contradict what authorities have been telling us. To hear a sacred site we must enter a site in a state of not knowing, innocence with childlike curiosity (p. 1).

Further, she suggests that we enter the sacred site with no expectations as to outcome, and that in a state of innocence, wonder and curiosity we allow the message to come to us. She advises that there are no right and wrong ways to enter a sacred site but that we need to be honest with ourselves and listen to our feelings. Messages are embedded in feelings. She cautions that we don't get the entire message at once, but that we should allow the story to build. She observes that spiritual archaeology can be just as much about hearing the site, as it is about listening inside ourselves.

At one level, Yaxk'in's (2003) thoughts provide us with an interesting insight into her work. However, they may also serve as a metaphor on which we may reflect and elicit learning about conceptualising career counselling from a constructivist worldview. So what can we learn from the previous metaphor that is illustrative of the constructivist worldview? First, it suggests the nature of the counselling relationship that is advocated by constructivists, specifically a relationship that is built on respect, collaboration, empathy and dialogue. Second, the metaphor suggests the relevance to the career counselling process of emotion and subjectivity, elements that have traditionally received little attention in the logical positivist story of career counselling. Third, it demonstrates the primary role of the site (the client) as an informer and expert of their own story. Fourth, it advocates a process that is driven by relationship and story rather than a process driven by prior expert knowledge such as that drawn from vocational psychology, counselling and career information. Indeed Yaxk'in suggests that where our prior knowledge dominates or intrudes on a process, it may drown out the message that is waiting to be heard. Thus the metaphor alerts us to a delicate balance in career counselling between not knowing and knowing, and between being learned and being a learner that is important if we are to accurately hear the stories of our clients.

The previous metaphor provides only one example of the power of metaphor as a tool through which meaning may be constructed within and about career counselling. However, Mignot (2004) cautions that metaphor may define but also confine constructions of reality in that the construction of a metaphor may produce conceptual boundaries "which serve to *edit-out* other ways of conceptualising the phenomenon concerned" (p. 457). For example, the metaphor of a cloud may be variously understood as dark, foreboding and threatening, as having a silver lining or as indicative of a change. In this way, the meaning ascribed to metaphors by clients may limit their possibilities, and it is the role of career counsellors to work with them to co-construct a variety of possible meanings.

Practical application

Story and metaphor also provide exciting and interesting teaching opportunities for those working in counsellor education settings. Further, they provide opportunities for addressing the "how to" question in relation to teaching and also in relation to counselling. Many constructivist learning processes used in the classroom may also be replicated or modified for use with clients, thus providing a theoretical consistency between counsellor learning and counselling practice.

Title/topic
Working with story tellers

Aims/learning objectives
As a classroom or group process, this activity draws on the work of Savickas (1997) to provide participants with an opportunity to identify life themes that have been present throughout their lives and that are reflected in the stories they tell about their lives.

Client group with whom you use it
Counsellor education students, career practitioners.

Work setting recommendations
This activity could be used in a classroom setting in a counsellor education programme or in a professional development training setting. Career practitioners may use some or all of the activity in their work with clients.

Recommended time
1 hour.

Materials/equipment needed
Each participant will need a copy of the working with storytellers handout (see Example 2.4)

Recommended background reading
Savickas (1997).

Step-by-step outline of the process or programme

1 Tell participants to think back to when they were growing up. In particular, they are going to think about the games they played, their role models and favourite book or TV characters. Tell participants to make a few notes on each of these in the space provided in the handout.

2 Invite participants to join with a partner and take turns to share their stories about growing up. Remind them to share only what they feel comfortable sharing and what is appropriate to share in the setting. Remind them also about issues of confidentiality.

3 Next invite each partner to provide feedback on themes they identified in the stories they heard from their partners.

4 Next tell each partner to share information about their present life story, for example the kind of work they do, what they like or don't like about that work, their leisure interests or community contributions. As partners listen ask them to identify themes that are common to the present story that were also common to the past stories.

5 The final step in this process is for each participant to make some notes in the final quadrant of the handout under the heading "reflection about anything they have learned, found valuable or is important to them from the previous activity".

6 Debrief the activity with the participants. Questions such as the following may be useful.
   • What was the process of connecting with games, role models and favourite characters like for you?
   • What did you become aware of that you may not previously have been aware of?
   • What have you learned from this that you could apply in your work?

Conclusion

I will begin this conclusion with a metaphorical reflection on our work as career counsellors that I have used previously (McMahon, 2003, 2004) by thinking about the story of Dorothy and her friends the lion, the tin man and the scarecrow from *The Wonderful Wizard of OZ* (Baum, 1900). After a cyclone Dorothy ends up in a place she's never been before and sets about finding her way home. Along the way she met her new friends the lion, the tin man and the scarecrow. Together they embark on a journey to see the wizard because they think he may have some answers for them. Dorothy

Example 2.4 Working with the storytellers

After you have read the questions in the boxes below, take some time to reflect on each and jot down what you remember as notes.

What was a game you liked to play when you were young? What excited you about this game? What role did you assume in this game? What qualities did you perceive yourself as having? Was this a game that you played with others or alone? Were there any aspects of this game that you did not like?	When you were growing up, who was your favourite book, TV or movie character? What was it that you liked about that person? What were the characteristics of that person that you admired? How did you feel when you were reading/watching stories involving that person? Were there any things about that person that you did not like?
When you were growing up, who was your role model, the person you most wanted to be like? What was it you liked about that person? What characteristics did you admire? Do you have a favourite story about that person? Was there anything about that person that you did not like?	Reflection

wanted a way home, the lion wanted the courage to face things, the tin man wanted a heart so that he could love and be happy and the scarecrow wanted a brain because he didn't want to be regarded as foolish.

Metaphorically, in many ways the needs of our clients are similar to those of Dorothy and her friends – they want to find direction, they want to be taken seriously and not be regarded as foolish, they want the courage to continue their journey and they want to be happy. While we are not the wizard and our clients are not Dorothy and her three friends, if we can listen to the stories of our clients and provide them with a space for reflection where they are treated with respect and care, an opportunity to find what they love and what makes them happy and the affirmation and courage to enact their future stories then we will have served our clients well.

As evidenced throughout this chapter, the use of story and metaphor provides a rich source of meaning and possibility in career counselling. However, just as the lives of individuals are composed of stories, so too is the profession of career counselling. The traditional positivist story has served us well and lives on. However, new and different constructivist stories are now being told about career counselling, and just as our lives are multi-storied, so too is our profession. Indeed, as evidenced in this chapter, "working with storytellers" may be emerging as a possible new metaphor for career counselling. Thus a challenge for all career counsellors is to understand the stories and metaphors that are being used about career counselling, and to begin to construct their own.

References

Albert, S. W. (n.d.) *Story Circle Network*. Retrieved 13 March 2005, from www.storycircle.org/main.shtml.

Amundson, N. E. (1998) *Active Engagement*. Richmond, Canada: Ergon Communications.

Amundson, N. E. (2003) *Active Engagement* (2nd edn). Richmond, Canada: Ergon Communications.

Baum, L. F. (1900) *The Wonderful Wizard of OZ*. Chicago, IL: Geo M. Hill.

Brott, P. E. (2001) 'The storied approach: a postmodern perspective for career counseling'. *The Career Development Quarterly*, 49(4), 304–13.

Bujold, C. (2004) 'Constructing career through narrative'. *Journal of Vocational Behavior*, 64, 470–84.

Campbell, C. and Ungar, M. (2004a) 'Constructing a life that works: Part 1, blending postmodern family therapy and career counseling'. *The Career Development Quarterly*, 53, 16–27.

Campbell, C. and Ungar, M. (2004b) 'Constructing a life that works: Part 2, an approach to practice'. *The Career Development Quarterly*, 53, 28–40.

Christensen, T. K. and Johnston, J. A. (2003) 'Incorporating the narrative in career planning'. *Journal of Career Development*, 29, 149–60.

Cochran, L. (1997) *Career Counselling: A Narrative Approach*. Thousand Oaks, CA: Sage.

Freedman, J. and Combs, G. (1996) *Narrative Therapy: The Social Construction of Preferred Realities*. New York: Norton.

Hale-Haniff, M. and Pasztor, A. (1999, August) Co-constructing subjective experience: a constructivist approach. Paper presented at the Mind-4 Conference, Dublin City University, Dublin, Ireland.

Hoskins, M. and Leseho, J. (1996) 'Changing metaphors of the self: implications for counseling'. *Journal of Counseling and Development*, 74, 243–52.

Inkson, K. and Amundson, N. E. (2002) 'Career metaphors and their application in theory and counselling practice'. *Journal of Employment Counseling*, 39, 98–108.

Law, B. (2003) 'Guidance: too many lists, not enough stories', in A. Edwards, (ed.), *Challenging Biographies: Re-locating the Theory and Practice of Careers Work* (pp. 25–47). Southborough: Canterbury Christ Church University College.

Lyddon, W. J., Clay, A. L. and Sparks, C. L. (2001) 'Metaphor and change in counselling'. *Journal of Counseling and Development*, 79, 269–75.

McMahon, M. (2003) *Life Career Journeys: Reflection, Connection, Meaning and Learning*. Australian Association of Career Counsellors Inc. 12th National Conference. Adelaide, Australia.

McMahon, M. (2004) *An Inn on the Journey to Tomorrow*. Building Tomorrow Today – 10th Annual Consultation for Career Development. Edmonton, Alberta, Canada.

McMahon, M. and Patton, M. (2001, April) *The place of qualitative assessment in career counselling*. Workshop presented at the Australian Association of Career Counselling Inc. 10th National Conference, Hobart, Australia.

McMahon, M. and Patton, W. (2002) 'Assessment: a continuum of practice and a new location in career counselling'. *International Careers Journal*, 3(4), (The Global Careers-Work Café). Available: http://www.careers-cafe.com.

Mignot, P. (2004) 'Metaphor and "career"'. *Journal of Vocational Behavior*, 64, 455–69.

Monk, G. (1997) 'How narrative therapy works', in G. Monk, J. Winslade, K. Crocket and D. Epston (eds), *Narrative Therapy in Practice: The Archaeology of Hope* (pp. 3–31). San Francisco, CA: Jossey Bass.

Morgan, A. (2000) *What is Narrative Therapy? An Easy to Read Introduction*. Adelaide, Australia: Dulwich Centre Publications.

Patton, W. and McMahon, M. (1999) *Career Development and Systems Theory: A New Relationship*. Pacific Grove, CA: Brooks/Cole.

Peavy, R. V. (1995) *Constructivist Career Counseling*. ERIC Document Reproduction Service No. ED401504.

Peavy, R. V. (1998) *SocioDynamic Counselling: A Constructivist Perspective*. Victoria, Canada: Trafford.

Peavy, R. V. (2000) 'The SocioDynamic perspective and the practice of counselling'. *Proceedings of International Career Conference, 2000, Perth, Western Australia*.

Peavy, R. V. (2001) *Part 1: A Brief Outline of SocioDynamic Counselling: A Constructivist Approach on Helping*. Retrieved 15 March 2005, from http://www.sociodynamic-constructivist-counselling.com/brief_outline.pdf.

Peavy, R. V. (2004) *SocioDynamic Counselling: A Practical Approach to Meaning Making*. Chagrin Falls, OH: Taos Institute.

Savickas, M. L. (1992) 'New directions in career assessment', in D. H. Montross and C. J. Shinkman (eds), *Career Development: Theory and Practice* (pp. 336–55). Springfield, IL: Charles C. Thomas.

Savickas, M. L. (1993) 'Career counselling in the postmodern era'. *Journal of Cognitive Psychotherapy: An International Quarterly*, 7, 205–15.

Savickas, M. L. (1997) 'The spirit in career counselling', in D. P. Bloch and L. J. Richmond (eds), *Connections Between Spirit and Work in Career Development* (pp. 3–26). Palo Alto, CA: Davies-Black.

Yaxk'in, A. J. (2003) *Spiritual Archaeology: A Holistic Approach to Archaeology in Palenque, Mexico*. Retrieved 10 November 2004, from http://www.kachina.net/~alunajoy/2003june.html.

Chapter 3

Usefulness and truthfulness

Outlining the limitations and upholding the benefits of constructivist approaches for career counselling

Hazel L. Reid

In a "postmodern" world where notions of secure and linear career progression have been overturned, career counsellors need new ways of working with their clients. Many established theoretical models seem narrow, overly classified and at odds with the dynamic realities of real lives in a rapidly changing world. Constructivist approaches appear to offer alternate ways to understand the diverse meanings given to behaviour and action. Constructivist, interpretive, narrative and biographical approaches emphasise the need to explore "meaning" and perceptions of "truth" from the client's worldview. Such approaches score highly in terms of truthfulness as lives, *pre-occupations*, context and subjective experience are placed in the foreground. Constructivist perspectives are not new (Collin and Young, 1986) but they are gaining credence in the career development literature. Savickas (1997a) refers to this development as located within a twenty-first-century preoccupation with meaning, in contrast to a twentieth-century focus on facts.

Beyond the appeal of truthfulness, this chapter will consider the usefulness of constructivist approaches in a "quick-fix", postmodern world. It will do this by posing the type of "nagging" questions that policy makers, service-funders and practitioners might ask. Before moving on to evaluate the limitations and strengths of constructivist approaches, it will begin by considering the importance of "meaning". The chapter will then progress to consider one area where constructivist approaches can be developed and will end with a specific example: the use of first person narratives in the training of career counsellors.

The importance of "meaning"

There is room for confusion when looking at the terms constructivist, interpretive, narrative and biographical approaches to career counselling. Interpretation suggests making sense of something, giving what already exists, for example a "foreign" language, meaning. When applied to behaviour we interpret intentional meaning from that behaviour; we look for intended goals in the action observed or described. A narrative is not the straightforward telling of an event but is a *re-presentation* of the event imbued with meaning from the teller's perspective. The teller wishes to convey a particular meaning within a certain context, and it is here that the links with identity can be found (Collin and Young, 1992). Biographical approaches take the aspect of identity further. For example, Law (2003) sees biographies as learning tools to help both learners and advisers to understand career better when considering their own career identity. West (2003) uses "biography" in research settings where stories, "auto/biographies", are important to find purpose and direction for the development of a life project.

All of the terms have the concept of meaning at their core and how that meaning is socially constructed, suggesting that "constructivist" may be appropriate as an "umbrella" term. In a range of contexts, that is career counselling, career education and research into career formation, this story telling "is not a reproduction of events but a construction" (Valach and Young, 2004, p. 64), an interactive construction.

The above approaches question the "taken-for-granted" views of the purpose, process and outcomes of career counselling. Constructivist approaches are concerned with taking an ethical and moral position in relation to how we gather information about an individual who seeks help from a career practitioner. In other words, these approaches attend to the key concept of who owns the story by focusing on who determines the sense of a story and who makes decisions about the development of career goals and career action.

A core condition of constructivist approaches includes listening to the client's story. This is more than displaying empathy; this is a profound listening from a self-aware and politically aware counsellor. It is a listening that believes that the client's understanding of the meaning of events, and how they think, feel and construe the impact of them on their lives, is *the* important meaning. This deep listening skill links with another core concept, that of helping people to speak for themselves in their own words and in their own way. In so doing we may hear "tales" that are outside of our experience, that lead us to question the story to clarify our understanding, but not to doubt the meaning or "truth" of the story for the individual.

Constructivist approaches recognise that in encouraging the client to "tell their story", clients do not provide us with a list of experiences or facts. Rather they tell us about events. These events are not a series of unrelated occurrences but present us with patterns formed from how we construct a view of ourselves in the world, past, present and future. Constructivist approaches score highly in terms of resonating with what individuals view as truthful. But for career counselling practice I can hear the pragmatists cry, "All very interesting, but tell me how to do it!" So, whilst convinced of the value of a narrative approach in terms of its truthfulness, what about its usefulness? This is not an argument against theory but it does highlight the tension created when elegant and eloquent abstract ideas fail to resonate with their intended objects. In other words, can constructivist approaches connect with the day-to-day realities of career counselling practice?

Are constructivist approaches too abstract, esoteric and unconnected to day-to-day realities?

There may be a perception that constructivist approaches involve story telling that is fanciful and unconnected to "harsh reality". In the context of career counselling, practitioners may ask where "reality-checking" sits within this approach. For example, a realistic opportunity for a young person living in an area where unemployment or underemployment is endemic may be participation in the informal or illegal economy. This opportunity may provide more money and status than a government sanctioned employment and training opportunity. So whose reality are we upholding when we insist on the need for reality-checking?

That said, practitioners may understand but may not want to collude with such choices. It is a hard world for many people and that harshness intrudes and shapes the degree of choice for clients. Roberts (2002) would argue that career choice is always determined by the opportunity structures available for individuals, and that this choice is inevitably linked to class status.

However, *how* we engage in reality-checking is the key. Effectiveness of engagement rests on the relationship developed between the counsellor and client. When trying to construct a new identity, individuals can be overwhelmed by the problems they face and will find approaches that do not engage with the social interchange of their lives outside the counselling room, as unrealistic. If approaches do not move beyond an approach which sees the individual as the sole author of their story (Gergen, 1994), then they will fail to resonate with "reality".

Narrative approaches may be viewed as leaving the client "stuck in the past". But an exploration of the past is helpful in order to identify interests and life themes for the future (Savickas, 1997a). Attention to the past avoids ignoring or discounting experience and is about looking back in order to move forward in a meaningful way for the client. The client decides "what to bring forward into the new story and what to leave behind" in the old (Savickas, 1997a, p. 177).

The reality-test of constructivist career counselling, then, needs to focus on the humanistic self but also on significant others, in order to recognise that action occurs in a social context and in an interactive world. Further, negotiating action moves constructivist approaches out of a retrospective past. Young and Valach (2000) note that "once we bring narrative into fields like action and culture, we begin to address the problem of the separation of narrative and reality. Narrative is more than persons spinning stories as they sit in their armchairs" (p. 186).

Peavy's (2000a) SocioDynamic model moves away from reductionist interventions designed to adapt behaviour to the majority norm, to an environment that is "co-operative, hopeful, and clarifying" (Peavy, 2000b, p. 5). When listening to clients' stories we need to acknowledge that in telling their stories we are being presented with an interpretation. However, if a genuine trust has been established, whether this is an accurate interpretation or not, is not important. What is important is the significance for the individual, in other words, his/her perception of how the event affects the current situation. We also need to engage with our clients' cultural context in order to understand their "world view" (Sue, Allen and Pedersen, 1996). Within the same culture it is easy to assume we understand another's position when differences in socioeconomic class, age, gender, sexuality, religious beliefs, ability and disability can result in very different perspectives on choice and decision making.

In career counselling, such an approach emphasises the importance of a partnership where ownership of the outcomes is in the individual's hands. Before any goals can be discussed, a shared understanding of the situation must be developed and nurtured, and clarity sought about meaningful goals and action. As Peavy (2000b, p. 7) notes, "any recipe for resolving your issue should be personally meaningful to you and should not come from my 'cookbook'".

If not a cookbook, practitioners need a model if constructivist approaches are to avoid appearing abstract and esoteric, appealing more to academics and researchers than to practitioners. To extend the usefulness of existing models for career counselling interventions, trainers and practitioners will need to investigate examples of practical applications, such as those provided in this book, and adapt them for their own working contexts.

Are constructivist approaches too focused on understanding with not enough attention paid to action?

As indicated earlier, it is in the action that constructivist approaches move into the future. However, how do the approaches compare with solution-focused approaches (O'Connell, 1998)? The latter, cognitive approaches are often favoured as they can incorporate measurable interventions such as assessment, action-planning, monitoring and management. They appear to offer effective ways of "fixing" people quickly. That said, cognitive approaches operate on small achievable goals, which give people a sense of achievement quickly via the emphasis on the positive. However "problem free talk" in solution-focused approaches includes selective summarising of what is heard in the story, which can lead to the client feeling "unheard". "Reframing" the event can move meaning too far away from the client's view of what is significant, and the resulting action may lead to short-term solutions rather than long-term change. This can lead to clients returning for more doses of help when existing life outside the cocoon of the counselling interview intervenes and derails good intentions: a kind of "revolving door" syndrome.

A narrative approach would also advocate changing behaviour immediately in order to enhance motivation and confidence. Savickas (1997a, p. 178) suggests that if, for example, the desired future is to become an artist then "one starts painting tonight". These activities help to bridge the gap between the current situation and the possible future. This need for immediate action can be thwarted if the mechanisms are not in place to support the individual. At a basic level, will clients "start painting tonight" if they do not have access to the materials or an environment within which to enact their future possible selves?

How can practitioners integrate the challenges of constructivist approaches into existing practice? There is much in constructivist approaches that is not new, as Valach and Young (2002) point out "Goal and goal-directedness are not novel concepts in career counselling" (p. 98). How the client and helper arrive at career goals is the key to constructivist approaches. Working alongside a client, not assuming the role of expert who knows best, can lead to vocational goals that are "integrated with other, personally relevant or identity goal systems *to make motivation operational*" (Valach and Young, 2002, p. 102, my emphasis). Whether short or long-term goals are being discussed, motivation needs to be personally and socially embedded for the client, for the resulting action to be "operationalised" in a way that is meaningful.

Constructivist approaches are then focused on action but arrive at action by asking clients to *describe* rather than *explain* (Valach and Young, 2002). The former stays with the client's meaning, which may be challenged appropriately for greater shared understanding. The latter asks the client to justify their thoughts, feelings and actions. The counsellor must understand their own and their client's frame of reference for understanding the social world, and they must recognise that meaning may change according to context. Understanding is central but as a prelude to meaningful action. Valach and Young (2002, p. 106) comment that "In counselling informed by action theory, goals are not solely talked about, they are worked on".

Are constructivist approaches too dependent on therapeutic counselling?

"The heart of my counselling model is to identify a life theme by compre-hending how clients actively master what they have passively suffered" (Savickas, 1997b, p. 11). Savickas is describing a *counselling* model used with clients who may have chosen career pathways that are, or have become, dysfunctional. The word "suffered" has close associations with therapeutic counselling, however, even those clients looking for career advice rather than career counselling get stuck, temporarily, in their story, hence their need for advice. Seeking help suggests a desire for change. The practitioner's task is to help clients understand the choices made that are causing dysfunction in their lives, not just their careers.

Once we start to use words like "suffer" and "dysfunctional" we start to label clients and cast them in a negative light. In so doing we risk applying deficit models that can ignore or underestimate how problems are socially constructed. The narrative counselling approach of White and Epston (1990) actively seeks to avoid this by "externalising" the problem, as emphasised in the statement, "The person isn't the problem; the problem is the problem" (Epston, 1989, p. 26).

When we move from looking at the individual to looking at the context that gives rise to the problem, we begin to question assumptions about the ability of individuals to change their circumstances. Such issues related to power will be considered in a later section of this chapter.

How do constructivist approaches fit with integrated models?

In a transitional period of doubt for career theory and research (Collin, 2000), approaches will need to be integrated in localities of practice. In keeping with constructivist theory, constructivist approaches will operate in connection with existing frameworks or models. Savickas (1997b) does not view a narrative approach as replacing the benefits of using established approaches, for example trait/factor theory. Rather how constructivist approaches "fit" will be decided by practitioners who will adapt and create models for their own career counselling context. The appeal of integrated approaches is that they avoid a "one-size-fits-all" approach to the use of theory, and to the connection between theory and practice.

Again, a cautionary note is needed, as integration is less likely to happen via academic papers and research articles, however "truthful". For usefulness to be assessed by practitioners, the ideas need to be unpacked and introduced via initial and on-going training opportunities. It is important that training opportunities are provided to assist career counselling practitioners to integrate constructivist and traditional models of career counselling, and to maximise effectiveness of their practice in all settings.

How useful are constructivist approaches for diverse groups in diverse situations?

The question could be asked: is this all still a touch middle class, this notion of building a career narrative? For many, work is a job, a means to an end, where notions of choice and "vocation" are foreign concepts. Securing a job is often the focus in a world where for many *enhancing* employment is a secondary concern, or of no concern. Nevertheless, those that seek or are sent to career counsellors for assistance have every right to expect to be listened to by a committed helper who may not be able to change the client's world, but who can work alongside them to encourage a sense of agency and choice, however restricted (West, 2003).

Working with narrative may be a better way of helping any client to enhance self-esteem, through working toward a culturally appropriate and positive self-identity in order to research life/career possibilities. When working with diverse clients in diverse settings we need to recognise that there is more than one way to tell a story. Not all clients can or wish to articulate their story in words; other media, for example art, sculpture, drama and less formal media, such as graffiti, video diaries or rap can be used. However, when we begin to think in more creative ways, constructing a story begins to sound expensive.

What about resources?

Ways of hearing a story and constructing a story that use resources other than the communication skills of the helper and client will involve additional resources. Building trust and rapport is relatively easy when the client shares the same language, culture and values as the helper, and is traditionally "articulate". Such a client, who probably also seeks help rather than being "sent", is likely to respond well to models that can get to their life theme in a relatively short space of time (Savickas, 1997a). Conversely, clients from different cultures, or the same culture but with different values, will need time. Time will be needed to build trust and rapport and this is an expensive resource. The question then arises, is it practical?

The answer probably depends on what is meant by practical. If policy makers are serious about inclusion, a definition of practical needs to go beyond the implied "how cheaply can we do it?" Money is of course important and "value for money" more so. "Is it practical?" is also linked to the discourse of "what works". Many practitioners in the field are weary of constant initiative implementation in careers work, and find the space to exercise their own reflective use of new ideas squeezed by top-down impositions on their time. It may be a simplistic desire to want a model that is "tested", but who can blame practitioners for wanting this when working in an environment which is target driven. For many practitioners, constructivist approaches for careers work will fascinate, but I can still hear that cry of "Tell me how to do it!"

How liberating are constructivist approaches?

Constructivist concepts are located within a broader movement within the social sciences that is shifting the discussion away from positivistic notions of truth and meaning. This turn towards narrative approaches is also associated with poststructuralist thinkers such as Foucault (Besley, 2002b). The importance of language and meaning in counselling is acknowledged in the work already cited, however issues of power have not been so widely addressed in the counselling and career counselling literature.

There are exceptions. The narrative therapy developed by White and Epston (1989, 1990) is influenced by Foucault's notion of the power of discourse and how discourses shape language and meaning. Narrative therapists are acutely aware of their powerful positions and do not assume that counselling is a benign or politically neutral activity. In other words, how people perceive and tell their stories and how those stories are received and acted upon is heavily influenced by the social, cultural and political context. Besley (2002a, 2002b) draws on the work of Foucault and White and Epston in order to challenge humanistic and traditional forms of counselling. She demonstrates how counselling becomes a disciplinary force for both clients and advisers in the way prevailing discourses shape what is viewed as "common sense" or "truth" (Besley, 2002a).

Humanism in counselling may be built on notions of person-centred practice (Rogers, 1961) but places the individual in the centre, somewhat removed from the constraints of their context. Locating meaning in action and meaning in career counselling practice is neither certain nor uncontested from a viewpoint informed by discourse theory. A discursive perspective that examines the macro concepts of power-knowledge and the location of meaning moves away from universal explanations and solutions and points to the essential need to understand individual meaning-making in a social context.

Employing the concept of discourse, Usher and Edwards (1998) remind us that a notion of self-development and autonomy can often mask the tension between the formation of self-identity and the influence of power and politics. The need for enhanced guidance or counselling for certain individuals in an inclusive context can be seen as an aspect of postmodern life that purports to extend involvement, but only within parameters that accord with more powerful views of what kind of work or lifestyle is seen as meaningful.

A "one-way process" that keeps the focus on the individual and their deficits can be avoided by using constructivist approaches. The aim of constructivist approaches is to locate help in the wider context of the individual's life, interests and desires, and to avoid myopic views of what is possible. Thus, an exploration of Foucault's ideas can help us to question some of the "taken-for-granted" assumptions that operate in guidance and counselling (Reid, 2002). Concepts taken from Foucault's work can help us to question practice that may not be liberating but may be reinforcing rather than reducing social inequalities. Further work at the micro level is needed to make the insights from discourse theory accessible for career guidance and counselling practice.

Conclusion

While not new, constructivist approaches are "a work in progress". In gaining ground in the twenty-first century they offer real potential to develop career counselling practice for the demands of a postmodern society with all its risks and uncertainties. There is no one simple model that can be applied to all practice. That said, a shift to placing meaning at the forefront of career counselling is a good foundation upon which academics, researchers, trainers and practitioners can build. In terms of truthfulness and usefulness constructivist approaches seem like the way forward for a more holistic, ethically motivated and politically aware form of practice.

A specific constructivist example – using first person narratives in training

This final section will offer an example of how a first person narrative can be used in initial training and for continuing professional development. The training arena offers the opportunity to work from the ground up, and constructivist approaches can be encompassed in the way we support learners, in the way we assess learners, in the way we conduct research (and encourage students to conduct research) and in the way we teach (Reid, 2003). In career education sessions with clients we often use case studies. Working with narrative can achieve far more than working with case studies. By using other people's stories, young people, who often have difficulty in articulating ideas about themselves, can be helped to identify their own life themes and interests. This approach is not restricted to work with young people, we all learn through hearing stories. We can encourage practitioners to use narrative by using the approach in our teaching. On the other hand, the difference between case study work and using narratives is not immediately apparent.

The authentic voice in a narrative has an immediacy that is lost when the story becomes written into a case study, which can diminish the goal of active learning as the value of the story is weakened. The narrative voice has a veracity that situates the reader as direct recipient of the story. Put another way, the story speaks uniquely to each listener. Un-interpreted, the raw story opens up thinking to the possibility of further and often deeper interpretation. It is difficult to argue with: clarity, ambiguity and first-voice speech give authenticity. We need to recognise of course that language is not neutral, but culturally determined. However, the language in narratives is "original", connections and meanings are explanation free and are not forced upon the reader in the same way as in case studies (Merttens, 1998).

When learning through narratives rather than case studies, our career advisers appeared far more interested and engaged (Reid, 2003). They produced perceptive comments, less held back by feelings that they were being "tested". What follows is a first person narrative unencumbered by the interpretation of the case study writer. Initially I gave advisers questions to guide their discussions, but opened up the possibility that they could ignore these and just work with the text. Many did, and now I give just the narrative, without intended learning outcomes, and ask them to reflect on the story. Here, the general aim was to consider vocational choice, development and decision making.

Mark's story

As you get older you come to realise, know what I mean, that you shouldn't do it, it's not worth it. I didn't realise before about insurance, running someone over, but I weren't one of those crazy ones, you know. I can drive properly. I ain't not getting into a car and going Brrwhrrrrrrrr (Mark made extremely loud and realistic car revving noises) 90 miles round the corner and all that. I drive like a proper driver. Fair enough, you think (he interpreted my thoughts correctly) "they all say that!" but you know, most people in a car, they go speeding. That's what joyriding is all about. For me it weren't like that. For me it was more getting used to being in a car and driving the car. I'll take my test now, I'm learning, and then I'll probably buy a car ...

It's hard getting back on the straight and narrow. Here they've got house rules. You have to abide by them, sign an agreement. There is rules at home but I break them. Sounds silly. Bang doors ... I love my Mum but I've had problems all over my life, it's not easy (Mark raised his voice, as if indignant). People have different upbringings, do you understand. Some people are different towards their mums from others, know what I mean – so there you go (and he seemed to relax again).

Mark's story (cited in Curtis, 1999, p. 60) is powerful and engaging. There is a sense of the real, active voice, which speaks more directly than a case study. You have to work with it, ask your own questions, and make your own interpretations. Our discussions have included the meaning Mark placed on his behaviour, his self-concept, his relationship with others, his understanding of his situation, what was important to Mark, his growing sense of responsibility and what it was like to be "looked after". We have thought about which career theories helped to explain all of the above, and identified where they failed to do so. Only after this did we consider what else we would want Mark to tell us, and how we might be able to help him script a possible future. When using this story our active engagement with the material and the enjoyment and ownership of the learning that took place appeared significant. Certainly by not determining what to learn, it seemed that more learning took place.

We all know Mark or someone like him. Trainees and experienced professionals, have many tales they can tell which help to relate theory to the experience of practice. We can all tell stories and can adapt real stories (whilst protecting confidentiality for our clients) to open up our thinking, our interest and our ability to learn from one another. If we do this in the training of practitioners we can practice what we preach, and *demonstrate* the usefulness and truthfulness of constructivist approaches.

References

Besley, A. C. (2002a) 'Foucault and the turn to narrative therapy'. *British Journal of Guidance and Counselling*, 30(2), 125–43.

Besley, A. C. (2002b) *Counselling Youth: Foucault, Power and the Ethics of Subjectivity*. Westport, CT: Praeger.

Collin, A. (2000) 'A reconceptualisation of career: implications for careers guidance and education', in K. Roberts (ed.), *Career Guidance: Constructing the Future* (pp. 31–44). Institute of Career Guidance, Stourbridge: Trotman.

Collin, A. and Young, R. A. (1986) 'New directions for theories of career'. *Human Relations*, 39, 837–53.

Collin, A. and Young, R. A. (1992) 'Constructing career through narrative and context: an interpretive perspective', in R. A. Young and A. Collin (eds), *Interpreting Career: Hermeneutical Studies of Lives in Context* (pp. 1–12). Westport, Canada: Praeger.

Curtis, S. (1999) *Children Who Break the Law*. London: Waterside Press.

Epston, D. (1989) *Collected Papers*. Adelaide, Australia: Dulwich Centre.

Gergen, K. J. (1994) *Realities on Relationships: Soundings in Social Construction*. Cambridge, MA: Harvard University Press.

Law, B. (2003) 'Guidance: too many lists, not enough stories', in A. Edwards (ed.), *Challenging Biographies: Re-locating the Theory and Practice of Career Work* (pp. 25–47). Southborough: Department of Career and Personal Development, Canterbury Christ Church University College.

Merttens, R. (1998) 'What is to be done? (With Apologies to Lenin!)', in I. Parker (ed.), *Social Constructionism, Discourse and Realism* (pp. 59–74). London: Sage.

O'Connell, B. (1998) *Solution Focused Brief Therapy*. London: Sage.

Peavy, R. V. (2000a) 'A SocioDynamic perspective for counselling'. *Australian Journal of Career Development*, 2(2), 17–22.

Peavy, R. V. (2000b) 'The SocioDynamic perspective and the practice of counselling'. *Proceedings of International Career Conference, 2000, Perth, Western Australia, 3–5 April*.

Reid, H. L. (2002) 'Are you sitting comfortably? Stories and the usefulness of narrative approaches', in K. Roberts (ed.), *Constructing the Future: Social Inclusion, Policy and Practice* (pp. 51–66). Stourbridge: Institute of Career Guidance.

Reid, H. L. (2003) 'Turning to narrative in the training of careers education, guidance and advice workers: could this be a way forward?' *Career Research and Development, The NICEC Journal*, 10, 3–9.

Roberts, K. (2002) 'Introduction: right approach for the wrong reasons', in K. Roberts (ed.), *Constructing the Future: Social Inclusion, Policy and Practice* (pp. 1–9). Stourbridge, UK: Institute of Career Guidance.

Rogers, C. R. (1961) *On Becoming a Person*. Boston, MA: Houghton Mifflin.

Savickas, M. L. (1997a) 'Constructivist career counselling; models and methods'. *Advances in Personal Construct Psychology*, 4, 149–82.

Savickas, M. L. (1997b) 'The spirit in career counselling: fostering self-completion through work', in D. P. Bloch and L. J. Richmond (eds), *Connections Between Spirit and Work in Career Development* (pp. 3–25). Palo Alto, CA: Davies-Black.

Sue, D. W., Allen, E. I. and Pederson, P. B. (1996) *A Theory of Multicultural Counseling and Therapy*. Pacific Grove, CA: Brooks/Cole.

Usher, R. and Edwards, R. (1998) 'Confessing all? A "postmodern guide" to the guidance and counselling of adult learners', in R. Edwards, R. Harrison and A. Tait (eds), *Telling Tales: Perspectives on Guidance and Counselling in Learning* (pp. 211–22). London: OU/Routledge.

Valach, L. and Young, R. A. (2002) 'Contextual action theory in career counselling: some misunderstood issues'. *Canadian Journal of Counselling*, 36(2), 97–112.

Valach, L. and Young, R. A. (2004) 'Some cornerstones in the development of a contextual action theory of career and counselling'. *International Journal for Education and Vocational Guidance*, 4, 61–81.

West, L. (2003) 'Challenging auto/biographies: careers and guidance in a 5 to 9 world', in A. Edwards (ed.), *Challenging Biographies: Re-locating the Theory and Practice of Career Work* (pp. 8–22). Southborough: Department of Career and Personal Development, Canterbury Christ Church University College.

White, M. and Epston, D. (1989) *Literate Means to Therapeutic Ends*. Adelaide, Australia: Dulwich Centre.

White, M. and Epston, D. (1990) *Narrative Means to Therapeutic Ends*. Adelaide, Australia: Dulwich Centre.

Young, R.A. and Valach, L. (2000) 'Reconceptualising career theory and research: an action-theoretical perspective', in A. Collin and R. A. Young (eds), *The Future of Career* (pp. 181–96). Cambridge: Cambridge University Press.

Part II

Constructivism, culture and career counselling

Career counselling theory, culture and constructivism

Mark B. Watson

Career theory has always guided career counselling. It provides a conceptual framework for the career choice process from its initial stages to the developmental adjustments that individuals need to make throughout life. Over the last century this conceptual framework has modified as career theory has reflected macro changes in the economic, social and political spheres. These changes have impacted on the nature and role of work in individuals' lives, thus challenging earlier conceptual understandings of career behaviour. The last century has seen career theory and counselling move from a dominant trait-factor approach to what was considered a radical new psychologically-based theory of career development by mid-century. While this reflects a movement from a more static to a more dynamic, lifelong developmental approach, the underlying philosophical position of logical positivism has remained entrenched in most career theory and counselling. Core assumptions of logical positivism are that individual behaviour is observable, measurable and linear, that individuals can be studied separately from their environments and, consequently, that the contexts within which individuals live and work are of less importance than their actions.

Underlying more recent developments in career theory and counselling has been the philosophical shift toward constructivism, the belief that individuals construct their own reality, their own truth. On a philosophical level, the movement from logical-positivism to constructivism mirrors the earlier shift from a static to a more dynamic approach in career theory and counselling, as constructivism challenges both the more scientific approach of earlier career theories as well as the lesser emphasis these theories have placed on the environment. As such, Patton and McMahon (1999) believe that constructivist approaches in career theory represent one of the most significant challenges that career counsellors trained in positivist approaches need to face.

This chapter starts with a clarification and a description of constructivist core assumptions. It then examines how a constructivist perspective may impact on career theory. The following section examines the influence of culture on career theory from a constructivist viewpoint. In particular, the endemic influence of culture on the career counselling process is considered in terms of the role of both the career counsellor and the client. The final section of the chapter provides career counsellors with an opportunity to examine the construction of their own career counselling process.

Constructivism

A starting point in defining constructivism is to look at the context in which it has developed. Like most approaches in career theory, constructivism reflects a reaction to and an interaction with the macro changes of recent decades. Certainly, the world of work has undergone systematic restructuring in the last two decades. Yet, Savickas (2003) argues that most career theories continue to reflect the values that characterised the modern industrial era with its bureaucratic and hierarchical organisational structures. The post-industrial era calls for new theoretical approaches that reflect the realities of the present working world. One such reality has been a shift in perception concerning career management, with the responsibility for individual career management increasingly lying less with the corporate world and more with individuals themselves (Sharf, 2002). Similarly, Savickas (1993, 1994) refers to the movement away from fitting individuals into the world of work toward understanding how the world of work fits into individuals' lives.

Constructivists believe that there is no absolute truth, that truth lies where individuals are and in how they derive meaning from their environment and their experiences with others. In this sense, constructivism represents a perspective that more traditional career theories have struggled to address, that is the persistent call for attention to context and for the inclusion of factors in the client's environment as well as the client's interaction with such factors. Clearly then, a constructivist approach would require that the career counsellor accommodates the cultural contexts in which clients live and work. For if truth lies where the person is, then truth may be culturally embedded.

As with previous developments in the field of career psychology, the present literature on constructivism, career theory and career counselling offers diverse opinions and definitions. The *Journal of Vocational Behavior* has recently devoted a special issue to constructivism, social constructionism and career. Within this issue, Stead (2004) provides an in-depth theoretical debate on the emergent terminology in this field which illustrates how complex the constructs can be as well as the inherent danger in simplifying terminology. In the same issue, however, Cohen, Duberley and Mallon (2004) acknowledge that "the intricacy of this debate is a fascinating topic in its own right" (p. 409) but choose to provide their own take on this approach. My approach to this chapter is similar to the latter authors. There is a need to be clear about one's terminology and to try to avoid simplistic approaches, but there is also a need to contain the academic debate in a chapter of this nature and to attempt to translate some of this debate into the reality of one's career counselling practice and the lives of one's clients.

What is important is to recognise that the adoption of a constructivist approach by career psychology requires the adaptation of its core assumptions. Mahoney (2003) argues that there are five basic assumptions inherent across diverse theories of constructivism. These are: active agency, order, self, social-symbolic relatedness and lifespan development. *Active agency* implies that individuals are actively engaged in constructing their lives. Much of this activity is focused on *ordering processes*, that is on patterning one's experiences so that they provide meaning. The third assumption is that this ordering of personal activity is mainly *self-referent*, that the focus is on personal identity. The fourth assumption is that the development of self is embedded in the *social and symbolic systems* that surround the individual. A final core assumption of constructivism is that the activities of the previous assumptions are embedded in an ongoing developmental process that emphasises meaningful action by a developing self. All these assumptions have meaning for career theory and counselling, with the fourth assumption about social systems being of particular importance for the present chapter.

Constructivism and career theory

There has been considerable debate in the career literature on how a constructivist perspective impacts on career theory and counselling. Some authors have chosen to look at the philosophical implications while others have translated such implications into the realities of the counselling process. In terms of the former, Brown (2002) has translated four assumptions for career theory from the core assumptions of constructivism. The first of these is that everything is interrelated, that it is "impossible to separate figure from ground, subject from object, people from their environments" (p. 14). Given this relatedness, the second assumption that we must consider is that nothing is absolute, that individuals' career behaviour cannot be reduced to a set of laws. This leads to the third assumption that individuals' behaviour is relative to the contexts in which it occurs. Finally, the previous three assumptions imply that career theory and counselling should accept that the most objective perspective is the subjective frame of reference of an individual.

The adoption of these philosophical assumptions into career theory and counselling implies that we need to deconstruct existing ways we have perceived career behaviour as well as the counselling processes we have used. This leads to a second focus in the career literature on the practical implications of translating constructivist assumptions into the realities of the counselling process. An example that illustrates this latter focus is the use of career measures. Career assessment tools operationalise certain theoretical perspectives. For instance, a career maturity measure can provide the counsellor and client with the opportunity to assess the client's state or stage of career development. In practice, career assessment often provides structured boundaries for career exploration and has remained a major factor in defining the career counselling process (Patton and McMahon, 1999). The original goals of career assessment were to make objective what constructivism tells us is a subjective experience. Thus, constructivism requires us to deconstruct the results of career measures within the realities of a client's life. While such deconstruction makes for good counselling practice, the issue becomes more complicated when cultural perspectives are considered. For career measures are themselves constructed from a certain cultural perspective and the more this differs from that of the client, the more deconstruction of the measure may be required. It begs the question as to when deconstruction of a career measure invalidates the construct the measure purports to assess.

A constructivist approach to career theory and counselling clearly implies that the client would play a more significant role in the career counselling process than in a traditional approach. This suggests another practical implication of adopting this perspective in that the role of the career counsellor would change from that of an expert to that of a facilitator. Also, much of the material that would enhance this process would come from the client rather than from a predetermined battery of measures and techniques that the career counsellor may be comfortable with.

Constructivism, career theory and culture

There is an academic debate to consider here as well when it comes to the definition of culture. Stead (2004) makes the point that the career literature has largely limited the definition of culture to race, ethnicity or language. He argues that we need to go beyond this to the actual relationships that provide culture with its meaning and how this relational process occurs over time and space. Such an argument reinforces the need to define culture from a constructionist perspective. To do this, we need to return to the core assumptions of constructivism described earlier in the chapter and apply them to an understanding of the role of culture in career theory and counselling. These assumptions would tell us that culture is what the individual perceives it to be and that the influence of culture is variable as individuals actively engage with their cultural contexts, order their cultural experiences into meaningful patterns and relate to these in an ongoing developmental process. Clearly then, culture in career theory and counselling should be seen as an interactive rather than a static dimension of the career process.

There is a dilemma in discussing culture and career theory and counselling from a constructivist perspective where the only valid viewpoint would be to accommodate an individual's perceptions and experiences of cultural influences. This makes sense in the counselling process but it is difficult to accommodate in a theoretical discussion. There are cultural influences in any individual's life and, while recent debate warns us against simplistically describing culture and career psychology in a holistic fashion, the career literature continues to explore aspects of culture that impact on individuals' career development. While it would be wise to consider this literature, I would add a constructivist rider that the discussion that follows needs to be interpreted from a constructivist perspective, that is the influence of culture on an individual's career development depends on the meaning that individual ascribes to such influences.

Complicating the discussion of culture and career counselling is the fact that a constructivist viewpoint suggests that culture is endemic to the career counselling process itself (Fouad and Bingham, 1995; Stead, 2004). This implies that both the counsellor and the client bring cultural perspectives into the career counselling process. Traditionally there has been a greater emphasis on exploring the cultural perspectives of the client but this broader definition of culture requires career counsellors to examine their "cultural" role in the career counselling process. Thus, the roles of both the career counsellor and client in defining the culture of career counselling need to be considered.

The career counsellor may prescribe the process in choosing to work within certain theoretical perspectives (with their accompanying measurement). There has been an increasing recognition in the literature that career constructs and counselling approaches reflect the cultural beliefs of westernised culture and, in particular, those of Americans. At the core of career psychology at present are American theories and counselling approaches. Further, much of the commentary and development in career psychology is in relation to fellow Americans' work, a sort of circular development with citation firmly sited in an inner circle. Clearly, there is a predominance of American perspectives in career psychology and one way to understand this is to examine ourselves as role players in the field.

We need to be grateful that much of this frontier work has established a core to career psychology. We also need to accept that established career theory, assessment and techniques have not been prescribed to us. Watson (2004a) argues that it is not so much that a westernised, almost exclusively American, definition of career psychology has been imposed on us but rather that we have not sufficiently and proactively responded to our own national and cultural contexts within which we counsel. Thus most of us have mainly adopted and often not even adapted the core culture of career theory and counselling. This dependence on an American culture of career theory and counselling also raises questions for those of us who career counsel in different national contexts, particularly as the universality of core career beliefs has been questioned (Stead, 2004; Watson, 2004a; Watson and Stead, 2002). In the language of constructivism, we need to *deconstruct* existing career theory and counselling approaches in order to *reconstruct* them within the realities of the clients we serve.

A question we could ask ourselves as career counsellors is whether we would classify ourselves as synthesisers and commentators of mainstream

American career psychology. Put differently, how much of how we counsel is simply a reworking or reapplication of what already exists? How much of the US is in us? Savickas (2003) believes that there is a movement away from the exporting of American career theories and counselling and their subsequent translation in different national contexts. His call for us to develop indigenous models, methods and materials requires us to act as innovators, that is, to refocus career theory and counselling to reflect our clients' experiences of their own national and cultural contexts. Refocusing career theory requires us to initially establish what the core tenets of extant career theory and counselling are. In doing so, we may become more sensitised to the beliefs and perceptions that our clients bring into the career counselling process.

Central to career theory and counselling has been the tenet that the individual makes the choices, the belief in *individualism and autonomy*. Stead (2004) argues that this prominent dichotomy in cross-cultural career psychology of individualism–collectivism is simplistic as it fails to reflect the cultural diversity that can be found within it. Similarly, Savickas (2003) believes that macro-cultural beliefs about individualism versus collectivism need to be interpreted differentially within the micro world of the individual client. Clearly, a career counsellor needs to be sensitive when counselling a client who does subscribe to a collectivist cultural tenet. Watson, Duarte and Glavin (2005) discuss such examples across different national contexts. Take, for example, the career counselling of a Black South African who may subscribe to a collectivist definition of self. The belief in a self/community identity, that "a person is a person through others", locates the self not *inside* the person but *at the point of contact* with other human beings. If a client subscribes to this cultural belief then the career choice process tends to be greatly influenced by the individual's family and community, with decision-making more external than internal in its locus of control. In short, collectivist decision-making may represent career maturity rather than developmental lag.

The latter point about career maturity reflects Patton and McMahon's (1999) discussion of the use of career assessment from a constructivist perspective. These authors argue that assessment data, rather than being objectively presented, needs to be subjectively interpreted with the client. Such an assessment step in the career counselling process may help to address questions about the construct validity of a measure. Conceptual equivalence (i.e., whether constructs are meaningful in the culture being studied) is a psychometric issue that is aptly illustrated in the measurement of the construct of career maturity. Career maturity is defined as an individual's readiness to make career or educational decisions. Western culture measures this construct by examining the extent of planning, thought and exploration an individual has undertaken in relation to a future career. As such, career maturity implies independent thought and planning, self-sufficiency and individual achievement, all of which are valued in individualistic cultures. However, individuals in collectivist cultures grow up valuing interdependence, group goals and group rewards. Indeed, embedding one's career identity in one's family and community is perceived in Black South African culture as a "definition of personhood par excellence" (Akhurst and Mkhize, 1999, p.172). Glavin (2004) has argued that such an individual may score low when given a westernised career maturity measure.

The discussion of career maturity brings us to another core tenet of career psychology, that is the belief in the *centrality of work*. While much has been done to shift the predominant focus on the work role by examining other life roles and life space, the central assumption still remains in career counselling that individuals may choose the salience of their life roles. This reflects the constructivist assumption of agency, that individuals are actively engaged in constructing their lives. That their opportunity to do so may be restricted by the social systems that surround them, is not readily recognised by another core tenet of career theory, assessment and practice, that there is a *structure of opportunity for all*. This tenet reflects a counselling philosophy of internal locus of control, but it ignores the toll that discrimination has taken in the creation of social, psychological, institutional, political and economic barriers that have systematically eroded control over individuals' career choice and satisfaction.

Thus individuals' career behaviour may be "tightly tied to the social practices in which they are forged" (Savickas, 2002, p. 164). International research indicates that various ethnic groups may view family, home and the community as the centre of their existence. As Savickas (2002) states, individuals construct their careers within a particular social ecology that is multilevel in nature. Career counsellors need to be sensitive to a client who believes not only that the family community is of critical significance but also that this family is not solely nuclear. It could consist of a community of relatives that includes the living and the dead. The importance of the family and community in all life roles is well illustrated by South Africa's iconoclast role model, Nelson Mandela (1994), who has stated that an individual has a life role "obligation to his people, his community, his country" (p. 615).

A further career counselling tenet that has been increasingly challenged is that career counselling reinforces the *orderly, rational and linear developmental process* of career choice. While the linear nature of work is becoming less true for all workers as we move to short-term and disrupted work, this is especially so for working-class and racial/ethnic minorities. Yet this assumption continues to guide much of our current career theory and counselling. It certainly reflects the underlying structure of most career measures. Glavin (2004) has argued that the constructs measured by career tests are not endogenous to all human beings and that career measures should be considered as psychosocial tests that assess an individual against externally defined goals such as career maturity, career adaptability, life role salience and career self-efficacy beliefs. If one accepts this argument, then career constructs are not universal and consequently cannot be generalised or measured across different cultural groups. Such findings question the construct validity of a measure and thus how we construct the career counselling process in using them. Glavin's viewpoint is that the equivalence of constructs needs to be examined within the culture to which they are applied, that is whether constructs are meaningful to the cultural perspectives of the client. Career assessment thus becomes less an objective and more a subjective career counselling tool.

All these challenges call for career counsellors to deconstruct and reconstruct the theoretical and assessment frameworks they may have been comfortably counselling within. It requires career counsellors to move from applying "one grand narrative to everyone" (Savickas, 1993, p. 211) to helping our clients construct the local narrative as they perceive it to be. This calls for both the career counsellor and the career client to reflect on the perceptions that they bring into the career counselling process. In so doing, we can move away as career counsellors from traditional to empowering approaches, away from what has been referred to as the "cultural encapsulation" (Gysbers, Heppner and Johnston, 1998, p. 40) that characterises much of what we do in career psychology at present.

The following section gives a practical application that may provide career counsellors with an opportunity to explore their present construction of their own career counselling approach. It is adapted from Ivey, Ivey and Simek-Morgan's (1997, p. 416) text that explores multicultural perspectives on counselling and psychotherapy and readers are advised to read this excellent text. This exercise proved useful with a large group of Australian career counsellors who were able to deconstruct and reconstruct their perceptions about career counselling (Watson, 2004b).

Culture and career counselling: deconstructing and reconstructing your practice

Aims and objectives

This practical application provides career counsellors with an opportunity to explore the theoretical and counselling assumptions underlying their career counselling practice. The aims mirror the five core assumptions of constructivism described earlier in this chapter:

- Active agency. Career counsellors can actively engage in deconstructing and reconstructing their present career counselling approach.

- Ordering processes. Career counsellors have the opportunity to order the pattern of their own experiences and how this may have impacted on the present meaning of their career counselling.
- Self-referent. The ordering of their career counselling practice provides the opportunity for career counsellors to explore their own identity within their career counselling practice.
- Social and symbolic systems. Career counsellors are provided with the opportunity to explore their own social systems and how this may impact on their career counselling.
- Lifespan development. This practical application should be reapplied as career counsellors develop in their profession.

Client group

The following exercise can be used by career counsellors, their clients or for high school and tertiary students. In the present application it has been described for use with career counsellors. The questions would need to be reformulated for other group usage.

Work setting

One possible setting could be in a workshop format with a group of career counsellors when they meet to further their own professional development. Another work setting could be the career counselling process itself where the exercise could be used as part of a more holistic exploration of the client's career development. A third setting could be in a career education context such as a guidance class.

Recommended time

The time taken for this exercise is dependent on the setting in which it is applied. For the self-growth of career counsellors, a workshop of two to three hours would provide individual career counsellors both with the time to reflect on themselves as well as with the opportunity to share in a group context. When used as part of the career counselling process, this exercise could be contained to one session or expanded to further sessions depending on the client's needs. If this application is used for career education, then it would be wise to spend several class periods on this activity.

Materials needed

This application only requires a handout of the questions with the space provided to fill in answers. If used for group activity then a flip board or white board would help in content theming individual responses.

Outline of the process

Introduction

There would need to be an introduction that contextualised the exercise for the group or individual. When applying the exercise to career counsellors, one could point out that who one is determines what career counselling approach one uses. In a sense, one counsels from one's own being, one makes career counselling choices from what might even be subconscious family and multicultural experiences. Thus, career counsellors should have an understanding of their own values and assumptions about human beings, including their cultural values, biases and attitudes that might limit their role as career counsellors.

Career counsellors' understanding of their clients is affected by their own cultural norms, their own stereotypes and their own prejudices. In short, career counsellors need to be aware of the cultural baggage that they bring into the career counselling process. The following self-exploratory questions based on Ivey, Ivey and Simek-Morgan (1997, p. 416) provide career counsellors with an opportunity to explore their present construction in terms of the cultural perspective of their career counselling. They also allow career counsellors to explore where they are, where they are going and how their family and cultural history may influence their career counselling practice.

Handout: what is your career counselling worldview?

1   How do you see the goals of career counselling?

 • What are your key goals and values for career counselling?
 • What do you want to have happen for your career client?

2   Where do your values and beliefs come from?

 • How are these values and beliefs influenced by your life-span developmental process?
 • How do your family, your gender and your multicultural background affect your values?

3 How might your worldview of career counselling limit some of your clients?

- What types of groups do you need to learn more about?
- What types of values and behaviours might be difficult for you as a career counsellor?

4 What additional questions would you want to ask of yourself and of others in the workshop?

Conclusion

Some concluding remarks are needed in order to provide closure both to the exercise and the chapter as a whole. Answering the questions posed in the practical application section of the chapter allows us to explore our role in the culture of career counselling. It provides us with the point we need to start with if we are also to explore the cultural perspectives that our clients bring into the career counselling process. It is the interaction of this exploration of both role players in the career counselling process that will lead to more effective career counselling.

In general, a constructivist approach towards career theory and practice challenges career counsellors to understand and accommodate the cultural contexts in which their clients live and work. Further, it challenges career counsellors to consider how they have constructed their understanding of the career choice process and whether they need to reconstruct their role in this process. It is a challenge to which we all need to respond.

References

Akhurst, J. and Mkhize, N. J. (1999) 'Career education in South Africa', in G. B. Stead and M. B. Watson (eds), *Career Psychology in the South African Context* (pp. 163–79). Pretoria: J. L. Van Schaik.

Brown, D. (2002) 'Introduction to theories of career development and choice', in D. Brown and Associates, *Career Choice and Development* (4th edn, pp. 3–23). San Francisco, CA: Jossey Bass.

Cohen, L., Duberley, J. and Mallon, M. (2004) 'Social constructionism in the study of career: accessing the parts that other approaches cannot reach'. *Journal of Vocational Behavior*, 64, 407–22.

Fouad, N. A. and Bingham, R. P. (1995) 'Career counselling with racial and ethnic minorities,' in W. B. Walsh and S. H. Osipow (eds), *Handbook of Vocational Psychology. Theory, Research, and Practice* (pp. 331–65). Mahwah, NJ: Erlbaum.

Glavin, K. (2004, June) 'Generalizing constructs versus adapting psychological tests for global use', in M. B. Watson (Chair), *Techniques and Assessment*. Discussion group of the Symposium on International Perspectives on Career development, San Francisco.

Gysbers, N. C., Heppner, M. J. and Johnston, J. A. (1998) *Career counseling: process, issues, and techniques.* Needham Heights, MA: Allyn and Bacon.

Ivey, A. E., Ivey, M. B. and Simek-Morgan, L. (1997) *Counseling and Psychotherapy: A Multicultural Perspective.* Needham Heights, MA: Allyn and Bacon.

Mahoney, M. J. (2003) *Constructive Psychotherapy.* New York: Guildford.

Mandela, N. (1994). *Long Walk to Freedom.* London: Little, Brown.

Patton, W. and McMahon, M. (1999) *Career Development and Systems Theory: A New Relationship.* Pacific Grove, CA: Brooks/Cole.

Savickas, M. L. (1993) 'Career counseling in the postmodern era'. *Journal of Cognitive Psychotherapy: An International Quarterly,* 7, 205–15.

Savickas, M. L. (1994) 'Vocational psychology in the postmodern era: comment on Richardson (1993)'. *Journal of Counseling Psychology,* 41, 105–7.

Savickas, M. L. (2002) 'Career construction: a developmental theory of career behavior', in D. Brown and Associates, *Career Choice and Development* (4th edn, pp. 149–205). San Francisco, CA: Jossey-Bass.

Savickas, M. L. (2003) 'Advancing the career counseling profession: objectives and strategies for the next decade'. *The Career Development Quarterly,* 52, 87–96.

Sharf, R. S. (2002) *Applying Career Development Theory to Counseling* (3rd edn). Pacific Grove, CA: Brooks/Cole.

Stead, G. B. (2004) 'Culture and career psychology: a social constructivist perspective'. *Journal of Vocational Behavior,* 64, 389–406.

Watson, M. B. (2004a). *Career Counselling through a Cultural Lens: North, West, South's Best?* Keynote address delivered at the 13th Australian Association of Career Counsellors National Conference, Coolangatta, Gold Coast, Australia, 13–16 April.

Watson, M. B. (2004b) *Culture and Career Counselling: Reflecting on your Practice.* Experiential workshop presented at the 13th Australian Association of Career Counsellors National Conference, Coolangatta, Gold Coast, Australia, 13–16 April.

Watson, M. B., Duarte, M. E. and Glavin, K. (2005). 'Multicultural perspectives on career assessment'. *The Career Development Quarterly* 54, 29–35.

Watson, M. B. and Stead, G. B. (2002) 'Career psychology in South Africa: moral perspectives on present and future trends'. *South African Journal of Psychology,* 32, 26–31.

Chapter 5

Infusing culture in constructivist approaches to career counselling

Nancy Arthur

Cultural influences are inextricably woven into people's career development. The meanings of career and career development, people's career issues, and career counselling must be understood through the historical and cultural location of these constructions (Young and Collin, 2004). Rather than controlling for culture as a "nuisance variable" (Stead, 2004, p. 389) or artificially categorising people according to group membership, culture must be understood through the meanings constructed across cultures and across relationship contexts. A key implication is that theorists, researchers and career practitioners need to "infuse their work with cultural issues more than they have to date" (p. 390). Arthur and Collins (2005) have developed a conceptual model of multicultural counselling based on the premise that culture needs to be located centrally in the principles and practices of counselling with all clients. "Culture-infused counselling ... is the *conscious and purposeful infusion of cultural awareness and sensitivity into all aspects of the counselling process and all other roles assumed by the counsellor....*" (p. 16).

This chapter focuses on ways for counsellors to infuse culture in the practice of constructivist approaches to career counselling. First, career counsellors are challenged to examine carefully the career development theories and models that guide their practice. Second, career counsellors are challenged to examine their views of culture and their views of clients considered to be culturally diverse. Third, the cultural background of career counsellors is emphasised in light of personal and professional influences on interactions with clients. Fourth, the discussion turns to the working alliance between counsellors and clients. A key principle espoused in this section is that culture is an essential consideration in the relationship constructed between counsellors and clients. Fifth, counsellors using constructivist approaches to career counselling are challenged to consider their roles and responsibilities towards social justice. Career interventions need to be expanded from individual to systemic levels to address cultural influences that lead to social inequities and sources of oppression. The overriding goal of the discussion is to illustrate ways that career counsellors can infuse culture into constructivist career counselling in working with individuals and for addressing cultural forces that constrain people's career development. The chapter ends with examples of a cultural auditing process to support counsellors in reflecting about their roles and relationships in career counselling.

Representations of culture

The mobility of people between and within countries is changing the fabric of societies through the introduction of diverse cultural norms and customs. In response to these changing demographics, career counsellors need to expand their perspectives from a "monocultural" or a singular knowledge base, to "multiculturalism" in which pluralistic perspectives are acknowledged and incorporated into practice (Hartung, 2002; Leong and Hartung, 2000). This is consistent with a fundamental tenet of social constructivism that stands against a singular reality, suggesting that there are multiple "truths" which are formed through relationships and internalised through experience in various cultural contexts (Stead, 2004). Rather than adhering to one worldview, counsellors need to be skilled at understanding and negotiating multiple realities – their own as well as the similarities and differences in meanings held by their clients. Therefore, career counselling may be better characterised as a cultural process of meaning-making (Stead, 2004), in which counsellors and their clients co-construct understandings about past and present career influences, and future possibilities.

Theoretical tenets that guide career counselling practice

As part of their professional socialisation, career counsellors are trained in particular paradigms that espouse specific "truths" about career development. There are debates about how well theories of career development incorporate contextual influences such as cultural diversity, the social and institutional forces that impact career pathways and the interactions between individual and larger systems (Arthur and McMahon, 2005). A shift in emphasis is needed from focusing solely on personal variables, such as interests and abilities, to include more emphasis on environmental and contextual variables like gender, ethnicity, socioeconomic status and cultural values (e.g., Brown, 1996; Constantine and Erickson, 1998; Cook et al., 2004; Fouad and Bingham, 1995; Hartung, 2002; Patton and McMahon, 1999). Person-environment models of occupational matching (e.g., Holland, 1997; Swanson, 1996) need to give more attention to contextual forces that impact career development (Constantine and Erikson, 1998; Hartung, 2002), and provide directions for career counsellors to intervene through environmental change (e.g., Hotchkiss and Borow, 1996).

In examinations of traditional career development theories, theoretical tenets such as individualism, the centrality of work, the presumption of affluence, freedom of choice and equal opportunity have been deconstructed for issues of representation and cultural validity (Constantine and Erickson, 1998; Gysbers *et al.*, 2003). Major concerns have been raised about the problems of applying Western, middle-class frameworks of career development theories and counselling techniques that do not take into account contrasting values and the cultural contexts of people's lives (e.g., Fitzgerald and Betz, 1994; Leong and Hartung, 2000; Leung, 1995). It is debatable whether these theories can be adapted to diverse populations without further consideration and explication of the cultural influences on people's career development.

Another concern is that many theories and models utilised by career counsellors were developed in a social context in which notions of career development were linear and the world was characterised as stable and secure (Hudson, 1999; Savickas, 2003). Many clients who experience employment as chaotic, unpredictable and/or unstable require career counselling to find meaning in their work roles and in their lives. As noted by Mark Watson in Chapter Four of this book, "we need to *deconstruct* existing career theory and counselling approaches in order to *reconstruct* them within the realities of the clients we serve" (p. 49). In other words, rather than fitting people into existing career development theories, we need to consider how well our theories explain and support the worlds of our clients (Savickas, 1993, 1994).

Who are our clients?

As career counsellors we need to examine our views of culture and our views of clients defined as "culturally diverse". We need to expand our discussions about culture from a focus on ethnicity and race to a fuller range of dimensions such as gender, sexual orientation, ability and age, along with their intersections in the identity construction of clients (Arthur and Collins, 2005). An "emic" or group specific perspective calls attention to the influences of social and political forces on people's career development, due to group membership. However, according to constructivist principles, it is not group membership per se that imbues understanding, rather it is the meanings and interpretations of culture derived by individuals that are emphasised. This is consistent with advocates of an "etic" or universalistic position who argue that every client must be considered to have a unique cultural background and that all forms of counselling are multicultural (Pedersen, 1991; 2001). Taking a universalistic perspective implies going beyond group membership to exploring culture as internalised by the individual to understand the relationships between worldview and people's unique career development needs (Ho, 1995; Williams, 2003). The appeal of the universalistic perspective for constructivist approaches to career counselling is that an individual's experience is not tied to one cultural identity bounded by group membership. Rather, it opens up the possibility of exploring multiple cultural identities that are fluid and adaptable across relationships and responsive to multiple contextual influences (Stead, 2004).

The influence of culture on counsellors and the counselling relationship

Infusing culture in career counselling also requires attending to cultural influences on the meaning-making and interpretations of counsellors (Arthur and Collins, 2005). A fundamental competency domain in multicultural career counselling is awareness of the impact of personal and professional social-isation (Hargrove *et al.*, 2003) in shaping counsellors' values and internalised notions about concepts of career, "on-track" and "off-track" career develop-ment and how they define career problems, interventions and actions in helping clients to access career resources. There are several innovative frameworks that draw attention to career counsellors as cultural beings, emphasising how cultural influences of both counsellors and clients are relevant for the career counselling relationship. These frameworks are instructive for helping counsellors move beyond cultural constructs of "self" and "other" to focusing on the interactions between clients and counsellors.

The Systems Theory Framework (STF) (Patton and McMahon, 1999) places emphasis on the system of the career counsellor and how personal culture is carried into professional values and roles. Career counsellors need to be reflective about their personal culture and how socialised beliefs and values influence their professional behaviours and interactions with clients (Arthur and McMahon, 2005). Patton and McMahon (1999) suggest a process of reflection to help career counsellors reflect upon their own experiences of career development and their personal values and attitudes towards others. Further, the STF provides a means of analysing the career counselling relation-ship, or therapeutic system, in which the interplay of cultural influences *between* counsellor and client is taken into consideration. Essentially, the counsellor and client create a new culture by coming together to exchange perspectives and create new meanings about career issues. The STF provides career counsellors with a framework for analysing the career counselling relationship and incorporating cultural influences between counsellor and client into career counselling.

Career counselling models developed by Fouad and Bingham (1995), Leong and Hartung (1997) and Leung (1995) are also noteworthy for the attention paid to cultural influences on the counsellor, career client and culturally appropriate process and outcome goals in career counselling. Arthur and Collins' (2005) framework of culture-infused counselling emphasises practitioner knowledge of self, understanding about clients from culturally diverse backgrounds and the influence of culture on the therapeutic alliance. Their suggestions for infusing culture in the goals of processes of multicultural counselling are relevant for career counselling. Launikari and Puukari's (2005) collection of articles on multicultural guidance and counselling in a European context offer many examples of cultural influences on the working alliance that can be used to avoid cultural misunderstandings and to strengthen effective working relationships. These models are important resources for career counsellors to become informed about cultural influences on the construction of counselling relationships and how interaction processes between counsellors and clients influence meaning-making (Stead, 2004).

From individual action to social justice

Career counselling using constructivist approaches requires counsellors to examine the linkages between culture and social justice. Stead (2004) notes that, "Culture provides access to resources for some but also creates boundaries and limits resources to people inside and outside the culture" (p. 394). Culture may pose as constraining forces to exclude some members of society in a fuller range of occupational choices, while providing privileges to others, e.g., members of equity groups such as women, persons with disabilities, visible minorities and Aboriginal people (Arthur et al., 2003; Fitzgerald and Betz, 1994; Patton, 1997). Constructivist approaches to career counselling allow for a focus on the career experiences of non-dominant groups in our society while appreciating the heterogeneity of within-group experiences to avoid generalisations and stereotypes.

Career counsellors using constructivist approaches can help clients to better understand the influence of culture on their career experiences, which may unfortunately contain discrimination and other forms of oppressive practices, including historical oppression such as racism, sexism and heterosexism. Career counsellors encourage clients to give voice to their experiences of oppression and to examine how dominant discourses have framed their career experiences (Blustein et al., 2004). Blustein et al. suggest that the surfacing of non-dominant discourses is a powerful intervention for helping clients gain new understandings and options. Through the relationship formed between counsellors and clients, multiple perspectives are considered and narratives are co-constructed in a process of empowerment.

Social constructionists would consider an examination of power disparities as an important agenda to introduce into counselling to help clients better understand external influences on their career development. This raises the question of how counsellors frame client concerns and their responsibilities for introducing social justice themes into the narrative that defines client issues. It could be implied that career counsellors should let the meanings and interpretations of cultural influences on career development emerge from clients rather than introducing systemic interpretations. However, career counsellors have responsibilities for addressing oppression, privilege and distribution of social resources that are powerful forces for the career experiences internalised by clients (Arthur,

2005). Career counsellors are in positions to help clients gaining understanding about systems that influence career development, including societal inequities and oppression. This is not to remove the focus from guiding clients to tell their career stories as the main actor to gain insights into their individual behaviour, relationships and feelings about their career development. Rather, multiple influences are considered in the framing of client issues to avoid an overemphasis on intrapersonal causes and inadvertently blaming clients for their situations. The main point is that an overfocus on individual factors to explain behaviour decontextualises the person from influential environmental contexts (Cook *et al.*, 2004; Herr and Niles, 1998). Incorporating a social justice perspective into career counselling positions client issues as something experienced by clients as opposed to locating the source of client problems internally (Arthur, 2005).

Incorporating consciousness-raising as part of the meaning-making process is a valid intervention. However, action needs to be directed at the contextual influences on people's career development; otherwise career counsellors run the risk of helping clients to discover new meanings but clients must continue to deal with adapting to oppressive social and employment conditions. Counsellors using constructivist approaches need to consider their responsibilities for addressing the social conditions that manifest in problems experienced by clients. Arthur and McMahon (2005) suggest ways for career counsellors to expand their repertoire of interventions, by incorporating social action and advocacy roles. For example, career counselling may take on the form of coaching clients to address systemic inequities that directly impact them as individuals or helping groups of clients to take collective action to improve employee benefits or working conditions. Career counsellors might leverage their professional status to lobby on behalf of clients for increases in programme funding, or to change institutional policies or practices to improve the availability of career development services for clients. Career counsellors may also expand their community profiles to better understand the career development needs of and work in conjunction with community members to design relevant programmes and services. These examples illustrate how cultural influences on people's career development need to be taken up in ways that actively address social inequities.

Cultural auditing in career counselling

Collins and Arthur (2005a) advocate that counsellors incorporate cultural auditing as an ongoing process in culture-infused counselling.

> The intent of *cultural auditing is to provide counsellors with focused reflection about the influences of culture on their work with individual clients, groups, and systems. Cultural audits may be formal processes*

embedded in formative and summative evaluation protocols but they are more often part of an individual practitioner's daily practice of cultural reflection (p. 141).

Cultural auditing is not intended to be cumbersome or time-intensive in the delivery of counselling services. Rather, it is recommended as a reflective process to integrate during interactions with clients and for case planning. Cultural auditing supports the development of cognitive complexity (Pedersen & Ivey, 1993), or counsellors' capacity to manage the ambiguity resulting from multiple sources of information in counselling. "This skill enables counsellors to keep track of a number of cultural variables and counselling hypotheses concurrently, as well as assess the number of variables that change as the counselling relationship unfolds (Collins and Arthur, 2005b, p. 81). The model of cultural auditing is organised using 13 steps or topic areas that are linked to establishing and maintaining an effective working alliance. Questions and probes for reflection associated with each step are designed to help counsellors negotiate effective counselling processes and outcome goals with clients (see Table 5.1).

The cultural auditing process is intended to guide career counselling practices with all clients. Career counsellors are invited to incorporate the framework as a tool for enhancing their multicultural counselling competencies. For example, in reviewing the topics and prompts, counsellors can reflect about individual cases to consider salient areas to emphasise for enhancing the therapeutic alliance. During supervision sessions, the cultural audits are incorporated as the basis of discussion about client issues, counsellor reactions, the therapeutic alliance and/or planning interventions. To facilitate specific competency development, counsellors might choose to focus on one topic area or specific prompts for monitoring practice and invite feedback during case consultation or when reviewing client tapes. Alternatively, the cultural auditing process may help counsellors to reflect about commonalities between client issues and how interventions may better be designed to address systemic constraints and barriers that impact people's career development. These examples illustrate some ways of incorporating cultural audits through ongoing reflective practice in career counselling.

Summary

This chapter has offered several perspectives about ways that culture is infused in constructivist approaches to career counselling. A central point is that culture is represented in career counsellors' discourses about career development, including perceptions about client issues, perceived barriers and opportunities, and the directions of career interventions. Stead (2004) argues that "career counselling is cultural and not merely a variable in the process" (p. 402). Several implications have been outlined in the discussion.

Table 5.1 Structure and prompts for conducting a cultural audit of counselling practices

Steps in cultural auditing	Topics for reflection
Reflect on the potential influences of culture on …	
1. Establishing initial rapport in the career counselling relationship	• Gender dynamics, differences in age, sexual orientation, ethnicity, or range of ability between counsellor and client • Conflicts in values and beliefs • Prior history of working with clients from a similar cultural group • Client's cultural norms about privacy and preferences for informal versus formal relationships, degree of directiveness and communication styles • Client's previous experiences with people in authority • Language barriers
2. Development of a relationship of trust and respect	• Information about the career counselling process • Share values, beliefs and perspectives· Style of counselling • Types of cultural inquiry, direct or indirect • Ways to enhance the counsellor's credibility • Communicating cultural empathy • Addressing client's expressed needs early to increase efficacy for success in counselling • Establishing a collaborative interaction
3. Counselling conventions	• Structuring the environment and the career counselling session • Norms and counselling conventions that require adaptation
4. How counsellor views clients from this particular cultural group or groups	• Assumptions about client and client's cultural background • Assumptions about counsellor and client similarities and differences • Counsellor's beliefs, values or worldview that are challenged or in conflict • Initial hypotheses about the impact of culture on client's presenting concerns
5. How counsellor views client's presenting issues	• Beliefs about career development • Assumptions about career problems and how change occurs • Common presenting concerns from client's cultural group(s) • Assumptions about the nature of client's career problems that might reflect cultural encapsulation • Stereotypes or biases in assessment
6. Client's views about presenting career issues	• Client's rationale for career issues • Client's view of causality (internal or external), and beliefs about positive change • Client's cultural identity and similarities/differences in views about career development and change processes • Compatibility of views with counsellor's theoretical orientation
7. Broader social, economic and political systems and client's presenting concerns	• Presenting career problems and impacts from family, subcultural group, community and larger social systems • Sociopolitical oppression • Experiences of oppression • Expanded roles in career counselling to address multiple influences

continued …

Table 5.1 continued

Steps in cultural auditing	Topics for reflection
8. Definition and negotiation of client goals	• Match between counselling goals and presenting issues • Level of client's acculturation and cultural identity and impact on goals for counselling • Counsellor's level of identity development in facilitating or hindering client goals • Insuring that client goals are consistent with the changes that client wishes to make • Compatibility between conceptualisation of career issues, expectations about appropriate solutions and counsellor's repertoire of career intervention strategies • Ethical considerations or personal/professional values in negotiating career counselling goals
9. Associated tasks or subgoals and the negotiation of career counselling interventions	• Counsellor's repertoire of intervention strategies and techniques to address client's presenting concerns • Counsellor's preferences for career interventions and need for modifications • Levels of interventions to address client's presenting career concerns • Matching interventions with client's preferred ways of help-seeking • Openness to incorporating indigenous healing practices or resources • Choosing appropriate cultural supports or healers
10. Evaluating client's progress in counselling	• Counsellor's views of desirable change • Indicators from client's cultural context of effective change • Negotiating indicators with client that career counselling work is finished
11. Termination and follow-up	• Cultural meanings of endings for counsellor and for client • Impact of client's and counsellor's cultural context on the termination process • Potential hazards and benefits of continuing contact in a non-counselling role • Strategies and safeguards for public contact
12. Links between client's experience and other clients in career counselling	• Common career concerns raised by clients from specific groups that are culturally diverse • Common career concerns raised by clients between groups that are culturally diverse • Levels of intervention to best address individual client issues • Levels of intervention to ameliorate the social conditions that lead to career counselling concerns
13. Continued competency development	• Current level of multicultural competence • Feedback from client about the working alliance, the counselling process and the outcomes of counselling • Targeting learning goals for working more effectively in career counselling with clients in the future

Source: Arthur, N. and Collins, S. (2005) *Culture-Infused Counselling: Celebrating the Canadian Mosaic*, Calgary: AB: Counselling Concepts. Adapted and printed with permission from the authors.

First, culture must be moved from the periphery and infused centrally in career development theories and practices. Career counsellors need to examine the cultural tenets explicitly or implicitly embedded in the foundation of knowledge that guides their practices with clients. Second, cultural influences on both counsellors' and clients' knowledge and interpretations are equally important considerations for career counselling. Career counsellors are challenged to examine the ways that culture frames their personal and professional positions espoused in the counselling role, including their view of clients, and their view of client's career issues. The position advocated in this chapter is that cultural forces surround the unique needs and circumstances of all clients.

Third, a key principle of constructivist career counselling is that meaning-making is constructed and negotiated within a counselling relationship. The relationship between counsellors and clients is pivotal for helping clients generate new understandings and meaningful plans for their career development. The relationship formed between counsellor and client is constructed from prior understandings that combine to generate new understandings and narrate future possibilities.

Fourth, career counsellors are challenged to expand their understanding about systemic and environmental forces that impact people's career development. In order to help clients overcome systemic barriers, career counsellors need to be willing to engage in dialogue about dominant and non-dominant discourses and to expand their expertise for systemic interventions.

Lastly, career counselling using constructivist approaches requires that counsellors actively engage in reflection about culture. Cultural auditing is suggested as an ongoing process for reflective practice about the ways that culture is infused in career counselling practices.

References

Arthur, N. (2005) 'Building from cultural diversity to social justice competencies in international standards for career development practitioners'. *International Journal for Educational and Vocational Guidance*, 5, 137–48.

Arthur, N., Brodhead, M., Magnusson, K. and Redekopp, D. (2003) 'Employment equity career counselling in Canada'. *Guidance and Counselling*, 18(2), 52–8.

Arthur, N. and Collins, S. (2005) 'Introduction to culture-infused counselling', in N. Arthur and S. Collins, *Culture-infused Counselling: Celebrating the Canadian Mosaic* (pp. 3–40). Calgary, AB: Counselling Concepts.

Arthur, N. and McMahon, M. (2005) 'Multicultural career counseling: theoretical applications of the systems theory framework. *The Career Development Quarterly*, 53(3), 208–22.

Blustein, D. L., Schultheiss, D. E. and Flum, H. (2004) 'Toward a relational perspective of the psychology of careers and working: a social constructionist analysis'. *Journal of Vocational Behavior*, 64, 423–40.

Brown, D. (1996) 'Brown's values-based, holistic model of career and life-role choices and satisfaction', in D. Brown and L. Brooks (eds), *Career Choice and Development: Applying Contemporary Theories to Practice* (3rd edn, pp. 337–72). San Francisco, CA: Jossey-Bass.

Collins, S. and Arthur, N. (2005a) 'Enhancing the therapeutic alliance in culture-infused counselling', in N. Arthur and S. Collins, *Culture-infused Counselling: Celebrating the Canadian Mosaic* (pp. 103–50). Calgary, AB: Counselling Concepts.

Collins, S. and Arthur, N. (2005b) 'Multicultural counselling competencies: a framework for professional development', in N. Arthur and S. Collins, *Culture-infused Counselling: Celebrating the Canadian Mosaic* (pp. 41–102). Calgary, AB: Counselling Concepts.

Constantine, M. G. and Erickson, C. D. (1998) 'Examining social constructions in vocational counseling: implications for multicultural counseling competency'. *Counseling Psychology Quarterly*, 11(2), 189–99.

Cook, E. P., O'Brien, K. M. and Heppner, M. J. (2004) 'Career counseling from an ecological perspective', in R. Conyne and E. Cook (eds), *Ecological Counseling* (pp. 219–42). Alexandria, VA: American Counseling Association.

Fitzgerald, L. F. and Betz, N. E. (1994) 'Career development in cultural context: the role of gender, race, class, and sexual orientation', in M. L. Savickas and R. W. Lent (eds), *Convergence in Career Development Theories: Implications for Science and Practice* (pp. 103–17). Palo Alto, CA: CPP Books.

Fouad, N. A. and Bingham, R. P. (1995) 'Career counseling with racial and ethnic minorities', in W. B. Walsh and S. J. Osipow (eds), *Handbook of Vocational Psychology: Theory, Research, and Practice* (2nd edn, pp. 331–65). Mahwah, NJ: Lawrence Erlbaum Associates.

Gysbers, N., Heppner, M. J. and Johnston, J. A. (2003) *Career Counseling: Process, Issues, and Techniques* (2nd edn). New York, NY: Allyn and Bacon.

Hargrove, B. K., Creagh, M. G. and Kelly, D. B. (2003) 'Multicultural competencies in career counseling', in D. B. Pope-Davis, H. L. K. Coleman, W. M. Liu and R. Torporek (eds), *Handbook of Multicultural Competencies in Counseling and Psychology* (pp. 392–405). Thousand Oaks, CA: Sage.

Hartung, P. J. (2002) 'Cultural context in career theory and practice: role salience and values'. *The Career Development Quarterly*, 51(1), 12–26.

Herr, E. L. and Niles, S. G. (1998) 'Social action in behalf of purpose, productivity, and hope', in C. C. Lee and G. R. Walz (eds), *Social Action: A Mandate for Counsellors* (pp. 117–36). Alexandria, VA: American Counseling Association.

Ho, D. Y. F. (1995) 'Internalized culture, culturocentrism, and transcendence'. *The Counseling Psychologist*, 23(1), 4–24.

Holland, J. L. (1997) *Making Vocational Choices: A Theory of Vocational Personalities and Work Environments* (3rd edn). Odessa, FL: Psychological Assessment Resources.

Hotchkiss, L. and Borow, H. (1996) 'Sociological perspectives on work and career development', in D. Brown and L. Brooks (eds), *Career Choice and Development: Applying Contemporary Theories to Practice* (3rd edn, pp. 281–334). San Francisco, CA: Jossey-Bass.

Hudson, F. M. (1999) *The Adult Years: Mastering the Art of Self-renewal*. San Francisco, CA: Jossey-Bass.

Launikari, M. and Puukari, S. (2005) *Multicultural Guidance and Counselling: Theoretical Foundations and Best Practices in Europe.* Finland: Centre for International Mobility CIMO and Institute for Educational Research.

Leong, F. T. L. and Hartung, P. J. (1997) 'Career assessment with culturally different clients: proposing an integrative-sequential conceptual framework for cross-cultural career counseling research and practice'. *Journal of Career Assessment,* 5, 183–202.

Leong, F. T. L. and Hartung, P. J. (2000) 'Adapting to the changing multicultural context of career', in A. Collin and R. A. Young (eds), *The Future of Career* (pp. 212–27). Cambridge, UK: Cambridge University Press.

Leung, S. A. (1995) 'Career development and counseling: a multicultural perspective', in J. G. Ponterotto, J. M. Casas, L. A. Suzuki and C. M. Alexander (eds), *Handbook of Multicultural Counseling* (pp. 549–66). Thousand Oaks, CA: Sage.

Patton, W. (1997) 'Women's career development', in W. Patton and M. McMahon (eds), *Career Development in Practice: A Systems Theory Perspective* (pp. 37–46). Sydney, Australia: New Hobsons Press.

Patton, W. and McMahon, M. (1999) *Career Development and Systems Theory: A New Relationship.* Pacific Grove, CA: Brooks/Cole.

Pedersen, P. (1991) 'Multiculturalism as a generic approach to counseling'. *Journal of Counseling and Development,* 70, 93–5.

Pedersen, P. (2001) 'Multiculturalism and the paradigm shift in counselling: controversies and alternative futures'. *Canadian Journal of Counselling,* 35, 15–25.

Pedersen, P. and Ivey, A. (1993) *Culture-centered Counselling and Interview Skills: A Practical Guide.* Westport, CT: Praeger.

Savickas, M. L. (1993) 'Career counseling in the postmodern era'. *Journal of Cognitive Psychotherapy: An International Quarterly,* 7, 205–15.

Savickas, M. L. (1994) 'Vocational psychology in the postmodern era: comment on Richardson (1993)'. *Journal of Counseling Psychology,* 41, 105–7.

Savickas, M. L. (2003) 'Advancing the career counseling profession: objectives and strategies for the next decade'. *The Career Development Quarterly,* 52, 87–96.

Stead, B. G. (2004) 'Culture and career psychology: a social constructionist perspective'. *Journal of Vocational Behavior,* 64, 389–406.

Swanson, J. L. (1996) 'The theory *Is* the practice: trait-and-factor/person-environment fit counseling', in M. L. Savickas and M. B. Walsh (eds), *Handbook of Career Counseling Theory and Practice* (pp. 93–108). Palo Alto, CA: Davies-Black.

Watson, M. B. (2006) 'Career counselling theory, culture, and constructivism', in M. McMahon and W. Patton (eds), *Career Counselling: Constructivist Approaches* (pp. 45–56). London: Routledge.

Williams, B. (2003) 'The worldview dimensions of individualism and collectivism: implications for counseling'. *Journal of Counseling and Development,* 81, 370–4.

Young, R. A. and Collin, A. (2004) 'Introduction: constructivism and social constructivism in the career field'. *Journal of Vocational Behavior,* 64, 373–88.

Chapter 6

The use of narratives in cross-cultural career counselling

Kobus Maree and Maisha Molepo

Despite the sustained efforts of law makers and those who implement policy, occupational landscapes across the globe are still characterised by a number of gross imbalances. Unemployment is rife; in South Africa, for instance, some people put the unemployment figure at an alarming 46 per cent (Jansen, 2004, personal communication). Furthermore, in many countries career counselling, often a metaphor for change (Davidson, 1989; Krumboltz, 1993), presents a non-threatening substitute strategy for receiving personal therapy, since it offers a "more legitimate frame within which adults can review past choices, reflectively rue or celebrate their consequences, and use that learning to better understand self in relation to occupational and family work, and that work in relation to life" (Krumboltz, 1993, p. 153). Yet in 2005, career counselling is accessible primarily to people who are able to afford this often expensive service.

In this chapter we aim to:

- contribute to the development of a theory base for our practice, as well as a strategy that is based on research and acceptable to education departments, tertiary institutions, career counsellors, clients and parents;
- further the investigation on the question about whether local contexts, in particular an African context, reflect a postmodern career counselling context (in this chapter, the term "narrative approach" is used interchangeably with the terms "alternative", "qualitative" and "postmodern"); and
- reflect on the following questions:
  - "Can a postmodern approach to career counselling be imposed in diverse contexts?" (Watson and McMahon, 2004, p. 170).
  - Can we "advance our theory base in career counselling to one that is more holistic, contextual and multicultural?" (Savickas, 2003, p. 89).

Concept clarification

From a *postmodern* perspective, individuals are treated as meaning-making persons, instead of being objectified and pictured as points on a so-called normal curve. A *narrative approach* implies that problems and difficulties are embedded in texts, words and stories, representing a lived experience which only exists in language in stories (Becvar and Becvar, 1996; Joffe, 1999). Using narratives is a natural way in which the inherent structure of personal experience is expressed (Barresi and Juckes, 1997). In constructivist assessment and counselling (Patton and McMahon, 1999), specific attention is paid to tracing the connections between clients' experiences and various elements from their respective systems of influences, and this includes the past, present and future: "The task of career counselling is to construct narratives a person can enact" (Cochran, 1997, p. 151). *Social constructionism* is based on knowledge as a social construct, language as a social phenomenon and the individual as a rational person. This approach ties in with a *qualitative* approach to counselling, "At a time when professional psychology as a whole is called upon to relate more effectively to persons of different cultural and ethnic groups, socioeconomic levels, sexual identities, and to people with disabilities" (Goldman, 1990, p. 206).

The University of Maryland definition of *diversity* (which is used inter-changeably with the word "(cross-) cultural" will be accepted for this chapter. Diversity implies human qualities, different from one's own, that manifest themselves outside the groups to which one belongs, and that are present in both individuals and groups. A distinction can be drawn between primary dimensions of diversity which cannot be changed, such as age, ethnicity, physical characteristics, race and sexual orientation, whereas secondary dimensions of diversity include matters that can be changed, such as one's educational background, geographic location, income, marital status, religious beliefs and work experiences (Diversity, 1995).

Career theory, practice and assessment have been accused of failing to address the needs of non-white, non-western, non-standard populations (McMahon and Patton, 2002). Stead (2004, p. 5) opts for a social constructionism approach to defining culture instead of a (post-) positive approach and notes that "social constructionism views people who share meaning-making in their relationships as being part of a culture (they could also be in other cultures as well), so race, ethnicity and language are not necessarily the only ways we can conceive of culture". In any diverse setting, quantitative measurement, observation of behaviour and a qualitative analysis of test results should be combined to enable psychologists to enter the phenomenological world of the client.

Rationales for the current chapter

Six rationales are proposed for the current chapter.

I. Relevance to theory building

We need empirically based career counselling ideas and data that support our judgement with practical ideas (Whiston, 2003). Until recently, counselling theories were essentially developed by and for white, male, upper middle-class, persons and are based on the assumption that "individuals have the freedom to choose any career and that most careers are viable options for many individuals" (Evans and Larrabee, 2002, p. 24).

2. Problems with the traditional approach to career counselling in dealing with diverse clients

The traditional approach to career counselling is based on a logical positivist worldview. Tlali (1999, p. 36) argues that it has become inevitable that ethnopsychology (or indigenous psychology) be established on account of the following:

- frequent communication breakdowns between client and counsellor;
- counsellors making negative judgements of their clients;
- counsellors harming their clients instead of helping them;
- both counsellor and client experiencing the counselling process as frustrating and anxiety-provoking; and
- counsellors setting inappropriate therapy and process goals.

3. Relevance of diversification in a changing international context

Radical changes in people's lifestyles and career planning as a result of the phenomenal technological advancement and the information explosion of the twenty-first century have brought career counselling practice to a crossroad. Career counsellors play an increasingly important integrating role in the effective planning of an individual's career since new skills are constantly required.

4. Possible value of a narrative approach to career counselling in a diverse setting

Chen (2001) indicates that individual psychology theorists (e.g. Adler), person-centred theorists (e.g. Rogers), and existential philosophy theorists (e.g. Frankl) all contributed to the growing notion of meaning-making in career psychology. Hickson and Christie (1989) explain that Western psychology has been dominated in the past by psychoanalytic, behaviourist and humanist paradigms, and that each of these is based on an idiosyncratic worldview, which defines, explains and predicts cause and effect, human behaviour and psychopathology. Worldview is defined as "the way in which people perceive their relationship to nature, institutions, other people and things" (Hickson, Christie and Shmukler, 1990, p. 171) and codetermines the way in which individuals think, make decisions and define matters. Hickson and Christie (1989) explain that a person's worldview includes a dynamic interaction between matters such as race, sexual orientation, state of health, ethnicity, age, lifestage, gender, lifestyle, social class, degree of acculturation, level of education, ordinal family position, marital status and geographical situation.

5. The need for innovative assessment strategies in a diverse setting

To be able to function effectively in a diverse setting, counsellors need to accomplish at least the following:

- reaching an understanding of their own values and assumptions about human behaviour and becoming able to identify and accept differing values;
- becoming aware of generic characteristics of counselling and their relation to matters such as class and culture;
- being willing to act on the basis of a critical analysis of their own conditioning, that of their clients, and of the sociopolitical system in which they find themselves;
- becoming culturally aware of adequately understanding the bases for worldviews and to accept worldviews that differ from their own; and
- being willing to be eclectic in administering counselling, as well as striving to create the widest possible array of microcounselling skills which may have relevance for the idiosyncratic lifestyles of individual clients (Hickson and Christie, 1989, pp. 167–8).

6. Combining approaches to career counselling in a diverse setting

There is a clear need for multiple and flexible approaches to the collection of data, and to combine a number of approaches, since both objective and subjective data are necessary for making a well-informed or appropriate career decision.

Facilitating a narrative approach to career counselling in a diverse setting

Chen proposes the following guidelines or "helping strategies" for career development professionals (Chen, 2001, pp. 326–8).

1 The need to facilitate subjectivity. Career counsellors need to engage clients in becoming subjectively involved in the career counselling process, emphasising: "What do these results mean *to me*?"
2 Clients need to develop a personal intention, namely personal goals, objectives and outcomes. In order to do this, clients first have to internalise meaning of their personal life career journey experiences.

3   Clients and counsellors need to develop a keen understanding of the career counselling or development context. For this to happen, counsellors need to keep in mind the need to consistently remind themselves to put clients' narratives into perspective, that is to interpret and perceive clients' expressions in "the very experiential context in which such meaning exists" (Chen, p. 327).

4   Counsellors need to support clients in making sense of their experiences, that is, promoting and facilitating a sense of flexibility and creativity in their perception of meaning.

5   Counsellors need to help clients construct meanings for planning the future. In this sense the career counselling process becomes a possible opportunity for "active engagement" (Chen, p. 327).

Congruence and appropriateness of the narrative approach in an African setting

A narrative approach to career counselling which embraces the environment and the social experiences of individuals in their stories and draws meaning from them has brought some perspective to the need to co-construct (reveal), deconstruct (unpack) and (re-)construct (re-author) (Brott, 2001) the experiences and career wishes of African communities. The appropriateness of the narrative approach in an African context will now be exemplified.

The storied or narrative approach gives diverse individuals the opportunity to recollect, reflect and put their experiences together. It grants recognition to the many experiences gathered from school and childhood to the present time. African clients have a myriad of life experiences and patterns of life that may need to be recognised and unpacked in order to map out their future career lives. The following examples illustrate the lived experiences of many rural African people.

Rearing of siblings

Many children in rural areas have been forced by parental work conditions (e.g., migrating parents) to remain with their young brothers and sisters when their parents were kilometres away in the cities. They had to cook, wash and do all the adult work to keep going, while they were also expected to go to school and perform. Unacceptable as this practice sounds, counsellors may utilise it to assist such individuals to tell a life story that may shape and influence the client when mapping out a career. Since they have already cared for others, such clients have had premature adult experiences which they may use to build on after the necessary assistance has been given. They may thus have developed an interest in helping profession jobs such as medical doctors, nurses, HIV/AIDS caregivers or in jobs in the travel or tourism industry.

Tending livestock

Rural boys (sometimes girls too) have to tend the sheep, cattle and goats of their parents after school and during weekends. Much experience is obtained in the *veld* through taking responsibility for the welfare of the herd, caring for the sick, injured and maimed animals and feeding and milking them. Herdboys take dogs along to the *veld* for company, protection and hunting purposes. Such experiences could be recognised as the starting points for narrating stories to build or co-construct a profile that may help to investigate occupational interests such as those in environmental, agricultural, conservational and veterinary fields. Love for animals, and first-hand experience in dealing with them in their various environments, may facilitate involving clients in the narration of stories that are inextricably linked to these environments and that may impact significantly on the identification of career patterns linked to such fields.

Initiation school experiences

Initiation schools (circumcision schools) also feature in the cultural experiences of many rural school learners. While such schools have been largely portrayed as barbaric by their critics, many rural communities attach much value to them and as a cultural characteristic they cannot be ignored. Young men and women attend such schools and graduate with some cultural patterns of thinking that need to be recognised as possible influences during career counselling. Many African poets and storytellers have acquired their skills through *koma* (initiation). Experiences gathered through the process of *koma* often serve as the starting point of clients narrating their life stories. Interest category patterns that often originate from endurance training and other experiences gathered through *koma* rituals that emerge from these stories include the unconventional (e.g., museum curators), the artistic/linguistic (e.g., authors), the social community dimension (e.g., *ubuntu* facilitators) and the civil (e.g., defence forces).

The role of cultural influences on career choices

Career-related inhibitions may surface during narrative career counselling. First, in an African environment, some careers are traditionally reserved for females, for example, grinding maize meal, hoeing of fields, cooking/catering (men are not allowed in the kitchen) and building of houses, hand plastering and general house cleaning. If a male "deviates" and practises these chores he is referred to as "abnormal", usually called *mmabasading* (that is, "he is always associating with women"). Examples of occupations traditionally reserved for males include herding of cattle (including milking, kraaling, treating cattle wounds or injuries), hunting, fishing, roofing (thatching excluding building), and ploughing with cattle or donkeys (excluding harvesting).

Characteristics in an African context

We will now focus on a number of cultural characteristics that could be exploited by counsellors who deal with African clients in particular.

Telling stories

One of the proudest characteristics of Africans is their ability to *tell stories*. It is common practice to have a family gathering after supper and listen to stories told by elders with younger members of the extended family participating in discussions and fun. Admittedly, although this practice has to a certain extent and in varying degrees been affected by the introduction of radio, television and the internet, it is still practised in the vast majority of families (in many cases, families do not have access to electricity). Tapping into this practice constitutes a spontaneous way of introducing a storied approach to career counselling.

Cultural singing

Many African experiences have been expressed through *cultural singing*. Stories of battles, soil tilling and other ways of living have been expressed and developed through horns, drums, and oral singing and recitation. A storied approach to career counselling ties in exceptionally well with engaging a client in a relaxed mood of singing or dancing.

Cultural games

Various forms of *cultural games* (a powerful facilitator of self-expression) may be used to facilitate the narration of stories. African games that help to make the client tell stories include *umorabaraba mmabana* (using stories to portray normal family or community life), and *maruba* (which is a chess-like game played with tiny stones or, in fact, any type of accessory on any surface imaginable).

Working together

Letjema or *working together* is one way in which Africans create a situation of unity in action. Adults, for instance, come together in one family's land, either to plough (or harvest) through collective effort. Various family ox-spans are brought in on a given day to plough or till the soil of a certain person, without asking for payment or remuneration. Adults will enjoy food with *mageu* (home brew) while youths receive food and milk at lunch. The spirit of assisting that particular family is the major incentive and a goat may even be slaughtered to serve as relish for the day.

Family in action

Family in action is practised by girls during the puberty stage when they come together to grind *sorghum* or mealies to make *bupi* (for making porridge). They will grind simultaneously while singing songs, for example:

Silang mabele (grind the grain)
Silang mabele
Tsutri le phurmile! (the sun has set)
Bana ba Swerwe ke tlala (children have hunger)
Monna yo morwane (the thin man)

Facilitating valid and trustworthy counselling in a diverse setting

We will now turn our attention to the issue of facilitating valid and trustworthy counselling in a diverse setting. Using multiple data collection strategies (e.g., interviews, observation and documentation/records), requesting member checking for agreement on final results, monitoring the counsellor's own bias through continuous reflection, literature review and conversations with other practitioners and researchers in the field, as well as explicitly acknow-ledging the tensions that may exist in the data are some general strategies for facilitating trustworthiness in career counselling (Denzin and Lincoln, 2000). The following strategies may be included.

Adequate language usage

Adequate language usage ensures that individuals express themselves adequately and meaningfully in terms of their feelings and the interests they may wish to pursue (Herr, 1997). Clients should be afforded the opportunity to choose and use a language that will make them feel unthreatened and at ease when sharing their stories. Individuals who, for instance, are not fluent in English or the language being used by the counsellor, may withdraw and be unable to reveal their experiences or needs effectively, leading to misguided career mapping. Since clients need to have adequate language control to develop the confidence required to reveal life experiences, it seems essential for counsellors to acquire the assistance of interpreters in situations in which they do not know or understand the client's language.

Quality of the counselling relationship

In a diverse context the quality of the counselling relationship is of crucial importance (Brott, 2001) and stage fright syndrome (inhibition) needs to be considered. Due to the problem of inadequate facilities, most clients at schools are used to being taught or spoken to in groups. Because of the overcrowded conditions at most schools, implementing an individual approach is rare.

Counsellors could thus find it difficult to speak to individual clients as the latter may not be used to face-to-face types of interview or dialogue. It may thus be necessary to start the dialogue by proceeding from a group or game context. This may encourage clients to take counsellors into their confidence and become able to share their life experiences.

An increased emphasis on emotions and passions

Kidd (1998) notes that the major distinction between a traditional and a more subjective approach lies in the increased emphasis which the latter places on clients' purposes, emotions and passions. In an African context, it is especially important to elicit and to attend to narratives which elaborate clients' purposes, emotions and passions. Failure to gauge the extent of these matters would inevitably impoverish the counselling process. Indeed, "attending to the emotional realities of the setting in which career interventions take place brings the socio-political tensions and dilemmas inherent within provision into sharp relief" (Kidd, p. 286). In the light of South Africa's *apartheid* past, this matter acquires special significance. Failure to take the deeply ingrained significance of these and other related matters into account during the career counselling process would inevitably deny both counsellor and client an essential opportunity for growth.

Dealing with idiosyncratic cultural beliefs

Counsellors need to acquaint themselves with prevailing cultural beliefs, such as the African belief with regard to greeting another person. A younger person normally greets first in order to show respect. In most Northern Sotho cultures, people greet by calling the greeted person by his/her respecting traditional name (*soretho*) or praise name such as *mahloko* or *mogoshadi* (or *letuba*, and *orphogole* in the case of females).

Sometimes token instead of surnames are used to greet others. In the case of the surname Molepo, for instance, the word *tlou* (elephant) is used; in the case of Mojapelo the word *mohalerwa* (wild dog). Such greetings are normally followed by sharing current affairs between individuals. The greetings serve as ice-breakers for information sharing such as issues about rain (abundant or lack of it), plowing times, opportunities and deaths in the village.

Mohlala (2000, p. 32), for instance, refers to the prevailing fear of witchcraft and black magic, which is still rife in black communities: "It is believed diseases and ailments such as severe headaches, insanity and death emanate from witchcraft and black magic." During a recent workshop, the following anecdote was shared.

At the age of five, I was living with my parents and five siblings in a small village. One day I was tending cattle in the *veld*, and it started to rain. Our hut was struck by lightning, and, upon my return, my parents had already begun to move out, as it was clear that someone had put a spell on our abode. We moved to another village, but soon after that the same thing occurred. This was a most unsettling affair, and we moved house on several occasions. Today, still, I am aware that many forces that are beyond my control, shape our lives. The most we can do is to care for those that are entrusted to us (male, aged 43, in the counselling profession).

Understanding of the role of humour

In developing an understanding of the role of humour, it should also be realised that jokes and expressions in different languages are not always readily appreciated. What is hilarious in English may for instance not be the case in Sepedi, even if the joke is interpreted idiomatically. Cultural differences and nuances clearly need to be noted meticulously when the interaction process between clients and counsellors takes place. If counsellors are from a culture other than that of their clients, the interactive process needs to be studied, understood and appreciated thoroughly. This endeavour should include the significance and idiosyncracies of body language in particular cultures.

Understanding the idiosyncratic view of academic achievement

Mohlala (2000) refers to the phenomenon whereby persons who achieve well academically fear that they might be victimised for standing out among their peers. These persons believe that they might become *zombies*. This matter leads achievers to refuse to have their academic achievements displayed on notice boards.

Appreciating the significance and scope of stereotyped sex roles

While boys play tough, hard games, and are encouraged to explore, girls are discouraged from participating in masculine activities. Likewise, by and large, girls are still discouraged from taking key subjects such as mathematics and physical science. This matter impacts severely on enrolment patterns at tertiary institutions and ultimately on individuals' career choices.

Developing a keen sense of the role of external locus of control which may impact on narratives

Matters associated with an external *locus* of control, which severely impede the achievement of disadvantaged learners, include under-resourced schools, impoverished communities, violence, an unsatisfactory family situation (e.g., broken homes, single-parent or no-parent families) and peer group pressure. Thematically derived narratives provide sufficient evidence that these matters impact negatively on personality development, as is evidenced by low motivation, an inadequate self-concept, illness and fear of failure or achievement (Maree and Beck, 2004; Mohlala, 2000).

Implementing games

Implementing games such as Secret Identity, Critical Incidents and other career-related intercultural sensitisers (Pope and Minor, 2000) could go a long way towards facilitating mutual understanding and cultural sensitivity.

Limited value of certain assessment narratives in diverse settings

Researching and developing a deep sense of understanding of the limited value of certain assessment narratives in diverse settings is essential. In our experience, the *collage*, for instance, has extremely limited value in this particular setting. Member checking informs us that disadvantaged clients in particular are at a major disadvantage when they create *collages*, inter alia, because magazines and other materials that are typically employed when *collages* are created are rare luxuries and thus foreign to most of our disadvantaged communities. Furthermore, *collages* of the majority of the participants in our research reflect only their most basic needs, for example, the need for basic nutrition, healthcare and relaxation. *Drawing*, on the other hand, provides a natural mode of self-expression, and lends itself exceptionally well to empowering clients to "write" their life stories.

Conclusion

Sharing stories to create new and "healing" stories is the right of every person. Sensitising society in general, and the teaching and counselling fraternities in particular, to the specific counselling needs of the most vulnerable members of society and intervening in the case of these populations appropriately may help to ensure the continued success of generations to come in our country.

We have argued that local contexts for a postmodern, narrative approach to career counselling may indeed be accessed in such a way as to accommodate and reflect postmodern developments. If we hope to impact not only on career counselling, but also on the more generic and immediate ills of unemployment, the poverty cycle, the lack of education and spiralling crime levels, we will need to extend our theory base to one that is applicable to the entire kaleidoscope of diversity in our country. For adequate counselling to be facilitated, the idiosyncratic counselling needs of clients along the entire continuum of diversity need to be addressed, especially those in the furthest and most remote regions.

Focusing on and facilitating the strengths or characteristics of a narrative approach to counselling and, in doing so, exploiting the "natural" characteristics of diverse populations, is a crucial cog in the wheel we aim to set rolling: alerting the collective conscience of government, corporate business and the psychology fraternity at large, marrying the possibilities and characteristics of a narrative approach to the realities of diverse settings, working for the common good and, most importantly, believing in what we are doing. Clearly, research is essential for the refinement and development of postmodern narratives that could be used, in diverse contexts, for groups and individuals. This *modus operandi* should evolve into a cost-effective strategy that could have a significant influence on career counselling.

References

Barresi, J. and Juckes, T. J. (1997) 'Personology and the narrative interpretation of lives'. *Journal of Personality*, 65(1), 693–719.

Becvar, D. S. and Becvar, R. J. (1996) *Family Therapy*. Massachusetts: Allyn and Bacon.

Brott, P. (2001) 'The storied approach: a postmodern approach for career counselling'. *The Career Development Quarterly*, 49(4), 304–10.

Chen, C. P. (2001) 'On exploring meanings: Combining humanistic and career psychology theories in counselling'. *Counseling Psychology Quarterly*, 14(4), 317–30.

Cochran, L. (1997) *Career Counseling: A Narrative Approach*. London: Sage.

Davidson, S. L. (1989) 'Career counselling with adults: a metaphor for change'. *Career Planning and Adult Development Journal*, 5(3), 15–19.

Denzin, N. K. and Lincoln, Y. S. (eds) (2000) *Handbook of Qualitative Research* (2nd edn). New Delhi: Sage.

Diversity at UMCP: Moving Toward a Community Plan (1995) [Online], http://www.inform.umd.edu/EdRes/Topic/Diversity/ [2004, July 19].

Evans, K. M. and Larrabee, M. J. (2002) 'Teaching the multicultural counselling competencies and revised career counseling competencies simultaneously'. *Journal of Multicultural Counseling and Development*, 30, 21–39.

Goldman, L. (1990) 'Qualitative assessment'. *The Counseling Psychologist*, 18, 205–13.

Herr, E. L. (1997) 'Career counselling: a process in process'. *British Journal of Guidance and Counselling*, 25, 81–93.

Hickson, J. and Christie, G. (1989) 'Research on cross-cultural counselling and psychotherapy: implications for the South African context'. *South African Journal of Psychology*, 19(3), 162–71.

Hickson, J., Christie, G. and Shmukler, D. (1990) 'A pilot study of world view of black and white South African adolescent pupils: implications for cross-cultural counselling'. *South African Journal of Psychology*, 20(3), 170–7.

Jansen, J. D. (2004) Information given to J. G. Maree during a personal communication in 2004.

Joffe, S. E. (1999) 'A postmodern, narrative approach to career planning'. Unpublished Masters dissertation. Johannesburg: Rand Afrikaans University.

Kidd, J. M. (1998) 'Emotion: an absent presence in career theory'. *Journal of Vocational Behavior*, 52, 275–88.

Krumboltz, J. D. (1993) 'Integrating career and personal counseling'. *The Career Development Quarterly*, 42, 143–8.

Maree, J. G. and Beck, G. (2004) 'Using various approaches in career counselling for traditionally disadvantaged (and other) learners: some limitations of a new frontier'. *South African Journal of Education*, 23(4), 80–7.

McMahon, M. and Patton, W. (2002) 'Using qualitative assessment in career counselling'. *International Journal for Educational and Vocational Guidance*, 2, 51–66.

Mohlala, S. C. (2000) 'The identification of gifted in an under-resourced rural area'. Unpublished Masters dissertation. Pretoria: University of South Africa.

Patton, W. and McMahon, M. (1999) *Career Development and Systems Theory: A New Relationship*. Pacific Grove, CA: Brooks/Cole.

Pope, M. and Minor, C. W. (2000) *Experiential Activities for Teaching Career Counseling Classes and for Facilitating Career Groups*. Columbus, Ohio: National Career Development Association.

Savickas, M. L. (2003) 'Advancing the career counseling profession: objectives and strategies for the next decade'. *The Career Development Quarterly*, 52, 87–95.

Stead, G. B. (2004) 'Culture and career psychology: a social constructionist perspective'. *Journal of Vocational Behavior*, 64(3), 389–406.

Tlali, M. T. (1999) 'A review of the mono-cultural approach to psychology and various criticisms of cross-cultural counselling and psychotherapy in the South African context'. *Vital*, 13(1), 33–9.

Watson, M. B. and McMahon, M. (2004) 'Postmodern (narrative) career counselling and education'. *Perspectives in Education*, 22(1), 169–70.

Whiston, S. C. (2003) 'Career counseling: 90 years old and yet still healthy and vital'. *The Career Development Quarterly*, 52, 35–42.

Constructivist approaches to career counselling

Active engagement and the influence of constructivism

Norman Amundson

In recent years I have made a concerted effort to stand back and look at the career counselling process through fresh eyes. I have come to some new understandings with respect to client problems and the way in which clients and counsellors relate to one another. I have used the term "active engagement" to capture some elements of this new perspective (Amundson, 2003a). With this approach there is a critical evaluation of traditional counselling conventions and an emphasis on creativity, story telling, questioning techniques, action strategies and relationship building. There also is the recognition of the need to integrate personal and career counselling. In building this more active counselling approach I have relied heavily on constructivist notions of career counselling. I have placed at the centre the notion of meaning-making from both client and counsellor perspectives.

Supporting creativity and innovation

An important concept with active engagement is the recognition that many clients come forward with a "crisis of imagination". This is reflected through confusion, lack of self-confidence and a sense of hopelessness about new possibilities. Given this scenario, counsellors need to use their own energy and creativity to help clients create a new story for themselves where there is clarity, confidence and optimism. In achieving this objective the client's personal creativity needs to be fully engaged. In more traditional career counselling the term "career management" is used to describe this process. In active engagement, however, there is more emphasis on the creative and the term "career craft" seems to be a better fit (Poehnell and Amundson, 2002). The notion of craft combines the elements of functionality, skill and creativity. When one is involved in crafting a career there is ample opportunity for personal investment, energy and empowerment.

When one closely examines the counselling process it becomes apparent that there are many traditional elements or conventions that form the foundation for the career counselling process. A critical analysis of these conventions is necessary in order to support a counselling framework such as active engagement that values creativity and innovation. Counselling can be much more than two people sitting together in a room engaged in dialogue for a set period of time (repeated on a weekly basis). While verbal exchange is important it is also helpful to encourage visual imagery and physical activity. The simple addition of a flip chart in the room can encourage people to start to explore issues using drawings and written commentary. Counsellors can also take clients on walks, sit on park benches and use hallways to "walk their problems". The dialogue also does not need to be continuous. There are advantages to having reflective breaks and times for clients and counsellors to sit back and assess what is being accomplished. The length of sessions is another variable that can shift. Many counsellors no longer have the luxury of hourly meetings on a regular basis. Counselling strategies often need to fit into shorter segments and perhaps occur in open spaces where there might be 10 or 15-minute discussions. In a multicultural social context there are also many situations where family members need to be included in career discussions. Space needs to be adjusted to allow for group meetings. There are many ways in which career counselling can be conducted; counsellors need to be actively choosing the structures and strategies that best fit with the needs of the situation.

Establishing the counselling relationship

An important element in active engagement counselling is the personal stance of the counsellor as they enter into the counselling relationship. One way to look at the counselling relationship is through use of the term "mattering" to describe how clients interpret their connection with counselling. Schlossberg *et al.* (1989) define mattering as the beliefs people have that they are important or significant to others. Mattering is more than just words, it is the way in which people reach out to others to make them feel welcome. The counsellor plays a role in this, but it is important to recognise that the beliefs about mattering start from the first contacts that are made with the counselling office staff. Counsellors take this further in the discussion that follows as they attempt to listen and validate their clients' perspectives. At its highest level, clients come away with the feeling that they are more than just another "case" for the counsellor – that they indeed do matter.

The connection between client and counsellor is further enhanced when counsellors extend the opening discussion beyond the traditional boundaries of the expressed career counselling problem. Taking this extra time is usually a wise investment. One way of achieving this objective is through use of the "Twenty Things I Like Doing" exercise prior to engaging in problem-focused discussion (Amundson, 2003a). With this exercise clients are asked to begin by taking a piece of paper and writing up to 20 things that they enjoy doing. These activities can come from any part of their life. After the list has been composed there is some reflection about the activities with respect to the following considerations:

1   How long has it been since they did each activity?
2   What costs were involved?
3   Are the activities done alone or with someone else?
4   Are the activities spontaneous or planned?
5   How do the activities help them find overall fulfillment (mental, physical, emotional, spiritual)?

As the client and counsellor discuss the activities there is opportunity for some self-disclosure by the counsellor (i.e., finding common ground); there also is an opportunity for the counsellor to expand their view of the client in a more holistic manner.

Negotiating the counselling process

There are a number of different beliefs about career counselling that often confuse the process. A common belief is that counsellors have a special test that will provide all the answers (Amundson, Harris-Bowlsbey and Niles, 2005). Another belief focuses on the topic areas that will be addressed in career counselling, the assumption being that there are clear boundaries between career and personal issues. The expectation is that counsellors will only raise questions related to academic and work life experiences. If these beliefs are not clarified at the beginning there can be difficulties further along in the process.

One way of clarifying some elements of the career counselling process is to use a centric wheel to describe the various components of career counselling (see Figure 7.1) (Amundson, 1989; Amundson and Poehnell, 2003).

The process of defining career goals is complex and the career wheel can be used to explain how career goals depend on a wide variety of variables. Some of these segments have a more personal focus (skills, interests, values, personal style) while others address social and environmental concerns (significant others, learning experiences, work/life experiences, career opportunities).

Defining the client's career concerns

People enter counselling with concerns and often some confusion about what to do next. Patsula (1992) suggests that an important first step is to help clients tell their stories and formulate their problems as constraint statements. For example, if someone is unsure about their educational options they might be encouraged to describe their problem as follows: "I can't find a job because I haven't explored all the options." With a constraint statement there is a description of the problem and then a clause at the end describing the reason (from the perspective of the client) for the problem. At this point the counsellor is not trying to pre-judge the situation, rather it is a matter of

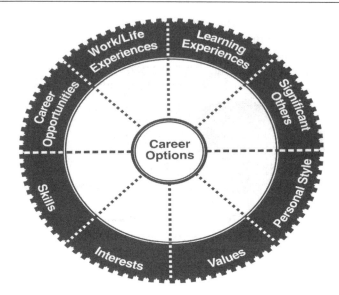

Figure 7.1 The wheel (Amundson and Poehnell, 1996, p. 14)

helping a client to state the problem clearly and to indicate what they perceive to be the reason for the problem.

For some people there might be a number of issues that emerge. The task then is to make choices about the order in which problems will be addressed. It is important here to ensure that there is a specific focus for the counselling. In other situations, the problems that emerge might be beyond the expertise or mandate of the counsellor. Career counsellors need to be prepared to discuss the appropriateness of the problems and also to make referrals when warranted.

Problems can also be conceptualised using a metaphoric framework. Some clients use visual images as part of telling their stories to describe their problems. These images can serve as a useful platform for further discussion and exploration. Metaphors are often based on familiar situations and help people to "pull things together" and to be more creative and proactive in their problem solving (Combs and Freedman, 1990; Inkson and Amundson, 2002). Taking the same example as above, the client might describe their situation as follows: "I feel like I've walked down a hallway to a nice room and now I am wondering what is in the other rooms that I passed along the way". In this situation the career exploration that would follow would be based on elaborating the various facets of the metaphor.

Exploring the problem

One of the metaphors that I use to describe the counselling process is the "backswing" (Amundson, 2003b). A backswing is something that is needed to generate power and to move an object forward. Whether a person is using a broom, a hammer or a golf club, there is a need to move backwards before going forwards. Applying this to counselling, many people come for help because they are discouraged and also confused about what steps they should take. They need to explore and clarify issues and also to remember some of their past accomplishments in order to rebuild their confidence and develop goals for the future.

There are many different ways of exploring the different facets of career problems. Within active engagement there is room for a range of systematic and more dynamic counselling methods. Systematic methods include various questioning strategies, self-assessment programmes, card sorts, information searches – often using the internet and standardised assessment. From the more dynamic perspective, there are strategies such as mind mapping, storytelling, games, drawings, dramatic enactment, metaphors and an array of chair techniques. The challenge for the counsellor is to use strategies that fit best with each individual situation.

A defining characteristic of active engagement is the willingness of the counsellor to use a wide variety of counselling methods. According to Gladwell (2000) one of the key factors in change is the experience of memorable and transformative experiences. As counsellors design intervention measures they need to focus on both the relevance issue and the need to involve clients in activities that will be memorable. For example, asking someone to walk their problem is something that is helpful and also a bit unusual, therefore likely to "stick" in their mind. With this exercise clients start with their problems at one end of the hallway and are asked to visualise the solution to their problem at the other end of the hallway. They are then told that a "miracle" has occurred (based on the miracle question – De Shazer, 1985; O'Hanlon and Weiner-Davis, 1989) and that their problem is solved. Without worrying about all the details they are asked to walk to the other end of the hallway, the place of solutions. From this new perspective they then look back at where they came from and consider what steps need to be taken to get to where they have arrived. Most people are used to solving problems in only one direction, from the problem to the solution. By starting at the solution there is the possibility of gaining new perspective on the situation. Walking the problem introduces physical activity along with cognitive reflection.

Another important element within active engagement is the focus on in-depth exploration of events. Many of the exploration activities are based on a close examination of a few critical experiences. The Pattern Identification Exercise (Amundson, 2003a) for example, starts with a full exploration of an interest. Clients are asked to describe a specific time when they really were pleased with their involvement and another time when they were not so satisfied. After carefully describing each event the client is encouraged to look for patterns in the stories that have been generated. The counsellor provides some support and guidance but the emphasis is on a client's own analysis of their experiences. In traditional assessment, if someone indicates an interest in tennis the assumption might be made that they like athletics. A fuller examination of the story, however, might reveal that the interest in tennis is fuelled by a desire for social relationships or a desire for physical fitness. It is only through a careful analysis of the situation that patterns are revealed.

The centrality of flexibility during all aspects of the counselling process ensures that there is a synchronisation between the goals of the client and the goals of the counsellor. There are times when there is a shift in the client's goals during the exploration phase. In active engagement the counsellor closely monitors any shift in direction and is always prepared to step back to problem clarification approach to ensure the proper alignment of client and counsellor goals. In the example that was used earlier the client indicated that they couldn't choose an educational programme because they didn't have enough information. Through exploration it became obvious that gathering information wasn't a problem. The client enjoyed doing research and was using this activity to avoid contacting employers. The revised constraint statement became: "I can't get a job because I am afraid of contacting employers." With the emergence of this new goal there was a need to explore other issues.

Consolidation, decision making and action planning

While the exploration phase is very important in terms of building confidence and clarifying issues, there also comes a time when clients need to consolidate information, make decisions and move forward. Returning to the image of the "backswing", there is a need to push forward with renewed energy and focus. It is important here to remember that a good backswing is something that is efficient and has focus. Some counsellors and clients get lost in the backswing and never take the next step of moving things forward. Others, of course, try to push ahead too quickly and don't give enough time to the backswing. Obviously, there is some middle ground here that helps to define good counselling.

As with the exploration phase there are a number of different activities that can be used to facilitate decision making. For some it is a more intuitive and holistic process, perhaps using the centric wheel that was mentioned earlier. Others prefer to make lists of advantages or disadvantages or use grids to compare various career options. The activities are designed to engage clients at different levels – verbal, visual and the physical. For some clients it is enough just to discuss options and make decisions. Others prefer diagrams and visual representations. There are also those who gain additional insight by physically walking their problems.

Many clients delay action planning because they want to have everything worked out before taking a first step. While it is important to have some long-term goals it is equally important to recognise that a first step needs to be taken in order to generate some momentum. Given the complexity of the current labour market it is often necessary for people to take a step and then work out other details as they move along. Each step that is taken results in a new perspective on the situation. Sometimes small movements can generate new insights.

As people develop plans for action there is a need to be concrete, to have back up plans, and to have a written contract specifying what is going to be accomplished (witnessed by another person). Sometimes action plans fail because insufficient attention is paid to working out the details. As people take steps it is important that they experience success and a real sense of moving forward. There also is a need for follow through to ensure that action plans are being integrated into the overall change process. Going back to the metaphor of the backswing, much of the effectiveness of the movement forward depends on the follow through that is put into place.

Practical application

Active engagement serves as an "umbrella" under which many different counselling techniques can be applied. As a counsellor educator I initially teach trainees the dynamics of these various techniques by involving them in experiential exercises where they do some self-reflection or facilitate the exploration of others in the training group. Following this experience, they then have the opportunity to use the various techniques as part of supervised counselling practice.

One technique that works well in the classroom and also in counselling practice is that of achievement profiling. In preparing for this activity it is helpful to have access to a flip chart or to some writing paper. The activity takes about half an hour and the time frame can be extended depending on the needs of the client. As a starting point, the person is asked to describe an achievement from any area of their life – leisure, education, volunteer or employment activities. It is important to encourage the telling of the story and to use supplementary questions to ensure that a full description of the situation is included. If, for example, a person pointed to an event where their team won a sporting prize, it would be important to "unpack" the details so that it would be clear how the person prepared themselves for participation in the event and also how they contributed to the overall team success. Listed below are some questions that might be helpful in fully describing the story:

1   What did you actually do? What made it successful?
2   What led up to it? What happened after it?

3   How does this relate to other aspects of your life?
4   What did you like or dislike while doing it?
5   Why did you do it? What was important to you?
6   What personal characteristics did you use?
7   Were others involved? In what way?
8   What prepared you for this accomplishment? (Amundson and Poehnell, 1998, p. 3)

Once a full story has been generated the client and counsellor can work together to identify some of the characteristics that are reflected in the story. In a classroom setting the other class members would also be encouraged to contribute to the analysis. Continuing with the example of the sporting event, there might be examples of hard work, athletic ability, willingness to follow a strict training plan over an extended period of time, an ability to follow strategy but also to be creative within that plan, teamwork, competitiveness and the ability to overcome obstacles. One way of describing this sequence is to take a blank piece of paper and put at the centre a small circle indicating that this is the sporting accomplishment. Around the outside of the circle it is then possible to make several "spokes" of a wheel. Each spoke reflects a certain characteristic. So, in this case, there would be the hard-working spoke, the athletic ability spoke and so on. By representing the story in this way it becomes clear to the person that each story illustrates a variety of different characteristics. These characteristics reflect skills, interests, values and personality style and represent one way of filling in the career wheel that was described earlier. Of course, one story is never enough to capture the full range of personal skills and qualities, thus the need to repeat the profiling exercise using different types of achievement experiences.

Conclusion

An active engagement approach to career counselling includes many ideas that are consistent with constructivist theory and practice. Certainly there is a valuing of the way in which each person makes sense of life experiences. It is these constructs that heavily influence both actions and emotions.

Many clients come to counselling in a state of confusion and despair. As they appraise their situation they feel hopeless and lack the ability to image new possibilities. It is this "crisis of imagination" that is at the heart of active engagement. The process of helping people to see new perspectives is one that requires active involvement of both client and counsellor. There are many ways of re-energising the situation, often involving a mix of verbal, visual and physical activities. The image of the backswing has been used to reflect this process. Through a measured backswing there is a rebuilding of self-confidence and a focus on new ways thinking and of taking action. Once this is achieved there is movement forward and attention given to follow through.

References

Amundson, N. E. (1989). 'A model of individual career counselling'. *Journal of Employment Counseling*, 26, 132–8.

Amundson, N. E. (2003a). *Active Engagement: Enhancing the Career Counselling Process* (2nd edn). Richmond, BC: Ergon Communications.

Amundson, N. E. (2003b). *Physics of Living*. Richmond, BC: Ergon Communications.

Amundson, N. E., Harris-Bowlsbey, J. and Niles, S. G. (2005). *Essential Elements of Career Counselling*. Columbus, OH: Pearson / Merrill Prentice Hall.

Amundson, N. E. and Poehnell, G. (1998). *Career Pathways Quick Trip*. Richmond, BC: Ergon Communications.

Amundson, N. E. and Poehnell, G. (2003). *Career Pathways*. Richmond, BC: Ergon Communications.

Combs, G. and Freedman, J. (1990). *Symbol, Story and Ceremony*. New York: Norton.

de Shazer, S. (1985). *Keys to Solution in Brief Therapy*. New York: Norton.

Gladwell, M. (2000). *The Tipping Point: How Little Things Can Make a Big Difference*. London: Abacus.

Inkson, K. and Amundson, N. E. (2002). 'Career metaphors and their application in theory and counseling practice'. *Journal of Employment Counseling*, 39, 98–108.

O'Hanlon, W. H. and Weiner-Davis, M. (1989). *In Search of Solutions: A New Direction in Psychotherapy*. New York: Norton.

Patsula, P. (1992). *The Assessment Component of Employment Counselling*. Ottawa: Human Resources Development Canada.

Poehnell, G. and Amundson, N. (2002). 'CareerCraft: engaging with, energizing, and empowering creativity', in M. Peiperl, M. Arthur and N. Anand (eds), *Career Creativity: Explorations in the Remaking of Work* (pp. 105–22). Oxford, UK: Oxford University Press.

Schlossberg, N. K., Lynch, A. Q. and Chickering, A. W. (1989). *Improving Higher Education Environments for Adults*. San Francisco, CA: Jossey-Bass.

Chapter 8

The Systems Theory Framework

A conceptual and practical map for career counselling

Mary McMahon and Wendy Patton

As the influence of constructivism has become more pervasive in career theory and practice, traditional theories reflecting the logical-positivist worldview have been challenged in relation to their capacity to adequately account for the complex career development patterns of a diverse client group in a rapidly changing society. In response to such challenges, career practitioners have turned to other professions such as counselling and family therapy for guidance in the application of constructivist approaches to their work. Correspondingly, the emergence of a career counselling literature derived from constructivism is now apparent and informing the work of practitioners.

In the development of a constructivist career counselling literature, three approaches by authors may be observed. First, attempts to apply counselling or family therapy modalities to career counselling have been described. For example, Cochran (1997) applied constructs from narrative therapy to career counselling, and applications of solution-focused brief therapy have been described by McMahon *et al.* (2002) and Miller (2004a, b, see Chapter 10 of this book). Second, specific counselling approaches have been proposed. For example, sociodynamic counselling (Peavy, 1998, 2004; Spangar, see Chapter 11 of this book) and active engagement (Amundson, 1998, 2003, see Chapter 7 of this book) actively encourage clients to locate occupational or work issues into the broader context of their other life roles and situations. Third, theory derived approaches such as that of Young and Valach's (1996, 2004) contextual action theory of career have been proposed. It is in this latter category that the Systems Theory Framework (STF) of career development (Patton and McMahon, 1999) presents as a map that may guide the work of career counsellors.

Presented as a metatheoretical framework, the STF provides an understanding of career development that is consistent with the emerging constructivist position on career development and on career counselling. Thus it is responsive to holistic understandings about career, the inseparability of career and life, debate about the fusion of counselling and personal counselling (e.g., Krumboltz, 1993; Manuele-Adkins, 1992; Subich, 1993), and also addresses concerns about a gulf between career theory and practice (e.g., Osipow, 1996).

This chapter will provide a brief theoretical overview of the STF and outline its capacity to provide a theoretical map or frame of reference with which to approach career counselling. For a more comprehensive description of the STF the reader is referred to Patton and McMahon (1999). The current chapter will also explore the practicalities of applying the STF to career counselling by expanding on the key dimensions of this approach, specifically, connection, reflection, meaning-making, learning and agency with their clients.

A brief introduction to the STF

The STF (McMahon and Patton, 1995; Patton and McMahon, 1997, 1999) is not a theory of career development. Rather it represents a metatheoretical account of career development that accommodates career theories derived out of the logical positivist worldview with their emphasis on objective data and logical, rational process, and also of the constructivist worldview with its emphasis on holism, personal meaning, subjectivity and recursiveness between influences. Indeed, one of the advantages of the STF is that it values the contribution of all theories. Clearly illustrated in the STF are the content and process of career development (see Figure 8.1). The content influences are presented as a series of interconnecting systems of influence on career development, specifically the individual system, the social system, and the environmental/societal system, while the process influences include recursiveness, change over time and chance.

Central to the STF is the individual system within which is depicted a range of intrapersonal influences on career development such as personality, ability, gender and sexual orientation, some of which have received considerable attention in the extant career theory and some of which have not. Individuals do not live in isolation, and so, connecting with the individual system are influences that comprise the individual's social system or the significant others with whom the individual interacts such as family and peers. Thus the individual system, and indeed all systems in the framework may be viewed as systems in their own right and also as subsystems of other systems. For example, the individual is a subsystem of the social system. The individual and social systems are located within an environmental or societal context, termed the environmental/societal system. While the influence of many of these factors such as geographic location and political decisions on career development is less well understood in the extant career theory, their influence on career development may be profound.

The STF presents career development as a dynamic process depicted through its process influences, recursiveness, change over time and chance. Fundamental to understanding the STF is the notion that each system is an open system. An open system is subject to influence from outside and may also influence that which is beyond its boundaries. Such interaction is termed

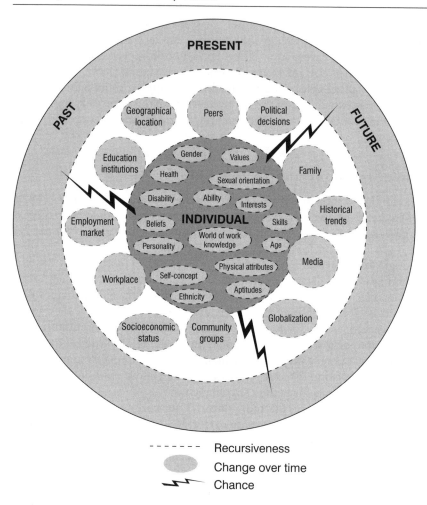

Figure 8.1 The System Theory Framework of career development (© Patton and McMahon 1999)

recursiveness in the STF which is depicted by broken lines that represent the permeability of the boundaries of each system. Significantly, the nature of the influences on an individual and their degree of influence may change over time. Perhaps the best illustration of this is the nature of the family influence during adolescence and the nature of the family influence during middle age. For example, in adolescence the influence of family may present to an individual as parental support or lack thereof, whereas in middle age the influence of family may present to the same individual as responsibilities to children and ageing parents. The final process influence, chance, is depicted on the STF as lightning flashes. As the influence of constructivism has become more apparent, and reliance on logical, objective and sequential accounts of career development has decreased, there has been increased recognition of the part chance plays in career development. All of the systems of influence are located within the context of time, past, present and future, all of which are inextricably linked; the past influences the present, and together past and present influence the future.

As a metatheoretical framework, the STF is applicable to theory analysis at a macro-level. For example, theoretical accounts of influences such as personality and family are variously explained in the extant literature. Through individual analysis at a micro-level, the meaning of such influences is elaborated by the individual. Essentially, the STF provides an opportunity for individuals to construct their personal theories of career development through the narration of their career stories and the elaboration of meaning in career counselling. Thus, in terms of career practice, systems theory lends itself to a theoretical and practical consistency.

The STF and career counselling

At a practical level, the STF provides a map to guide career counsellors as they encourage clients to relate the details and reality of their own maps through the telling of their career stories (McMahon and Patton, 2003; McMahon, Patton and Watson, 2004). Together, counsellor and client gain insight into the interconnectedness of systemic influences on the client's situation. While the STF may serve as a map of the possible elements of clients' career stories, it may also serve as a map of the counselling relationship as depicted in Figure 8.2. Career counsellors also exist within their own system of influences, and career counselling therefore constitutes the connection of two systems of influence, those of the client and those of the counsellor, and consequently the formation of a new dynamic system, the therapeutic system (Patton and McMahon, 1999). Of significance in Figure 8.2, is the incorporation of the organisational system of influence. Organisational systems should not be overlooked in career counselling as they may influence elements such as the nature of services offered by career counsellors, the nature of the client group, fees, record keeping and counsellor support.

In its relatively brief history, the STF has been applied to a range of cultural groups and settings (see Patton and McMahon, 1997), qualitative career assessment (McMahon *et al.*, 2004, 2005a; McMahon *et al.*, 2005b), career counselling (McMahon, 2005; Patton and McMahon, in press) and multicultural career counselling (Arthur and McMahon, 2005). In addition, its application across countries has been suggested (Patton *et al.*, in press; United Nations Educational, Scientific and Cultural Organisation, 2002). Thus it seems that the STF has much to offer career counselling. For example, Arthur and McMahon (2005) propose that the STF may be applicable to clients with individualist or collectivist worldviews because counselling "proceeds from the worldview represented by clients through the telling of their career stories" (p. 216). Further, these authors contend that the STF suggests the possibility of expanded roles and levels of intervention for career counsellors, particularly in relation to multicultural career counselling.

In applying the STF to career counselling, McMahon (2005) suggests a number of conceptual understandings and practical considerations that may guide the work of career counsellors. Conceptual understandings related to the individual, systemic thinking, story and recursiveness may provide a theoretical base for counsellors. Importantly, individuals are considered as experts in their own lives who seek to make sense of their lives through the telling of stories. Indeed, their lives are multi-storied. Individuals connect with career counsellors in a recursive system described by the STF as the therapeutic system (see Figure 8.2). Through counselling individuals may connect with a range of stories (see Chapter 2 of this book). For example, they may relate stories they commonly tell, stories told by others in their system of influence, stories they have long forgotten, stories they have never told, stories they have been afraid to tell and stories they did not know they could tell. In addition, they may connect with and co-construct future stories. On the surface, stories may appear discrete and unrelated; however, systemic thinking encourages counsellors and clients to take a holistic view by locating the individual within the context of their whole system of influences. In so doing, the recursiveness and connection between the influences of the system may be examined, and patterns and themes in and between stories may be uncovered. Recursiveness, or the interaction between elements of the system, necessarily means that the system is dynamic.

Practical considerations include facilitating connectedness, the use of story and the nature of the counselling relationship. Connectedness is a multi-leveled concept illustrated through the STF and essential for effective career counselling. At a fundamental level, connectedness is desirable between counsellors and their own systems of influence, clients and counsellors in the counselling relationship, and clients and their own systems of influence. The narration of career stories fosters connectedness between individuals and the elements in their systems of influence as well as connectedness between elements of the systems. In order that the telling of stories may be encouraged, it is important for career counsellors to facilitate relationships where a mattering climate is created (Schlossberg, Lynch and Chickering, 1989), a climate where clients feel valued, cared about and appreciated, and that they really matter. Amundson (1998) suggests that the Rogers' (1951) necessary conditions for counselling, genuineness, unconditional positive regard and empathic understanding are essential for such a climate.

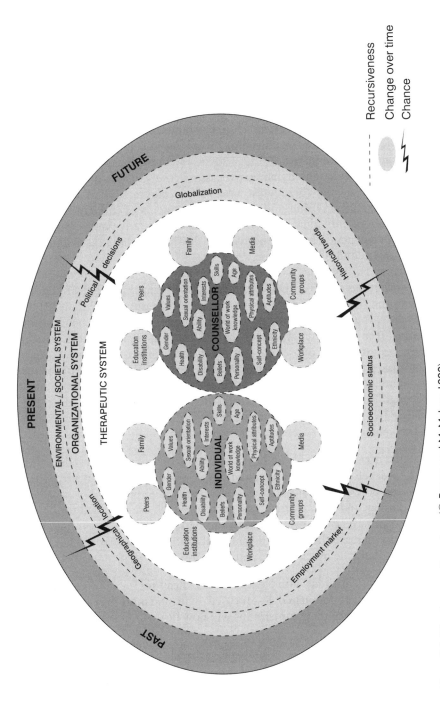

Figure 8.2 The therapeutic system (© Patton and McMahon 1999)

The STF and career counselling – practice dimensions

The STF not only provides a map to guide career counsellors in terms of the possible content of client stories, it also provides a lens through which to view the career counselling process. Through the lens of the STF key recursive dimensions of the career counselling process may be identified, specifically connectedness, reflection, meaning-making, learning and agency (McMahon, 2003). The dimensions of relationship, meaning-making and agency are not new concepts for career counsellors working within the constructivist paradigm. For example, Peavy (1992) advocated these dimensions along with that of negotiation. The dynamic process of recursiveness depicted in the STF, particularly the therapeutic system (see Figure 8.2), illustrates the interconnectedness within and between the systems of influence. Themes and patterns in individuals' life stories are also illustrative of the process of interconnectedness. Thus "connectedness" has been included as a dimension of the career counselling process.

Learning has also been proffered as a dimension of the career counselling process as it has been recognised as critical for managing life, learning and work in the twenty-first century (Cornford, Athanasou and Pithers, 1996; McMahon, Patton and Tatham, 2003). In addition, the importance of learning has long been recognised in career theory (e.g., Super, 1990). It is through the process of career counselling that individuals come to recognise or learn what is required for them to move towards their preferred future. Learning is facilitated through connectedness, reflection and meaning-making, and it is through learning that agency is fostered.

These five dimensions are consistent with what Peavy (1998) suggests are the three main tasks of a counsellor, specifically:

1 to enter into sensible and trustworthy communication with the other,
2 to develop a mutual understanding of the particular difficulty which the other faces, and
3 to plan and construct activity projects which are designed to:
   a) increase self-responsibility and personal control,
   b) increase the other's meaningful participation in social life, and
   c) help the other choose and move toward preferred futures (p. 50).

They are also consistent with Savickas' (1993) call for career counselling to become less expert dominated, less focused on fit, and more focused on stories than scores. Each of these dimensions will now be described in more detail.

Connectedness

Connectedness is an intricate and multidimensional construct (Townsend and McWhirter, 2005) that occurs on many levels in the career counselling process. First, it is advisable for career counsellors to connect with their own career stories in order that they understand their own history, values, biases, beliefs and prejudices, and the socio-political system in which they live and work. The awareness generated out of knowing and understanding their own career stories, may assist career counsellors to more appropriately respond to the needs of a diverse client group and also to be alert to situations where they could potentially impose elements of their own career story onto the counselling process. Exercises such as that detailed in Chapter 4 of this book and later in this chapter may foster awareness of career counsellors' personal career stories. In addition to connecting with their own career stories, career counsellors connect with a body of theoretical knowledge and practical skills that inform their work. Understanding the cultural applicability and appropriateness of this knowledge and skill may also assist career counsellors to be responsive to the needs of a diverse client group.

Second, career counsellors connect with their clients. Indeed, this is the relationship dimension of career counselling. Savickas (1993) suggests that supportive relationships help people to articulate their experience, interpret their needs and shape their lives out of a range of possibilities. Essentially, career counsellors enter the lifespace of another individual for the purpose of career counselling. The concept of lifespace is not new in the field of career development (e.g., Peavy, 1998; Super, 1990) and refers to the holistic nature of career development. At a fundamental level, connecting with clients involves meeting and greeting. However, connecting with clients should not be viewed as a process or step that occurs during the first few minutes of the counselling relationship. Rather, it is a recursive process through which the counselling relationship deepens and strengthens over time. It is a relationship where clients are viewed as experts in their lives, and where the curiosity of the career counsellor encourages them to tell their stories.

Third, connecting clients with their own system of influences is critical to the career counselling process. It is through this process that stories are remembered and told, and it is through the telling of stories that connectedness between the systemic influences is recognised. In terms of connecting with client stories, it is important for career counsellors to engage with clients at an appropriate level or to "start where the client is". Cochran (1997) suggests that clarifying the career issue or the gap between what is, "the existing state of affairs", and what ought/could/should be, "the desired state of affairs" (p. 16), is important in connecting with the client. Further, clarification of what is desirable (what the client wants from us) and what is possible (what we can offer) is also important. It should be remembered that a client's "existing state of affairs" and "desired state of affairs" are not static and may change over time as a result of the recursive process with elements of his/her system of influences and also with the career counsellor. With the STF as a map that may guide the possible content of career counselling, clients may be encouraged to tell stories from their past, from their leisure activities, or from their community service. It is not uncommon for clients to compart-mentalise their lives and to not recognise the themes and patterns that permeate their lives. Thus counselling may be viewed as a collaborative process in which Savickas (1993) suggests that:

> acting as co-authors and editors ... counsellors can help clients
> 1 authorize their careers by narrating a coherent, continuous, and credible story,
> 2 invest career with meaning by identifying themes and tensions in the story line, and
> 3 learn the skills needed to perform the next episode in the story (pp. 210–13).

Reflection

Peavy (1998) suggests that career counsellors model a process that creates care, hope, encouragement, clarification and activation. In so doing, they model a respectful, curious, tentative and non-expert approach that encourages clients to be "explorers in their own life" (p. 20). Amundson *et al.* (2002) suggest that people are active agents who "make sense of the world of work through subjective interpretation of their own career experience. In living through the complexity of economic life, they draw new insights and formulate new strategies that make sense of this complexity" (p. 27). Further, these authors suggest that there is "a continuing tension between leveraging past experience and positioning for future opportunity" (p. 27). The processes described by these authors are enhanced if career counsellors create a space for reflection whereby individuals feel safe to narrate their stories, where they are encouraged to elicit meaning and where they are supported in the co-construction of new or alternate stories. In today's busy world, experiencing a space for reflection or a time to think may be a new or rare experience for many clients.

Meaning-making

Career counselling produces a relationship that requires "both speaker and listener to enter an open communication interchange. What comes to be understood (shared meaning) is the result of negotiation. The two interpreters arrive at a fusion of understanding that takes the form of an agreement, understanding or shared knowledge" (Peavy, 2000, p. 8). Thus career counsellors facilitate a process where stories are elaborated, new meaning is invited or constructed, and possibilities for the future elicited. Morgan (2000) describes the process whereby clients relate "thin descriptions" (Morgan, 2000, p. 12) of their circumstances which produce "thin conclusions" (p. 12) and necessarily limit the possibilities for the future and frequently sustain problems. Therefore, it is the role of career counsellors to work with clients to explore alternative stories that might provide the possibility of change. Morgan (2000) suggests that the key question for counsellors is "how can we assist people to break from thin conclusions and to re-author new and preferred stories for their lives and relationships?" (p. 15).

Learning

Learning is the process whereby individuals construct and transform experience into knowledge, skills, attitudes, values, beliefs and emotions (Holmes, 2002). Thus meaning-making may be seen as an important element of the learning process. Increasingly, the need for individuals to continue learning throughout their lives in formal and informal settings is being recognised. Career counselling may be viewed as a learning environment that is consistent with understandings about lifelong learning. For example, Longworth and Davies (1996) define lifelong learning as "the development of human potential through a continuously supportive process which stimulates and empowers individuals to acquire all the knowledge, values, skills and understanding they will require throughout their lifetimes and to apply them with confidence, creativity and enjoyment in all roles, circumstances, and environments" (p. 22). In this way, career counselling may be viewed as a process of lifelong learning where stories of ability, strength, competence, hope and encouragement are co-constructed that may facilitate transition to the "desired state of affairs" (Cochran, 1997, p. 16). In this regard, Peavy believes that "As counsellors we have the privilege of hearing many stories and scripts and then joining the storytellers in the task of re-authoring them toward more preferred futures" (Peavy, 1998, p. 30).

Agency

Agency refers to a client's capacity to "act for themselves and speak on their own behalf" (Monk et al., 1997, p. 301). At a content level, fostering agency involves identifying and affirming clients' strengths, knowledge, attitudes and skills that will be helpful in creating their preferred futures. At a process level, fostering agency involves affirming, supporting, encouraging and creating an optimism around clients' capacity to create their preferred future. Peavy (1992) suggests that the career counselling process should be fruitful, that is "it should provide a re-construing or changed outlook on some aspect of life" (p. 221). In addition, he advocates use of the term "fruitfulness" rather than the term "outcomes".

These dimensions illustrate the possibilities offered by the STF to facilitate greater links between theory and practice. Further, these dimensions may also be used in the teaching of career counselling.

The STF – a practical application

One of the criticisms of constructivist approaches to career counselling, as discussed by Reid (see Chapter 3 of this book), is their failure to adequately address the "but how do we do it?" question that is frequently asked by students and practitioners. The STF lends itself comfortably to teaching, career counselling and career assessment. Indeed, the STF has been developed as a qualitative assessment instrument (McMahon *et al.*, 2004, 2005a). By presenting as a holistic framework that may be constructed in parts, the STF may be used as a teaching tool in group or classroom settings, or as a constructivist career assessment process with individual clients. The process outlined below, 'Reflecting on my career influences', serves as a template that could be used by counsellor educators or may be adapted for use by counsellors.

Title/topic: Reflecting on my career influences.

Aims/learning objectives
As a classroom or group process, this activity will provide participants with an opportunity to:
• reflect on the influences on their career development;
• examine changes in the nature and degree of influences over time;
• apply the STF in their own lives;
• understand the use of the STF with clients.

Client group with whom you use it
Students in a classroom setting. (The process may also be used with individuals in career counselling. To do so, career counsellors may consider appropriate variations, particularly in the debriefing.)

Work setting recommendations
It is desirable that the setting facilitates work in pairs or small groups. In working through the step-by-step process, it is useful for the facilitator to model the steps on a whiteboard or on a piece of paper.

Recommended time
1 hour minimum

Materials/equipment needed
Paper and pencil. If possible, felt pens or colouring in pencils may be used but these are not essential.

Step-by-step outline of the process or programme

1. Encourage students to reflect on their lives at school leaving age. Ask them to get a picture in their minds of where they lived, the type of person they were, the type of life they lived, and the significant others in their lives.

2. Ask students to draw a circle in the centre of their page and write the word *ME* in the middle of it. In that circle, write the intrinsic things about them that made them unique at that time, for example their personality, particular talents and skills they had.

3. Next ask students to consider the significant others in their lives at that time and to draw those people as small circles intersecting with the existing circle.

4. Now ask students to draw a much larger circle around all that they have previously drawn. Encourage them to reflect on the society in which they lived and significant aspects of that society or environment, for example did they live in a rural setting, were they from a socio-economically disadvantaged background or were they exposed to government policy that enabled or restricted their opportunities. Write these inside the larger circle.

5. Draw another circle around the previous one. Ask students to think about past and present at that time. For example, were they aspiring to a particular lifestyle, were they hoping to emulate the achievements of someone else, was an injury or past illness going to affect their opportunities.

6. Ask students to discuss their Systems of Influence in pairs, bearing in mind the need to keep their partner's information confidential. Remind students to share only that which they feel comfortable sharing and which is appropriate in the setting.

7. After this discussion, students are asked to consider their present career situation. Which influences are the same, which are different, which new ones need to be added. Preferably with a different coloured pencil, revise the System of Influences diagram to reflect their current situation.

8. Again with their partner, discuss what changes have occurred. How have these changes come about? Which changes have been for the better and which have not?

9. Debrief the activity with the whole group. Ideally, debriefing should occur at two levels, the personal experience of the individuals and the level of professional learning. The following questions related to the five dimensions of career counselling suggested by the STF could be used to guide the debriefing.

Questions related to connectedness

Personal: What have you come to understand about your own career story? For example are there any patterns or themes that you were not previously aware of?

Professional: What have you come to understand about career development in general?

Personal: What was it like for you to have the undivided attention of someone listening to your career story?

Professional: What strategies might you adopt in your own practice in order to facilitate a collaborative alliance with your own clients?

Questions related to reflection

Personal: What was it like for you to have a space where you could take time to reflect on your career story?

Professional: What strategies might you adopt in your own practice to create a space for reflection for your clients?

Questions related to meaning-making

Personal: What new or different understandings do you have about yourself as a result of this activity?

Professional: What were the strategies or processes that facilitated the generation of new meaning?

Questions related to learning

Personal: What is the most significant learning for you from this process?

Professional: What have you learned about the role of career counsellor? What have you learned about the role of client?

Questions related to agency

Personal: What steps may you take in your own life as a result of this process?

Professional: How might you use this activity with your clients?

At this point, counsellor educators could move into a discussion/ explanation of the STF of career development.

Conclusion

As discussed throughout this chapter, the STF's utility is becoming increasingly apparent (Patton *et al.*, in press) through its theoretical contribution to career development, and its application to a range of cultural groups and settings, qualitative assessment processes (McMahon *et al.*, 2004, 2005a; McMahon *et al.*, 2005b), career counselling (McMahon, 2005), and multicultural career counselling (Arthur and McMahon, 2005). A further strength of the STF is its capacity to facilitate the teaching of a constructivist approach to career counselling.

References

Amundson, N. E. (1998) *Active Engagement: Enhancing the Career Counseling Process.* Richmond, Canada: Ergon Communications.

Amundson, N. E. (2003) *Active Engagement: Enhancing the Career Counseling Process* (2nd edn). Richmond, Canada: Ergon Communications.

Amundson, N. E., Parker, P. and Arthur, M. B. (2002) 'Merging two worlds: linking occupational and organisational career counselling'. *Australian Journal of Career Development*, 11(3), 26–35.

Arthur, N. and McMahon, M. (2005) 'Multicultural career counseling: theoretical applications of the Systems Theory Framework'. *The Career Development Quarterly*, 53, 208–23.

Cochran, L. (1997) *Career Counseling: A Narrative Approach.* Thousand Oaks, CA: Sage.

Cornford, I., Athanasou, J. and Pithers, R. (1996) 'Career counsellors and the promotion of lifelong learning'. *Australian Journal of Career Development*, 5(2) 43–6.

Holmes, A. (2002) *Lifelong Learning.* Oxford: Capstone Publishing.

Krumboltz, J. D. (1993) 'Integrating career and personal counseling'. [Special section]. *The Career Development Quarterly*, 42, 143–8.

Longworth, N. and Davies, W. K. (1996) *Lifelong Learning: New Vision, New Implications, New Roles for People, Organisations and Communities in the Twenty-first Century.* London: Kogan Page.

Manuele-Adkins, C. (1992) 'Career counseling is personal counseling'. *The Career Development Quarterly*, 40, 313–23.

McMahon, M. (2003) *Life Career Journeys: Reflection, Connection, Meaning, Learning, and Agency.* Paper presented at the Australian Association of Career Counsellors Inc. 12th National Conference. Adelaide, Australia, 15–17 April.

McMahon, M. (2005) 'Career counseling: applying the Systems Theory Framework of career development'. *Journal of Employment Counseling*, 42(1), 29–38.

McMahon, M., Adams, A. and Lim, R. (2002) 'Transition in career counselling: what can solution oriented counselling offer?' *Australian Journal of Career Development*, 11(1), 22–6.

McMahon, M. and Patton, W. (1995) Development of a systems theory of career development. *Australian Journal of Career Development*, 4, 15–20.

McMahon, M. and Patton, W. (2003) 'Influences on career decisions', in M. McMahon and W. Patton (eds), *Ideas for Career Practitioners: Celebrating*

Excellence in Australian Career Practice (pp. 130–2). Brisbane, Australia: Australian Academic Press.

McMahon, M., Patton, W. and Tatham, P. (2003) *Managing Life, Learning and Work in the Twenty-first Century*. Subiaco, WA: Miles Morgan.

McMahon, M., Patton, W. and Watson, M. (2004) 'Creating career stories through reflection: an application of the Systems Theory Framework of career development'. *Australian Journal of Career Development*, 13(3), 13–16.

McMahon, M., Patton, W. and Watson, M. (2005a) *My System of Career Influences (MSCI)*. Camberwell, Australia: ACER.

McMahon, M., Watson, M. and Patton, W. (2005b) 'Qualitative career assessment: developing the My system of career influences reflection activity'. *Journal of Career Assessment* (in press).

Miller, J. H. (2004a) 'Extending the use of constructivist approaches in career guidance and counselling: Solution-focused strategies'. *Australian Journal of Career Development*, 13(1), 50–8.

Miller, J. H. (2004b) 'Building a solution-focused strategy into career counselling'. *New Zealand Journal of Counselling*, 25(1), 18–30.

Monk, G., Winslade, J., Crocket, K. and Epston, D. (1997) *Narrative Therapy in Practice: The Archaeology of Hope*. San Francisco, CA: Jossey-Bass.

Morgan, A. (2000) *What is Narrative Therapy?* Adelaide, Australia: Dulwich Centre Publications.

Osipow, S. H. (1996) 'Does career theory guide practice or does career practice guide theory?' in M. L. Savickas and W. B. Walsh (eds), *Handbook of Career Counseling Theory and Practice* (pp. 403–10). Palo Alto, CA: Davies-Black.

Patton, W. and McMahon, M. (1997) *Career Development in Practice: A Systems Theory Perspective*. Sydney: New Hobsons Press.

Patton, W. and McMahon, M. (1999) *Career Development and Systems Theory: A New Relationship*. Pacific Grove, CA: Brooks/Cole.

Patton, W. and McMahon, M. (in press) 'Connecting theory and practice: the Systems Theory Framework of career development'. *International Journal for the Advancement of Counselling*.

Patton, W., McMahon, M. and Watson, M. (in press) 'Career development and systems theory: enhancing our understanding of career', in G. Stead and M. Watson (eds). *Career Psychology in the South African Context* (2nd edn). Pretoria, South Africa: Van Schaik.

Peavy, R. V. (1992) 'A constructivist model of training for career counselors'. *Journal of Career Development*, 18, 215–29.

Peavy, R. V. (1998) *Sociodynamic Counselling A Constructivist Perspective*. Victoria, Canada: Trafford.

Peavy, R. V. (2000) 'The SocioDynamic perspective and the practice of counselling'. *Proceedings of International Career Conference, 2000, Perth, Western Australia, 2–5 April*.

Peavy. R. V. (2004) *SocioDynamic Counselling: A Practical Approach to Meaning Making*. Chagrin Falls, OH: Taos Institute Publications.

Rogers, C. R. (1951) *Client-centered Therapy*. Boston, MA: Houghton-Mifflin.

Savickas, M. L. (1993) 'Career counseling in the postmodern era'. *Journal of Cognitive Psychotherapy: An International Quarterly*, 7, 205–15.

Schlossberg, N. K., Lynch, A. Q. and Chickering, A. W. (1989) *Improving Higher Education Environments for Adults*. San Francisco, CA: Jossey-Bass.

Subich, L. M. (1993) 'How personal is career?' [Special section]. *The Career Development Quarterly*, 42, 129–31.

Super, D. E. (1990) 'A life-span, life-space approach to career development', in D. Brown and L. Brooks (eds), *Career Choice and Development* (2nd edn, pp. 197–261). San Francisco, CA: Jossey-Bass.

Townsend, K. C. and McWhirter, B. T. (2005) 'Connectedness: a review of the literature with implications for counseling, assessment, and research'. *Journal of Counseling and Development*, 83, 191–201.

United Nations Educational Scientific and Cultural Organisation (2002) *Handbook on Career Counselling*. Paris: UNESCO.

Young, R. A. and Valach, L. (1996) 'Interpretation and action in career counseling', in M. L. Savickas and W. B. Walsh (eds), *Handbook of Career Counseling Theory and Practice* (pp. 361–76). Palo Alto, CA: Davies-Black.

Young, R. A. and Valach, L. (2004) 'The construction of career through goal-directed action'. *Journal of Vocational Behavior*, 64, 409–514.

Chapter 9

Career narratives

Elizabeth M. Grant and Joseph A. Johnston

"Tell me a story" may qualify as one of the first and most often repeated lines we recall from childhood. Our fascination with "once upon a time" begins early in life. Campbell, Moyers and Flowers in the *The Power of Myth* (1991), point to how creation stories – taught in all religious traditions – are ones that captivate us early in our upbringing. We vary the topics, weave stories into our traditions and amend them to fit new situations. We read biographies and novels with a continued fascination and reframe our own stories as we raise our own children. Life can clearly be seen as simply a story or narrative; one told and lived with serious intent, developed early and continually amended to fit our sense of who we were, who we are and who we want to be. One's story or narrative can be shown to have importance that cannot be minimised. We are coached to tell our own story. It may be done independently; with parents, spouses, friends or in counselling or therapy. It is an on-going process, never really to be completed and surely never perfected.

The last century was dominated by a constant search for objective approaches to explain career ventures (e.g., through the work of Super, Holland, and others). Interest, aptitude, values and personality measures promoted a "test and tell" mentality, with all other approaches and techniques receiving only passing attention. There now emerges renewed interest and respect for attending to subjective and phenomenological input or explanations for career behaviour. Stories or narratives are to be studied and utilised with seriousness, as they may provide more explanation for the "how" and "why" of one's actions than can any objective explanation. When incorporated with objective material such as interest, aptitude and personality measures, subjective means can represent a much richer and accurate method of understanding how people actually engage in career planning. Such an approach also provides a whole new way of defining the role of the career counsellor.

This chapter focuses on the use of the narrative approach in career counselling. It aims to provide counsellors and counsellor educators with a theoretical basis for the topic, with a particular focus on explaining how the career narrative can be put into practice. Ideas, methods and techniques for implementing the narrative in practice and in counselling training programmes are included, as well as resources to use with clients and counsellors in training. The reader will gain an understanding of this important theoretically derived approach and will be able to apply it through interventions introduced at the end of the chapter.

Narratives defined

"Tell me a little about yourself", the classic line in career counselling, is not just a good opener but, if used appropriately, it is the only way to begin. When clients are left on their own, it is mostly what they can say about themselves subjectively that determines what they become. Providing objectivity to that is important; however, it is a helpful, but not necessary, part of the story. "Counselling may accomplish more quickly what time will eventually decode" (Campbell and Ungar, 2004, p. 29). If we believe that now is a time for a paradigm shift in the way we see people making their career plans, and there is evidence that such a shift is happening (Brott, 2001; Savickas, 1993, 1995), then we can almost begin anew designing appropriate interventions.

The last decade has foreshadowed this shift in focus (Brott, 2001; Christensen and Johnston, 2003; McLeod, 1996; Savickas, 1993, 1995). We might now give as much attention to "narrative" truth as, in the past century, we gave to establishing "historical" truth. Only now may we begin to establish the real importance of retelling and rehearsing stories and appreciating just how much that means to clients. It can introduce a whole new array of techniques for all of us. To make clear our interpretation of narratives, we borrow from the ideas of Antaki (1988) who describes narratives as the stories people construct to clarify, explain and understand elements of their lives. We can cite a definition that is more specific, and for our purposes, more to the point. A career narrative is basically a story about a career. Christensen and Johnston (2002) offer: "It is a story that connects the protagonist's (i.e., the client's) past to the present in the sense that it conveys how the protagonist came to be what he or she is presently" (p. 151).

Key ideas

In his article, "The emerging narrative approach to counselling and psychotherapy", McLeod (1996) gives us a sense of the common themes and concepts that need to be considered both in our theory and practice with narratives. Included in his article are: the notion of re-authoring; working with the life story; narrative truth vs. historical truth; developing a metanarrative; comparing different stories; deconstructing the meaning in stories; identifying themes; therapist as audience, co-constructor and editor;

drawing on cultural resources; and writing as a therapeutic act. A comment on each of these helps provide a comprehensive overview to the topic of career narratives.

Re-authoring

There is evidence that in counselling, as well as in almost any conversation, we recognise we are telling our story. At least, that is a way of framing what we say. "Let me tell you my story – what has happened…". Or, the counsellor says, "Tell me your story – your concern, your situation – and I'll try to respond in a helpful way." There may be reason to amend or affirm the story, and telling it will establish the appropriate response "path". Additionally, telling the story is often therapeutic in and of itself, resulting in change for the author. In many instances, the story is changed or needs to be changed because it is not a story the client wants to "own". As the counsellor makes input, the story is re-authored – it is still the client's story, but it is now something different from the original story. It might be defined as a re-authored story, and counsellors play an integral role in assisting in the re-authoring of clients' stories, as "good counselling helps clients develop the skills necessary to continually grow in and out of stories" (Campbell and Ungar, 2004, p. 37).

Working with the life story

A constructivist approach positions the "life story" as the central focus of counselling. Telling the story, in whatever manner, is the essence of counselling and thus the analysis of stories, however told, for whatever purposes, in whatever ways, becomes the essential focus of our work. Other professionals, for example, in medicine (Coles, 1989), history and philosophy, have made this the emphasis in what they teach prospective doctors and college students, respectively.

Narrative truth versus historical truth

We tend to accept what is said as truth, knowing full well that it is only one's perception of events, often distorted by circumstances. In law or medicine, one might feel more of a need to establish historical truth; in counselling, what is perceived to be the truth is what we accept as important. As previously discussed, the truth may change as the story is told and retold, but what, how or why it is perceived a particular way is the focus, not establishing objective truth. Holland, in the most recent edition of his book *Making Vocational Choices* (1997), writes about a theory of career intervention and change suggesting that everyone has a personal career theory. It may be "valid, complex and comprehensive"; it may not be. We listen and assess for this "personal theory" upon which one acts. No theory can incorporate all of the nuances or idiosyncrasies of objective thinking, and hence the narrative provides a greater context for action than the historical truth.

Developing a "metanarrative"

If we assume that clients seek help in changing their stories, then we must turn to our theories and successful practices for support and evidence of ways to rewrite or reframe stories. For example, we may impose Holland's (1997) theory on a story where one talks of himself as mismatched for his job or in a field where he doesn't find support for his interests, values or skills. Holland gives us a theory to help this client rethink or rewrite his story. We bring our theories to bear on stories and conscientiously help one rework what they say about themselves. In Alcoholics Anonymous, for example, one begins with a standard one liner, "I'm ..., and I'm an alcoholic." Thus begins a story that is to be rewritten, perhaps with help and practice from those in the group.

Comparing different stories

McLeod (1996) alludes to two types of stories that serve as a framework for most stories: "problem" stories and "solution" stories. We usually hear the former and look for the latter in counselling sessions. Clients come looking for solutions and often we are engaged in trying to move the client, as they become ready, towards telling "solution" stories. Again, Alcoholics Anonymous is a good example: disclosure of the problem is the first step towards finding a solution.

Deconstructing the meaning in stories

If we place the emphasis on telling stories, we then should make proper use of them in counselling. Deconstructing the story becomes the focus and we need to consider the skills that make this process most productive. For example, narrative skill derives from reading stories and hearing how others interpret them; from writing case notes; from staffing cases; and from reading journal articles and books. It takes practice with reading narratives before one becomes effective at using them in counselling.

Identifying themes across stories

Identifying the "big picture", plot or subplots in narratives is a skill developed through practice. Within McLeod's (1996) framework of problem and solution stories are literally hundreds of themes, that is, hundreds of problems and hundreds of solutions. A good way to appreciate one's ability to generate and make use of themes is to administer an occupational card sort (Gysbers *et al.*, 2003) and listen for the themes that emerge as clients tell you why and why not they would or would not pursue a particular career. Often their ability and insight is limited, but with some prodding or suggestion from the counsellor, they come to see and make use of what was not immediately conscious in their story.

Therapist as audience

As counsellors, we are providing clients with an audience – not just our singular self as audience member, but a vicarious collective audience consisting of the host of clients who came before with similar stories. Through our training and experience, we have learned to be good listeners. In that sense, we comprise a non-judgemental audience that listens and provides feedback from the many relationships in which we have previously engaged. We are a unique and appreciative audience that helps clients reconstruct their stories. However, listening to stories is more than establishing good rapport; our role as audience member helps clients retell their stories, which leads to meaningful and significant change. The audience a client chooses to tell her story to may determine the success of enacting that story. "It is important that individuals place themselves among others who will participate with them in authoring a new story while challenging those who maintain old and limiting stories" (Campbell and Ungar, 2004, p. 36). The counsellor may be the first audience member who collaboratively supports the client in imagining and acting upon new stories.

Drawing on cultural resources

We are often asked to help clients to construct or amend their stories to fit new life situations. Clients making transitions to new situations – jobs, relationships or moves to different parts of the country and into different cultural arrangements – all are examples of venues in which we are able to provide resources not as available to clients as they are to us. Career counselling can serve as a process in which clients are taught skills to manage their multiple life roles and stories during such transitions (Campbell and Ungar, 2004).

Writing as a therapeutic act

The act of writing out one's story is a powerful experience. For some, it brings clarity and insight to their story as talking does for others. Seeing one's life in black and white can be an eye-opening experience, as people make connections previously unavailable. It provides a means of understanding one's story in a new, fresh way, and it may be that to attain real insight, one needs to practise writing the story. We don't expect the first draft to be the final draft, and we should expect that each draft will be an improvement over the former one. Brown and Ryan Krane (2000) cite writing as one of the five kinds of career interventions that are positively correlated with successful outcomes. While counselling is a primarily oral process, it can be made more productive and focused for some clients by the reflection that comes from writing the story. The use of the diary, the log or the journal is therapeutic for some, with or without the adjunct of counselling.

Suggested actions

We should recognise how little attention is actually given to training counsellors to make use of narratives in counselling. The therapeutic interview, which is in fact a form of the narrative, is crucial in counselling. However, the analysis and creative use of the interview as a "script" to be examined and rewritten has been somewhat limited. Yes, it is used to facilitate exploration and understanding before defining goals and actions, but mostly as a means to help reach an understanding of the objective part of the story, not to assess and refine the subjective elements of the story. We need to examine more effective ways in which we can bring the two together, to identify practices that are confirmed as being helpful to our clients.

The last part of this chapter addresses such practices; they are practices that have been found to be particularly useful, are associated with successful outcomes, and pair naturally with the narrative approach. Many are described in Brown and Ryan Krane (2000) and are techniques that have the potential to promote seeing both the objective and the subjective sides of the story. These techniques include written exercises, individual attention through support building in individual counselling, information on the world of work and vicarious experiences. We describe techniques that address each of these. These approaches are designed to give us the "rest of the story".

Practical applications

Client population

Because stories are a primary way in which we make meaning of our experiences, the universal quality of the career narrative is well suited to virtually all client populations. The subjective nature of the narrative allows the storyteller to craft a story that is individually tailored to his or her unique experience. Therefore, the narrative is especially appropriate in working with clients from traditionally oppressed groups, such as women and racial and ethnic minorities, as the narrative literally "gives voice" to individuals in groups that have been silenced throughout history (Mair, 1988; McLeod, 1996). Indeed, "narrative therapy provides opportunities to look critically at how stories are privileged and by whom" (Campbell and Ungar, 2004, p. 22). In our multicultural society, the narrative plays an integral role in providing career counselling to diverse client populations, a process which can be viewed as helping people to remove obstacles that then allow them to "speak for themselves" through their narrative (Savickas, 1993).

Work settings

The authors have implemented the narrative in a university career centre providing service to college students as well as training for career counsellors. However, most of what is described below would be equally applicable in other settings.

College students

Writing narratives

The first of five career interventions identified by Brown and Ryan Krane that are positively correlated with successful career outcomes is written exercises. Career narratives can be integrated into the curriculum of career development courses in the form of a writing assignment, providing a prompt for students to tell their career story (see Appendix 9.1). "Writing (and to some extent talking) about an event forces structure onto thoughts and feelings that previously had not been clearly organised. Language provides an opportunity to develop new insights and coping strategies" (Baumeister and Vohs, 2002, p. 615). Indeed, it is through such exercises that clients become aware of the multiple influences that have shaped their career stories, as well as their personal and environmental resources and barriers (Campbell and Ungar, 2004). Upon writing their narrative, it is common for students to respond, "I had never put my story together in that way before". Previously silenced skills, abilities and feelings often emerge, and clients immediately begin viewing themselves in new, more hopeful ways. "Traditional approaches gather information, whereas narrative therapy generates a different experience" (Campbell and Ungar, 2004, p. 35).

In the career placement arena, résumé writing provides an additional written exercise in which experiences are constructed, deconstructed and reconstructed, as students tailor their story to specific employers, positions or professions. Résumés, then, can be viewed not only as a necessary document towards job acquisition, but also as a means to elaborate one's career narrative. This can be particularly salient for liberal arts students, who may not immediately see the connection between their academic and co-curricular experiences, and the world of work. Written exercises provide an opening space for storytelling, as résumé writing becomes a transcendent opportunity to develop one's story. Clients who are struggling to make a career choice will find writing the narrative, in whatever form, a particularly helpful exercise, as "connecting today's indecision to yesterday's experiences and tomorrow's possibilities makes meaning, allows comprehension, and creates new possibilities" (Savickas, 1995, p. 366). Conversely, "a client who is caught in the 'death grip' of certainty that there is only one preferred occupation can be encouraged to see his or her choice as embedded inside a much larger and more diverse narrative" (Campbell and Ungar, 2004, p. 29).

Reading narratives

Just as writing one's narrative can be a powerfully facilitative experience, so can reading others' life-career stories. The importance of understanding not only one's own narrative but also the stories of others in the forms of biographies, literature and fiction, is burgeoning in the profession (Hartzell, 2004). Listening to others' stories helps us to see our story in relation to another's, providing new perspectives. Reading collections of career stories, such as Po Bronson's (2002) *What Should I Do With My Life?*, helps clients feel that they are not alone in their struggles. Reading "assignments" can serve as a creative and effective intervention in helping clients to see their current issues and dilemmas in new ways, as well as generating solutions that may not have been previously considered. Asking clients what they are currently reading on their own may also provide clues as to the major questions that the client is currently struggling to answer through another's story. A client of the first author of this chapter recently noted that she was reading nothing but coming-of-age novels! Additionally, reflecting upon literary heroes and heroines from childhood can provide a rich source of information, as they highlight life themes and aspirations that still resonate today (Savickas, 1995, 2004).

After writing one's own narrative (see Appendix 9.1), the narrative can then be read and utilised in a variety of settings and situations. In a classroom or training setting, the author can read the narrative to the group, wherein the group acts as a collaborative co-author. The group listens for gaps in the story, and as these reactions are shared with the author, the story begins to take on an amended form. The group can also be asked to listen for themes that emerge while the story is being told. From the diverse voices of the group will appear themes that perhaps the author had not originally considered or heard. "Any story about a preferred future may be realised by travelling multiple paths. The postindustrial world and individual identity stories are far too indeterminate to have people lock into one particular way of performing their narrative" (Campbell and Ungar, 2004, p. 31). Group participation in the reading of the narrative expands the author's vocabulary, providing a new lexicon from which to continue the construction of the narrative. The second author of this chapter utilised the narrative in a group setting with counsellors-in-training as a professional development exercise.

Each student was asked to write his or her narrative, which were then collated and disseminated to the group. After the narratives were read, a discussion ensued which focused on the clarity of the narratives, as well as which parts of the narrative struck students the most.

Individual counselling

The narrative forms the basis of Savickas' (1993, 1995) model of career counselling, and Cochran (1997) conceives the career counselling process as bridging the gap between "what is" and "what ought to be". Therefore, the narrative forms the "backbone" of individual client sessions, helping clients to construct more meaningful and complete life stories. The counsellor can facilitate the storytelling process by using techniques such as challenging and interpretation (McLeod, 1996), accurate empathy, metaphor, fantasy, evocative language (Cochran, 1997; McLeod, 1996), and asking questions that highlight defining moments and important people in the client's story (Brott, 2001).

"Counselling, like any new experience, exposes the individual to alternate social constructions of reality through clinical conversation" (Campbell and Ungar, 2004, p. 21). It is through the counselling process that the client's story can be refined to help them arrive at their ideal future goal. Once the client has written their story (see Appendix 9.1), it can be revisited throughout counselling as the story develops. As previously stated, unrealised skills, abilities and feelings often emerge through the writing of the narrative. However, the client is often left wondering how to utilise this newfound information in working towards their goals. Campbell and Ungar (2004, p. 32) suggest posing the following questions to the client: "What internal and external resources do you have that will help you move towards your preferred future?" And, "What skills and experiences do you have that would move you as quickly as possible towards your preferred future?" These questions help the client begin linking their past, present and future together in meaningful ways.

The written narrative can also serve as a "canon" from which clients continually draw in counselling. "Counsellors play a crucial role helping clients to grow into roles in their new stories, frequently by revisiting similar past experiences that have been muted in clients' lives" (Campbell and Ungar, 2004, p. 36). The written narrative provides a "starting point" in counselling, from which past experiences and future possibilities can be explored. These experiences will be revisited time and again through the counselling interview, and new experiences will emerge from the periphery, which will be added to the canon and eventually morph into a new narrative. The first author frequently revisits the narrative when assisting students in creating their résumé. Often times, their résumé does not "match" their written narrative. Experiences that were highlighted as pivotal in the narrative are sometimes "muted" or nonexistent on the résumé. Through talking about this gap, both documents begin to change simultaneously.

Guided imagery through "fantasy trips" (Skovholt *et al.*, 1989), where counsellors assist clients in imagining what their life might be like in one, five, or 10 years, provide counsellors with excellent information regarding a client's storytelling "abilities". In addition, it helps clients to create a more cohesive story by focusing on such questions as: What did you do at work? With whom did you spend time with at work? What did you like best about your job? (Heppner *et al.*, 1994)? Counsellors are able to then see and help bridge the important gaps between the client's actual and imagined selves.

Counsellor educators

In adopting the narrative approach, the counsellor is asked to play the role of director, co-constructor, facilitator, educator and co-creator. However, perhaps the most important role the counsellor can learn is that of storyteller. While teaching clients to tell their stories is important, counsellors should be well rehearsed in telling their own stories. "Without a passion for telling, for telling it like it is for us, we cannot come to know the telling of others, or know from our own engagement what is involved in telling itself" (Mair, 1988, pp. 130–1). Career counselling training programmes should provide opportunities for counsellors-in-training to continuously practise and revise their narratives, in an effort to be more effective collaborators with their clients. Other disciplines have successfully espoused this approach, as many medical schools now require coursework in narrative medicine so that doctors can learn to listen more effectively to the stories that their patients are telling (Smith, 2003). Additionally, the continual telling of the narrative is important to students' professional development, as elements of the story are bound to change, while others remain constant during training. By having an awareness of one's narrative, students can gain a sense of continuity and change in their lives, providing an ongoing assessment of their growth.

Conclusion

While foundational coursework on career counselling theory and practice is vital to the future career counsellor's success, training programmes should consider integrating the narrative into the curriculum through both experiential and theoretical means. At the University of Missouri, career counselling students are encouraged to write and rehearse their personal narratives from the first day of classes. In an effort to train not only effective listeners but also effective storytellers, exposure to narrative theory and the elements of successful storytelling, such as those elucidated by McLeod (1996), ensure that students will be able to listen more adeptly to the stories that their clients tell.

References

Antaki, C. (1988) *Analysing Everyday Explanation: A Casebook of Methods*. London: Sage.

Baumeister, R. F. and Vohs, K. D. (2002) 'The pursuit of meaningfulness in life', in C. R. Snyder and S. J. Lopez (eds), *Handbook of Positive Psychology* (pp. 608–18). Oxford: Oxford University Press.

Bronson, P. (2002) *What Should I Do With My life?: The True Story of People Who Answered the Ultimate Question*. New York: Random House.

Brott, P. E. (2001) 'The storied approach: a postmodern perspective for career counseling'. *The Career Development Quarterly*, 49(4), 304–13.

Brown, S. D. and Ryan Krane, N. E. (2000) 'Four (or five) sessions and a cloud of dust: old assumptions and new observations about career counseling', in S. D. Brown and R. W. Lent (eds), *Handbook of Counseling Psychology* (3rd edn, pp. 740–66). New York: Wiley.

Campbell, C. and Ungar, M. (2004) 'Constructing a life that works: Part 1, an approach to practice'. *The Career Development Quarterly*, 53(1), 16–27.

Campbell, C. and Ungar, M. (2004) 'Constructing a life that works: Part 2, an approach to practice'. *The Career Development Quarterly*, 53(1), 28–40.

Campbell, J. (with Moyers, B.) and Flowers, B. S. (ed.) (1991) *The Power of Myth*. New York: Anchor.

Christensen, T. K. and Johnston, J. A. (2003) 'Incorporating the narrative in career planning'. *Journal of Career Development*, 29(3), 149–60.

Cochran, L. (1997) *Career Counseling: A Narrative Approach*. Thousand Oaks, CA: Sage.

Coles, R. (1989) *The Call of Stories: Teaching and the Moral Imagination*. Boston, MA: Houghton Mifflin.

Gysbers, N. C., Heppner, M. J. and Johnston, J. A. (2003) *Career Counseling: Process, Issues, and Techniques* (2nd edn). Boston, MA: Allyn and Bacon.

Hartzell, N. K. (2004, July) *Moving Beyond One's Story: Using Fiction and Non-fiction to Support Career Development*. Paper presented at the meeting of the National Career Development Association, San Francisco, CA.

Heppner, M. J., O'Brien, K. M., Hinkelman, J. M. and Humphrey, C. F. (1994) 'Shifting the paradigm: the use of creativity in career counseling'. *Journal of Career Development*, 21(2), 77–86.

Holland, J. L. (1997) *Making Vocational Choices: A Theory of Vocational Personalities and Work Environments*. Lutz, FL: Psychological Assessment Resources, Inc.

Mair, M. (1988) 'Psychology as storytelling'. *International Journal of Personal Construct Psychology*, 1, 125–37.

McLeod, J. (1996) 'The emerging narrative approach to counselling and psychotherapy'. *British Journal of Guidance and Counselling*, 24(2), 173–84.

Savickas, M. L. (1993) 'Career counseling in the postmodern era'. *Journal of Cognitive Psychotherapy: An International Quarterly*, 7(3), 205–15.

Savickas, M. L. (1995) 'Constructivist counseling for career indecision'. *The Career Development Quarterly*, 43(4), 363–73.

Savickas, M. L. (2004, July) *Meaning and Mattering in Career Construction: The Case of Elaine*. Paper presented at the meeting of the National Career Development Association, San Francisco, CA.

Skovholt, T. M., Morgan, J. I. and Negron-Cunningham, H. (1989) 'Mental imagery in career counseling and life planning: a review of research and intervention methods.' *Journal of Counseling and Development*, 67, 287–92.

Smith, D. (2003, October 11) 'Diagnosis goes low tech'. *The New York Times*, p. B9.

Appendix 9.1

Career narrative

Developed by Elizabeth Grant for use in the University of Missouri – Columbia, *College to Career Transitions*, a career development course for college juniors and seniors.

Most of you have probably written a career biography of some sort. It may have included information about you in a rather factual, chronological manner (I went to XYZ high school, I came to the University of Missouri to major in XYZ ...). However, chances are that most of you haven't written a *career narrative*. So, what's the difference, and why is it important?

Each of us has a special and unique life (hi)story. Part of this history can be thought of as facts: the positions we have held, our proven successes, skills, abilities, and goals. Each of us makes sense of these objective "facts" in different ways. In order to make meaning of these experiences, we must be able to understand the subjective aspects of our life-work. If the objective elements are thought of as "fact," then we can think of the subjective aspects as "opinion." *Why* was I drawn to my major? *How* did I get from "point A" to "point B?" By combining both the objective and subjective elements of your experiences, you construct a *career narrative*, which answers not only the "what" of your life (as a biography does), but also the "why" and the "how." This approach will give you access to some valuable information about yourself that you might not yet be aware of.

A career biography often reads like a résumé, whereas a career narrative reads like a story. *Your story*. The true richness in a story lies in the details. Because it is a story, your narrative will never be told the same way twice. You will alter your story for the needs of your audience. For the purposes of this class, creating a career narrative is important for two primary reasons:

1. *It will get you thinking critically and deeply about your experiences.* Since you must speak to not only the "facts" of your life, but how you make sense of those facts, you will be asked to reflect upon your experiences and ask yourself the "why" and "how" questions. As we continue with this course, you will be invited to talk about yourself and your experiences a great deal. This is the first exercise in learning more about yourself, as well as examining your experiences, beliefs, values, formative experiences, and guiding principles. The more confidently and specifically you can speak about yourself, in any arena, the better.

2. *Being able to "tell your story" will make you a stronger candidate, no matter what your post-graduation plans are.*

    Knowing your story is not only an important tool for growth, but a way in which to make yourself a better candidate for graduate school or the job market. You will be asked time and again to "tell me about yourself." There will be many other candidates who have similar experiences as you, but no one will have made sense of that experience in the same way. Having a career narrative highlights what is *uniquely you*. In addition, employers and graduate schools are looking for candidates who have thought about what they're doing, and why. If you can tell a story, rich in *detail* and *specificity*, that explains what has led you down your path, you will be ahead of the game! One of the most common missteps of candidates is not taking the time to learn about themselves. Before you can write a résumé or search for a job, you must know yourself.

    It is important to bear in mind that there is no one "right way" to do this assignment. You are simply telling a story. Some of you may want to focus on your college experience. Others may want to begin their story further back. *The only real requirement for this assignment is that you speak not only about what you've done, but that you also include some analysis/synthesis of your experiences, and that it be 3–5 pages in length.* You are not telling your life story, only a part of it. Also, remember that it will take some time to construct a meaningful narrative, so don't wait until the last minute to complete this assignment. Chances are you've never been asked to do something like this, and narratives are something that takes practice. Your narrative is a work-in-progress, continuing to evolve over time.

Here are some questions to help guide you as your write your story:

- What "pivotal points" or "defining moments" have guided your path?
- What is driving the "plot" of your life?
- Look for continuity in your story. What themes consistently play themselves out?
- How did you get from the beginning of your story to where you're at now? How will you continue your "plot line" into the future?
- What "script" did you receive from your family or other important people in your life regarding your career path?
- What's your personal philosophy? How have your experiences shaped that philosophy?
- What does the future look like? What would the title of the next "chapter" of your life be (aside from the obvious like "After College")?

Adapted from information in: Cochran, L. (1997). *Career Counseling: A Narrative Approach.* Thousand Oaks, CA: Sage.

Chapter 10

Using a solution-building approach in career counselling

Judi Miller

In this chapter, I describe the key principles of solution-focused counselling, and provide practical examples of its application to career counselling, that is solution-building career counselling. I will also discuss challenges for career counsellors who adopt this way of working with clients.

What is solution-focused counselling?

Solution-focused therapy was pioneered in the 1980s by the psychologist Steve de Shazer, counsellor Insoo Kim Berg and their colleagues at the Milwaukee Brief Family Therapy Center. Steve de Shazer's early writings were, apparently, influenced by hypnotherapist Milton Erickson's approach to psychotherapy (de Jong and Berg, 2002). Most accounts, however, indicate that the greatest influence on the development of a solution-focused way of working was the discovery made by the Milwaukee team when they observed counselling sessions and reflected upon what was most helpful to clients (de Jong and Berg, 2002). They noticed that even clients who presented with what they described as multiple problems could describe times when the problem was either less severe or absent. Further, when clients were encouraged to notice things that they were already doing during these times, they went on to make positive changes. From these discoveries, the Milwaukee team began to develop, and critically analyse, the use of techniques that focused on client change, client competence and client goals that were based on principles of collaboration and social construction.

A number of counsellors, researchers, coaches and teachers have welcomed the solution-focused approach and adopted the principles underlying this way of counselling. They have taken notice of what works best for their clients and adapted techniques in order to be most helpful to each of their clients. Since they are guided by the assumption that all clients seek positive change, the main focus in their work is to help clients clarify and express what it is they want, and discover and expand on what they are already doing to reach their objectives. Adaptations have included solution-focused work that incorporates different interpretations based on hypnosis (Dolan, 2000), narrative therapy (O'Hanlon and Beadle, 1996), neuro-linguistic programming (Te Ruru, 1998), motivational interviewing (Lewis and Osborn, 2004), systems theory (McMahon and Patton, 2000; Miller 2004a), and person-centred therapy (O'Connell, 1998). All of these approaches stand in opposition to therapies influenced by the medical model where the therapist is regarded as the expert who diagnoses problems and prescribes treatments.

In what ways is solution-focused counselling constructivist?

There are two main premises underlying constructivist approaches. The first is that individuals create their own reality based on their understanding of, and participation in, their own experiences (Brown and Brooks, 1996). The second premise is that the client's whole environment, and the interactions within it, influence behaviour. The solution-focused approach encompasses both premises. Solution-focused counselling is constructivist in that counsellors encourage clients to describe, reflect upon, make meaning about and interpret things that are important to them. Counsellors also invite clients to construct personally meaningful goals based on positive images of their own competence, achievements, resources, strengths and successes. The collaborative nature of the approach frees the counsellor from taking the burden of responsibility for the client's counselling outcomes and enhances the client's sense of self-helpfulness.

Since meanings are constructed and re-affirmed in social interactions (Blumer, 1969), a solution-building career counsellor recognises that every interaction has the potential to influence change. The counsellor therefore relies on therapeutic conversations to help the client shape and determine what kind of life the client wants, what the client is already good at, where desired change is already occurring and what will encourage further change (de Jong and Berg, 2002). The most important aspect of these conversations is that they are led by the "reality" of the client and the recognition that this reality is influenced not only by the interaction between the client and counsellor but also by the interactions clients have with themselves (see Blumer, 1969). Such conversations therefore involve the whole client (family, culture, society and relationships) and are grounded in the day-to-day activities and experiences of the client. The foundation of the solution-building model is the counsellor's unwavering confidence in the client's ability to make (construct) positive changes in his or her life by accessing and using inner resources and strengths (Miller, 1998). Important then, is the counsellor's ability to demonstrate his or her belief in, and hope for, the client's ability to change.

Principles of solution-focused counselling applied to solution-building career counselling

Gale Miller (1998) regarded solution-focused brief therapy as radically new because it is based on different assumptions about social reality, new practical concerns about the therapeutic process and new strategies for helping clients to change their lives. These same comments can be made about solution-building career counselling.

Guiding principles

- Change is inevitable and conversations are transformative.
- Clients have within themselves the capacity to consider new or different meanings, construct solution-focused realities and generate intrinsic motivation to change.
- When clients experience themselves as competent, they are more able to make positive changes (Durrant, 1995).
- When clients are able to express what they want, they can discover and expand on things they are already doing to get there.
- Rather than find a solution that fits the problem, counsellors need to help clients find the solution that fits them (O'Connell, 1998).
- If what clients are already doing is working, counsellors encourage them to keep doing that.
- If what clients are doing is not working, counsellors encourage them to do something different.

An essential element of solution-focused counselling is the paradigmatic shift in thinking, by client and counsellor, away from problems (what is going wrong) and toward possibilities and hope (what is wanted) (Friedman and Fanger, 1991). In keeping with this view, solution-building career counsellors consider that it is easier to help clients construct positive achievable goals and solutions than to dissolve concerns. Since many career clients expect counselling to involve talking about their interests, hopes and goals, it is relatively easy to elicit examples of client strengths and competences so that the counsellor and the client can gradually build an image of the client's career and preferred future. Thus, in solution-building career counselling, less time is spent on exploring the developmental career history of the client, or making interpretive statements, and more is spent on exploring a positive career goal and extending those times when progress toward achieving the career goal was made. The distinctive feature of solution-building career counselling is to help clients build their own life plans rather than fitting their characteristics and traits into a career profile.

Similar to other constructivist approaches, the solution-focused approach acknowledges the power of language to influence interactions, meanings and actions. Solution-building career counsellors therefore adopt a stance of curiosity, and ask many positively focused questions to demonstrate their respect for the client's resourcefulness and competence to succeed. Such questions enable the client to make sense of their current situation, recognise possible choices and envisage a preferred future (goal) through their answers to themselves. While questions help clients articulate their meaningful experiences, it behoves a solution-building career counsellor to listen carefully to responses for key phrases which, when amplified, help clients experience their own solution-building resources.

Using solution-building career counselling techniques

Overview of process

In solution-building career counselling, the counsellor uses many of the skills that are basic to all counselling but uses each with a different focus. These include: selective listening (for client responses that show optimism, demonstrate client self-determination, competence, self efficacy), speaking (with an emphasis on reinforcing evidence of client competence and on conveying hopefulness that the client will succeed), questioning (with an emphasis on meaning-making and solution-seeking) and respecting silence (providing time for the client to make sense of what is being created). Within a solution-building career counselling session, therefore, counsellors aim to help clients:

- clarify their reason for coming to counselling in terms of the preferred future that they want (goal setting questions);
- identify and amplify aspects of their lives that are working well (exception questions);
- re-discover important aspects of their context including resources, successes and strengths (self-helpfulness questions);
- clarify and envisage how life would be different if the problem were suddenly solved (miracle questions); and
- assess progress towards their goals (scaling questions).

Finally, the solution-building career counsellor can assist clients to connect past competencies with future goals by constructing a feedback message that will encourage success and self-helpfulness.

Solution-building questions

When practitioners first look at techniques used by solution-focused counsellors they are often deceived into thinking that mastery will only require learning a list of questions. Indeed, solution-focused counsellors do appear to ask a great number of questions. These are, however, questions with a particular focus; a focus to change the counselling interaction from being problem-saturated to being solution-oriented. Solution-building counsellors therefore adopt a stance of "not knowing" (Anderson and Goolishian, 1991) to enable clients to learn more about themselves and to create their own meaningful goals and solutions. Examples of questions include those that begin with; "I'm curious about ..." or "I'm just wondering how you managed that?" Second, since counsellors recognise that each interaction influences the client's sense of reality, they ask questions that anticipate client resourcefulness and competence to encourage client self-competence and self-helpfulness. Examples of such questions include "how did you realise that?" or "what do you know about yourself that will help you decide that?" Third, questions are often posed to help clients become aware of new distinctions (exceptions to their stuckness or their single view of their problem). Solution-building career counsellors formulate these questions because they know that solutions emerge from client recognition of even the smallest experiences of difference. Examples of such questions include "so is that new for you?" or "and how is that different?"

While questions that anticipate positive responses are important to solution-building career counsellors, to be effective, career counsellors need to be confident that they can also work with their clients' responses. The questions are part of the interaction, but paramount is the ability of the counsellor to hear or see within the client's responses details of exceptions, resources, strengths and successes. When these are amplified for the client, both counsellor and client can co-construct possible steps towards achieving client-defined goals.

Using prompts

When career counsellors are learning solution-building ways of working, it helps to use some process and language prompts as a guide. Such prompts include:

1 Clarify the problem by asking about goals (see scales later in this chapter).
2 Build up positive exceptions that are alternatives to the problem by asking questions that include "instead" or "suppose".
3 Encourage hope by asking questions about what, where, who and how NOT why? Also presuppose success by asking "when" NOT "if".
4 Encourage self-helpfulness by asking questions that include "how will you know?".
5 Encourage planfulness by constructing meaningful homework based on client-expressed goals, successes and resources.

Clarifying client-defined goals

Solution-building career counsellors often commence a counselling session with a question that helps the client articulate their goal. Such questions include "What would you like to get out of this counselling session?" or, to encourage a sense of client competence "what will tell you that coming here today was a good idea?". If a client responds to such questions with problem-talk, the counsellor respectfully acknowledges their difficulty and asks another goal-setting question. An example would be "given that [this issue] is what has brought you here, how will you know that you have changed it for the better" or "what will you be doing differently when it is not a problem anymore?". Paramount here is the ability of the solution-building career counsellor to ensure that the client's goals are self-identified and are expressed in terms of the presence of something rather than its absence.

Envisioning a preferred future

One solution-focused technique that is used to great effect in personal counselling is the so-called miracle question (de Jong and Berg, 2002). This is, in effect, a series of statements that encourage the client to imagine what they would be doing, and what other people would notice them doing if the concern that brought them to counselling no longer existed. Responses to the miracle question can elicit small details from which counsellor and client can construct client goals, or exceptions to their problems. Either will provide the building blocks for solution-building.

In solution-building career counselling, the miracle question can take a slightly different form, one in which the counsellor sets the context for clients to imagine how they would like things to be in (say) five years. Important here is both the pace and the language used to help the client experience such a future. Statements that start with "suppose you were talking to me in five years' time ..." or "let's pretend that we were able to turn the clock forward a few years ... and your career was developing well ... what would tell you that you were on track?". Responses to such questions help clients articulate their hopes for a particular quality of life and provide the counsellor with clues about client career goals. If the client responded by saying "I would be making reasonable money and I would feel valued" the counsellor hears the beginning of a career goal. The counsellor's role at this point is to help the client elaborate the detail of such a goal by asking questions that presuppose such a future is probable such as "and *when* you feel valued, what are you doing?" or "and *when* you are making reasonable money, what do your friends notice about you?" or checking that the statements are client goals by asking, "and would you find it useful for us to explore possible careers like that?".

A further example of using the client's vision of a preferred future is described by George *et al.* (2004). Here clients are encouraged to rehearse a difficult event from the standpoint of its successful, but still future, completion. This could be used effectively with a client who is anxious about an impending job interview. The counsellor might say "let's imagine that the job interview has just finished and you are getting up to leave. You are anxious, of course, because you don't know whether or not you have got the job, but you know that you have presented yourself really well in the interview. You feel very pleased with the way you presented yourself and you are remembering how you did it. What would you be remembering about how you were in the interview when you got outside the interview room?" A client's answer to this question can be heard, elaborated on and extended by the counsellor asking "what else?" often, and perhaps asking how the person conducting the job interview might describe the client in the interview or asking what the client was thinking and saying during the interview. Each of the client's answers has within it some clues to the solution to the client's concern about not presenting well at an interview.

Focusing on exceptions and progress

Each of the above future-oriented techniques allows clients to build up pictures of their own competencies with respect to their goals. The counsellor's role is to help clients see themselves clearly and identify useful resources they can use to help themselves move towards achieving their career goals. There are a number of practical techniques that the counsellor may use to assist this process. One is adapted from the empty chair technique often used within a Gestalt therapy session (Zinker, 1977). A solution-building career counsellor may use an outcome chair and assign it the name of the client's goal. The client can be invited to sit in the chair and then asked "from that outcome chair, what advice would you give yourself right now?" … "what else?"

A second practical technique is the use of questions relating to a scale that helps clients shift their perception from a problem focus to a goal focus. Essentially scales provide clients with clear images through which they can self-assess their own situations in terms of progress, seriousness, determination and hopefulness. When clients and counsellors are clarifying client goals, a scale can be drawn to help determine where clients want to be and where they are now relative to that goal. Solution-building questions help clients identify what needs to happen to help them move along the scale. The parameters of a scale are described in Figure 10.1.

This scale can take on a number of different formats. One format that encourages collaboration incorporates ideas from Kelly's (1955) personal construct theory by inviting clients to name the two end points of a scale. Suppose, for instance, in response to the initial goal-seeking question "what would you like to get out of this session?" the client responded "I'd like to feel confident that what I am studying will get me a good job". The counsellor could suggest a scale to help the client make the goal more concrete. The

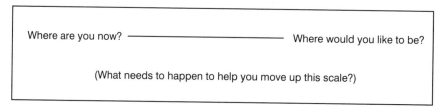

Figure 10.1 Parameters of a scale

counsellor might say "if I was to map your confidence on a scale where 10 depicts where you hope you can be and 1 depicts the opposite of that, what would you call those two points?" The client might describe a scale where 1 was "scared I'm taking the wrong subjects" and 10 was "doing well in my subjects will give me many options". Alternatively the client might describe a scale where "1" was "confused/stuck" and "10" was "clear about what to do".

Scaling questions are extremely useful to clients and maximum impact can be gained when the scale, and client descriptors are drawn, preferably on a whiteboard or large piece of paper. In the previous case, the counsellor might draw the second scale

    1   2   3   4   5   6   7   8   9   10
stuck/confused   Clear about what to do

Exposure to this scale, allows clients to observe, consider and assess all the nuances in their own scale. Once the scale is drawn, sensitive questioning on the part of the counsellor can help clients describe themselves at different points on the scale. The counsellor might ask clients to draw on the scale, "where would you have put yourself on this scale before you made the appointment to come here?" and, "the point on the scale that you would rather be" (goal clarification)?

Suppose in the previous case, the client indicates that a "3" describes her situation now, a "2" describes where she was before the counselling session and an "8" describes her preferred future. The client and/or counsellor would record the three points the scale:

    1   [2]   (3)   4   5   6   7   {8}   9   10
stuck/confused   Clear about what to do

Each of these points will be meaningful to the client and, to help her explore this meaning, the counsellor remains curious and asks the client to describe what she is (or would be) doing at each of these points. Questions that aid this process include:

- "What words would you use to describe that point on the scale?" (self-assessment)
- "What words describe what you would be doing differently at that point?" (self-helpfulness)
- "What would others say was different for you then?" (contextual meaning).

This client may use phrases such as, "I feel like I'm wasting my time" and, "I can't concentrate on anything" to extend her meaning for a "2". Further, she may add, "I want to check things out" to these descriptors to explain her difference at a "3" and she may use terms such as, "I would be confident in my course of study" and, "I would know where my qualification would lead" and "I would have a plan" to describe her "8". The scale could be built upon as follows:

    1   [2]   (3)   4   5   6   7   {8}   9   10
Stuck/confused   Clear about what to do

    [2]   (3)   {8}
    Wasting time   check things   confident
    Unable to concentrate   have a plan
                                                        know where
                                                        qualifications lead

When descriptors are written on the scale, those written below the preferred future are very important in the solution-building career process. The counsellor can use these in a number of ways. First, the counsellor may ask exception-building questions such as "has there been a time, recently, that you have felt just a little more confident about your course of study?". If the client is able to remember such a time, the counsellor asks questions that help the client acknowledge her own role in developing or maintaining confidence, "so, what was it that you were doing that made that possible?".

Another useful aspect of the counsellor and client reading the whole scale is that the counsellor can ask questions that encourage the client to recognise her agency in moving towards her self-identified goal. When the counsellor asks the client how she has managed to move from a 2 to a 3 the client's responses provide solution-building clues. Thus, if the client says "I decided to come to counselling" – the counsellor can write that on the board, immediately above the scale, and ask how the client expected counselling would help her move towards her goal. Say the client said "I wouldn't have to shoulder this on my own" the counsellor would help the client rephrase the statement in positive terms "I would look for support" and write that on the board. These statements provide what I like to call the parachute for the client who is feeling "stuck"; a list of successful strategies from which solutions may be built. The client can look at the list and see that she is already doing things (seeking support, looking at the internet, asking friends) that can help her move "up the scale". The counsellor might prompt this view by asking "So which of these 'successful strategies' would be useful for you to move from a 3 to a 4?". Such questions enable the client to break the goal into manageable pieces and to believe that their achievement is possible.

While the above examples describe a scale using 10 numerical points, it is just as effective to use other formats that incorporate images, steps or non-numeric text if these are more meaningful to the client. Consider, for example, how helpful it would be to some clients if they could be invited to examine past and present contextual influences and the possible effect of such influences as lifestyle and employment trends on their preferred future. The solution-building career counsellor can easily encourage this process by encouraging clients to use a systems theory framework such as that described by Patton and McMahon (1999) to explore and evaluate their own systems of influence on their career goals.

Suppose a client described himself as reserved, with an interest in photography and travel, and also as being good at maths and music and hoping for a career that would be exciting. He and his counsellor may draw a simplified diagram using colour, capital letters and size of circles to describe the importance of particular aspects (see Figure 10.2).

Once such a diagram was drawn, it can be used in much the same way as the points on a scale. It is easy for the counsellor to be curious about whether or not the client is happy with the appearance of the diagram, how it has looked at other times, ways the client would like to change particular influences and what it would take to make such changes. (For other examples of the use of systems models, see Miller, 2004a.)

Constructing meaningful feedback

In solution-focused counselling, there is an assumption that clients will work towards achieving their goals outside the counselling session. To help focus this work, counsellors finish counselling sessions with a formal procedure. First, they take a short break, preferably away from the room in which they are working, to quickly review things that the client has said during the interview. During the break, career clients can look through some relevant career information and counsellors consider three parts of their feedback: compliments, a bridge (or rationale), and usually a task.

Such feedback helps convey to clients that the counsellor has listened, acknowledged their problem, heard what they want to be different and agrees with steps they might take to achieve their goals. In order to compliment clients, counsellors need to recall and write down client strengths and successes. General, illustrative examples might include: making the decision to do something, coming to counselling, recognising that relaxation helps

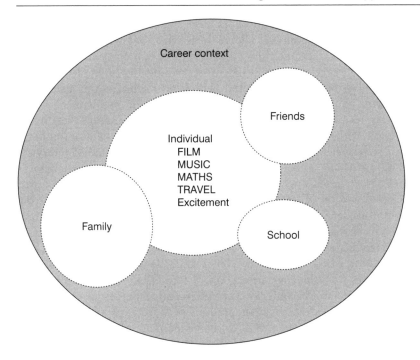

Figure 10.2 Example of the way a client could use a systems framework to describe career-related influences

make decisions easier, being clear about wanting a career that uses particular skills and training, working hard during the counselling session.

In order to formulate a task, counsellors should look at times, during the interview that clients recognised their own self-helpfulness, resourcefulness and hope that success would occur. The task itself can extend strategies, such as searching the internet, that clients are already using to move up the scale. If a task is perceived as logical, reasonable and relevant, it is more likely to be considered to be achievable. To ensure this, the counsellor links the task's relevance to the client's goal or exceptions. The suggested task is, therefore, shaped with phrases such as: "because you have said that you want ..." and, "since you have indicated that ...". Exemplars of feedback messages can be found in Miller (2004a and 2004b).

Challenges for career counsellors using solution-building in their practice

While I have just described a number of generic skills, it is inappropriate to reduce solution-building career counselling to simple, formulaic techniques. In solution-building, it is the uniqueness of clients that determines counsellors' questions, the alliance between clients and counsellors that allows this uniqueness to flourish, and counsellors' faith in clients' ability to reach self-identified goals that encourages clients' belief that they will make progress. The challenge for career practitioners is to respect that many clients come to them expecting a service related to identity, training and/or employment yet be able to delay their use of trait and factor approaches, adopt a stance of "not knowing" and recognise clients as experts in their own lives.

One way to achieve this balance is to engage the client's interest in co-construction at the outset, by explaining the rationale of solution-building. When there is sufficient time between appointment making and an interview, the solution-building career counsellor may include a rationale statement in an introductory letter. Such a statement makes it possible to include a pre-supposition question to encourage self-helpfulness: "in preparation for our interview, consider what you want, and what you are already doing to help yourself achieve this". When there is no time for a letter counsellors can include in their introductory statement a comment on the fact that when the client and counsellor work together to clarify the client's goals and discover client resources for achieving these goals, the counselling outcome is better than when the counsellor anticipates the goals and resources *for* the client.

This does not mean that career practitioners are expected to withhold information from the clients. Rather, it means that they delay producing such information until they have helped the client explore their needs, aspirations, strengths and skills first. The challenge is to restrain from offering information from the standpoint of the expert and to encourage client self-responsibility, by offering all suggestions and information tentatively. Questions at this stage might include "I wonder how this fits with your goal" or "I wonder if you are aware...".

Finally, adopting a solution-building approach does not mean discarding inventories and other assessment tools, rather, it means using them differently. Qualitative tools such as card-sorts, timelines and life-maps encourage clients to use their own language to self-reflect about vocational self-concepts and work roles and consider their own career themes. Such assessment tools can be used very effectively alongside scaling questions to help clients clarify goals or estimate progress towards achieving their preferred career future. Brainstorming can be used to help clients identify values and talents or clarify past successes that might give them clues about how to address current and future career quandaries. A solution-building career counsellor will use focused listening with each conversation to identify and amplify for clients those occasions that demonstrate client successes that may help clients move towards their chosen goal.

Conclusion

When Sexton *et al.* (1997) surveyed counselling outcome research, they concluded that clients preferred career counselling to last about three sessions, focus on specific career plans and decision making and provide them with a clearer sense of direction. Effective solution-building career counselling is brief, it focuses on clients' plans and it encourages them to leave the session with a clear sense of how to move towards achieving their goals.

My motivation for writing the chapter comes from my enthusiasm to encourage career practitioners to use solution-focused assumptions and techniques in their work. Further, I hope that when career practitioners adopt solution-building approaches in their work, they will generate the evidence that is so desperately needed to demonstrate the effectiveness of working this way in career practice. While I have only touched on some of the ways that solution-building procedures can be incorporated into the work of career-practitioners I anticipate that readers will begin to develop further exemplars.

References

Anderson, H. and Goolishian, H. (1991) 'Thinking about multi-agency work with substance abusers and their families: a language systems approach'. *Journal of Strategic and Systematic Therapies*, 10, 20–35.

Blumer, H. (1969) *Symbolic Interactionism: Perspective and Method.* Englewood Cliffs, NJ: Prentice Hall.

Brown, D. and Brooks, L. (1996) 'Introduction to theories of career development and choice', in D. Brown and L. Brooks (eds), *Career Choice and Development* (3rd edn, pp. 1–30). San Francisco, CA: Jossey- Bass.

de Jong, P. and Berg, I. K. (2002) *Interviewing for Solutions* (2nd edn). Pacific Grove, CA: Brooks/Cole.

Dolan, Y. (2000) *Beyond Trauma and Therapy: Steps to a More Joyous Life.* London: BT Press.

Durrant, M. (1995) *Creative Strategies for School Problems.* New York: W.W. Norton.

Friedman, S. and Fanger, M. T. (1991) *Expanding Therapeutic Possibilities: Getting Results in Brief Psychotherapy.* Toronto: Lexington Books.

George, E., Iveson, C. and Ratner, H. (2004) *Problem to Solution: Brief Therapy with Individuals and Families* (expanded edition). London: BT Press.

Kelly, G. (1955) *Principles of Personal Construct Psychology.* New York: Norton.

Lewis, T. F. and Osborn, C. J. (2004) 'Solution-focused counseling and motivational interviewing: a consideration of confluence'. *Journal of Counseling and Development*, 82, 38–48.

McMahon, M. and Patton, W. (2000) 'Beyond 2000: incorporating the constructivist influence into career guidance and counselling'. *Australian Journal of Career Development*, 9(1), 25–9.

Miller, G. (1998) *Becoming Miracle Workers: Language and Meaning in Brief Therapy.* New York: Aldine de Gruyter.

Miller, J. H. (2004a) 'Extending the use of constructivist approaches in career guidance and counselling: solution-focused strategies'. *Australian Journal of Career Development*, 13(1), 50–8.

Miller, J. H. (2004b) 'Building a solution-focused strategy into career counselling'. *New Zealand Journal of Counselling*, 25(1),18–30.

O'Connell, B. (1998) *Solution-focused Therapy.* London: Sage.

O'Hanlon, B. and Beadle, S. (1996) *A Field Guide to Possibility Land*. London: BT Press.

Patton, W. and McMahon, M. (1999) *Career Development and Systems Theory: A New Relationship*. Pacific Grove, CA: Brooks/Cole.

Sexton, T. L., Whiston, S. C., Bleuer, J. C. and Walz, G. R. (1997) *Integrating Outcome Research into Counseling Practice and Training*. Alexandria, VA: American Counseling Association.

Te Ruru. (1998) 'Specifying the miracle: integrating solution-focused approaches with NLP'. *Anchor Point*, 12(3), 23–30.

Zinker, J. (1997) *Creative Process in Gestalt Therapy*. New York: Brunner/Mazel.

Chapter 11

SocioDynamic career counselling

Constructivist practice of wisdom

Timo Spangar

This chapter is a tribute to Vance Peavy's legacy in the field of counselling. I am grateful for the support I received from Vance's wife, Judith Peavy in preparing the chapter.

I met Professor Vance Peavy, the father of SocioDynamic counselling, for the first time at the International Association of Educational and Vocational Guidance conference in Lisbon in 1991. The mutual interest we shared was our observation that fundamental changes have taken place in the world of work and new concepts and ideas about career counselling should be developed in order to meet those changes. The idea of new post-industrial and non-linear careers was one of the key concepts we both worked on at that time (Peavy, 1992; Vähämöttönen[1] *et al.*, 1994). From the Lisbon conference onwards our collaboration continued until the early death of Vance in 2002.

In this chapter I will first present my current interpretation of the essential conceptual ideas characterising SocioDynamic counselling. This will be followed by a description of the key starting points for understanding SocioDynamic counselling strategies. In the final practical section I will illustrate how the two counselling strategies, dialogic listening and life-space mapping, can be trained and practised. This section will also include examples of employment counsellors from the Finnish Public Employment Service context who have used SocioDynamic methods in their actual client work.

Typical of Vance's thinking that SocioDynamic counselling was a continuous "work in progress", he wrote hundreds of articles, manuscripts and different forms of teaching materials. Due to the restricted space I am not in a position to give a full picture of the development of the SocioDynamic approach, all of its concepts or the practical counselling methods Vance developed during the four decades he worked in the field of counselling.

Vance called his counselling approach "SocioDynamic". The concept originates from Greek words "socio" meaning "together", "companion" and "social". "Dynamic" stems from the Greek word "dynamiko" indicating continuous change and movement as well as an aesthetic equilibrium of parts. Through the concept of "SocioDynamic" Vance crystallised his basic philosophical approach to counselling as seeing humans as social beings, continuously changing and "at our best, we are a holistic, aesthetic equilibrium. A life well-lived is a work of art ... like a poem or dance" (Peavy, 1997b, p. 8). The SocioDynamic approach is closely linked with constructivist counselling, "constructivist-based" as Vance stated (Peavy, 1997b, p. 8).

The underlying philosophical ideas of the SocioDynamic approach

The SocioDynamic approach is not a traditional counselling approach in the sense that it would first create a theoretical framework, and then develop specific counselling methods and apply them in counselling practice. The SocioDynamic approach is rather a continuous dialogue with theorising and the experience of real counselling practice. However, there are certain strands of theorising that recurrently appear with the development of SocioDynamic counselling practice.

Perhaps most importantly, the SocioDynamic approach rests upon *philosophical ideas of human existence*. Human beings are seen as struggling for creating meaning in their lives and the counselling process is seen as a process of helping clients to make meaning in their lives through life-decisions, including their career decisions. The counselling process is a social process during which the client and the counsellor co-construct new ways for the client to go on with his or her life in a meaningful manner. In order to be able to help the client the counsellor must have the capability and attitude to step into the client's world. Referring to Kierkegaard's philosophy (Kierkegaard, 1859/1952) Vance wrote: "One [the counsellor, TS] must first take the pains to find the other where the other is and begin there" (Peavy, 1997b, p. 24).

The SocioDynamic approach as a response to social and working life changes is keenly related to contemporary *social theories*. Developing the SocioDynamic approach, Peavy initiated the need for a "New look" (Peavy, 1997a, p. 123) in career counselling reflecting the changes which had taken place as the industrial economies have moved to the post-industrial era (Hage and Powers, 1992), variously termed post-market era (e.g., Rifkin, 1995), late modern (e.g., Giddens, 1991) or post-traditional (e.g., Giddens, 1995). Whatever the current social transformation is called, the implications for individual citizens and their career decisions are profound. Citizens now have to make their career decisions in a "double-bind" context. On the one hand, the possibilities to shape their lives according to their individual needs have increased dramatically, the world (of work) is something that can be shaped and moulded, and the individual's relationship with work may be described by the term "plasticity"(Vähämöttönen, 1998,

p. 24). On the other hand, current social life is characterised by increased uncertainty and even risks (Beck, 1992). Career decision-making has now become more about citizens' self-construction where they need support of career counsellors. Vance saw that the "New look" career counselling should narrow the traditional gap between "life" and "career" indicating that citizens live single and holistic lives. Another key feature for "New look" counselling is that the current changes have an impact on how we understand the concept of "self". The SocioDynamic approach adopts the current ideas of the self as evolving, socially constructed, self-organising and entropic containing the ideas of complex selves (Hage and Powers, 1992), instead of structurally fixed and permanent over time and contexts as the traditional idea of the self has been.

Another important aspect of the SocioDynamic approach is that it sees citizens' lives and their relationships with working life inherently rooted in the *culture* where they live. Thus, the counselling process should always resonate with the client's own culture in order to be helpful for them. Vance developed the radically different SocioDynamic approach as a "practice of wisdom" (Peavy, 2004b, p. 26) and as a "culture of healing" (Peavy, 1996, p. 141). Based on the ideas of the cultural-historical school of psychology (Vygotsky, 1978), Vance stated that from the SocioDynamic perspective all humanly invented tools are called *cultural tools*. The cultural tools include *technical tools* such as computer, chair and pencil. *Mental tools* (psychological tools in Vygotsky's terminology) are symbolic including the phenomena of language such as words, sentences and sounds, as well as stories, texts, diagrams and maps. For the SocioDynamic approach the concept of tool, to a large extent, replaces the concept of psychological technique (Peavy, 2004a).

Through the adoption of a cultural orientation to the counselling process the SocioDynamic approach also integrates the idea of dialogue as a basis for human communication, also within the counselling process. Based on the Russian literary theorist Bakhtin (1984) Vance states that his idea of multiple voices, polyphony and multi-vocality (Peavy, 2004a) always present in human communication is vitally important for the career counselling process.

Reflecting in a holistic and heuristic manner on the social theories of contemporary social life, the existentialist philosophy of human beings as continuously creating their lives and struggling for meaning, and living in social and cultural contexts as well as today in the postmodern world, Vance proposed a new definition for career counselling. According to the Socio-Dynamic approach, *career counselling is a general method of life-planning*. Vance describes the concept of *life-planning* by referring in a holistic way to the wholeness of a person's life where he or she has a whole life to live rather than any single part or fragment (not even "career") of it. The concept of *general method* reflects this wholeness as any sphere of life cannot be separated from "life in general".

Vance's definition of career counselling was reflected in one of my client's descriptions of the counselling process I had with her: "The reason why I came to counselling was not necessarily what occupation is best for me but what kind of life will I have from now on ... counselling shouldn't necessarily deal only with something connected with an occupation" (Vähämöttönen, 1998, p. 88).

SocioDynamic counselling strategies

Congruent with the idea of career counselling as a general method of life-planning, Vance emphasised that the holistic and heuristic nature of the counselling process also calls forth a different idea of counselling methods. While traditionally determined methods have (ideally) paralleled theories and counselling approaches, Vance saw adopting the "counsellor attitude" more important than learning prescriptive methods for counselling. He called the SocioDynamic counselling tools "suggestive strategies" aiming at enhancing improvisation and spontaneity in the counselling process. These strategies are not meant to be used as formulas for counselling (Peavy, 2004a).

General SocioDynamic counselling strategy

The general SocioDynamic counselling strategy is a general template for instructing the counselling process. The counselling process is seen as a continuous *reflective dialogical feedback process* between the counsellor and the client. In any counselling process the counsellor and the client have some "joint resources" (Peavy, 2004a, p. 52) available. For example, such resources may be the old solutions the client has made, the client's reflections on his or her experience, knowledge of the constraints and opportunities of the situation and problem solving models.

Based on their joint resources the counsellor and the client enter into a counselling process that Vance called a "co-constructive mediating process" (Peavy, 2004a, p. 52), understanding the counselling process as a joint co-construction of the counsellor and the client. The co-constructive counselling process is emergent by its nature. It does not follow prescriptive phase-by-phase laws. The process mediates the client's past to his or her future.

The mediating co-constructive counselling process leads to "achievements of joint action" (Peavy, 2004a, p. 52). These achievements may be new or revised perspectives, new solutions or expanded choices, new reflections and critical thinking, strengthened self-identity, articulated life experience, increased capacity of building projects, reconstructed relationships, support of self-authoring and clarification of self-other-context interactions. Thus, the outcomes of the counselling process are not solely "placement" to vacant jobs or entry to educational institutes. The joint achievements of the process vary according to clients and their contexts.

Dialogical listening

The SocioDynamic approach emphasises the significance of listening to and genuine hearing of the client. Vance used to say that God gave humans two ears and one mouth so that they would listen twice as much as they speak. The counselling strategy which stresses the listening aspect of counselling is called "dialogical listening" (Peavy, 2004a, p 54). Enhancing the listening skills of the counsellor may be seen as a paradigmatic aspect of the Socio-Dynamic counselling. Vance elaborated the concept of dialogical listening by describing its three core aspects: *inner peace*, *harmonious relations* and *transformative learning*.

"Inner peace" is a state of mind where the counsellor meets the client in a genuine manner. The idea is to be really present for the client. Inner peace is a multi-dimensional phenomenon including elements like being receptive, still, concentrated, respectful, patient, empty of self, aware of one's mood and appreciative (Peavy, 2004a). Inner peace is not easily achieved, it requires conscious practise, it is "spiritual and psychological achievement". Vance gives a 15-page "repertoire" of fostering one's inner peace (Peavy, 2004a, pp. 55–70).

In addition to inner peace, genuine listening requires a harmonious relationship between the counsellor and the client. The idea is to listen to relate first, and only after that listen to the client's problem. The main road to problem-solving goes through relating with the client by attentive listening. The goal is to build up a common ground with the client to work on during the counselling process. A successful harmonious relationship between the counsellor and the client enables the counsellor to present a "human face", one of the key concepts in SocioDynamic counselling, reflecting "inward calmness, concentration, care, and responsibility" (Peavy, 2004a, p. 72) for the concerns the client has brought to counselling.

SocioDynamic counselling sees the counselling process as a space and environment for learning experience. The idea of transformative learning describes a learning process where the counselling process is a learning experience for the client (and for the counsellor) that can be transformed to another context so that it also makes sense in the new context. The transformative learning may be seen as a dialectical process of thesis, antithesis and synthesis (Peavy, 2004a).

Life-space

Another crucial concept for SocioDynamic counselling practice is the concept of "life-space". Vance encountered the concept through a colleague of Kurt Lewin (1948). Life-space is both the psychological and sociological space in which individuals live. It is the holistic state of mind and the individual, social and cultural context each individual inhabits. It may be also described as a "gestalt" of individuals' lives. Vance saw that the concept of life-space comes close to Bourdiueu's (2002) concept of "habitus" (p. 78), expressing the individual's way of being, his or her inclination or disposition. Generalising his experience of counselling experiences with clients, Vance divided the life-space into four semantic regions: relationships and intimacy, work and learning, health and body, and spirituality (Peavy, 1997a). This division is used as a platform for developing various graphic methods for mapping the client's life-space (Peavy, 2001).

For the practice of counselling it is vitally important that counsellors address, in one way or another, clients' life-spaces and recognise that there is always a wider context affecting clients' lives than only the problems clients have brought to counselling. Career concerns are viewed as being linked with other spheres of the client's life, just as career counselling is viewed as a general method of life-planning.

Two examples of SocioDynamic counselling methods

There are dozens of SocioDynamic counselling tools and Vance developed new ones continuously (Peavy, 1997a; 2001; 2004a; 2004b). In the present section I will describe two of perhaps the most important tools, "dialogical listening" and "life-space mapping". Both methods are accompanied by vignettes of Finnish employment counsellors' experiences of them in real client work. About 300 employment counsellors have now received training on SocioDynamic counselling tools in the National Professional Development Programme organised by the Ministry of Labour.

Dialogical listening

Dialogical listening can be rehearsed in the following manner. Two client workers (Counsellor A and Counsellor B) discuss in pairs.

1　Selecting a joint theme to be discussed: For example, "What things in the counselling process do I find challenging or difficult?" The discussion proceeds in a stepwise manner.
2　First A reflects and talks about the theme for five minutes.
3　Counsellor B listens to A. B tries to "empty his/her head", to stay in a position of "not knowing" and refraining from commenting on A. B reflects on what is going on in his/her mind while listening to A. B tries to recognise interrupting things that disturb the listening. B tries to get "behind the words" to the meaning of the words A is using.
4　B tells A how he/she understood what A was saying.
5　A comments on B's observations.
6　The turns are reversed. Now B talks while A listens for five minutes.
7　A and B discuss what it was like to talk and listen.

Depending on the teaching arrangements, the outcomes of the pairs activity may also be shared in the whole group.

The employment counsellors have experienced dialogical listening as a very powerful tool changing strongly the traditional working methods with job-seekers. The employment counsellors have also used dialogical listening in their contacts with employers. Two employment counsellors' self-reflections on using dialogical listening are given as examples of using dialogical listening.

Counsellor 1: visiting a "problem-employer"

The employment counsellor here uses dialogical listening at her visit to a small business. The business seems very problematic from the local employment agency's point of view as several job-seekers placed in the business had quit the job at an early stage of their employment complaining about poor wages and working conditions, as well as the personal behaviour of the owner. The employment counsellor tells of her experience:

> I was really afraid of visiting the company. I tried to keep in my mind the ideas of Kierkegaard and to listen to the employer from the employer's point of view, to start from where he stands. I tried to give up any "one-up" attitude, to be patient and admit that I do not know everything. I decided to abandon any prejudices I had for the employer … After coffee the employer asked why he can't hire a new employee and have state subsidy for it. I answered by asking him why he thought he cannot hire one without any subsidy. Having confronted him by my question I decided to take the role of active listener. I waited for the employer's response. There was a silence that seemed to last forever. Finally, the employer told his story as an entrepreneur and the difficulties he faced trying to keep the company alive. The employer's story was long and striking. I felt myself like a therapist without proper training and experience. I was empathic towards the employer. Afterwards I felt relieved. I felt that we had open, human, trustful, and equal contact with the employer. I noticed that I had never thought about the employer as a human being with problems and difficulties in his life as an employer. With active listening my role as a public official faded and the employer also noticed that "bureaucrats" are ordinary people who also feel compassion with their clients. I will certainly use this method in the future.

Counsellor 2: meeting with a 54-year-old immigrant

After having drawn a life-space map with the client, the counsellor takes the stance of dialogical and active listener and tells about her experience:

At first there was a total silence ... which was a little frightening although not a new experience for me. What is going to happen? Does she open up themes which she cannot handle without professional help, all by herself as she does not have any relatives nearby? However, I decided to trust the client's own willingness, my own intuition and long work experience. Compared to the earlier situations like this, now the client had the main role in the discussion. My role was to make observations, ask some elaborative questions and be genuinely present as an interested listener. At the end of discussion the client told me that she felt for the first time that she was really heard by public authorities and she is confident that she will get help for her problems. I concluded that earlier I had been too eager to impose the goals of the public authorities on the clients not listening to them in a sensitive enough manner. The dialogical listening rehearsal enabled the client to be genuinely heard and her service needs could then be immediately defined.

Reading the background materials of the training course I noticed that Peavy emphasises culturally sensitive communication and local knowledge instead of generalised theories. He writes about counselling as a practice of wisdom open to new experiences. Counselling is respecting the other, who he/she is and whom he/she wants to become ... Reading his book *Composing and Mapping My Life* [Peavy, 2001] and thinking about my own career I found it very easy to agree with his idea about the significance of listening in a dialogic conversation. The counsellor may be, in my opinion, seen as an expert of a process where the counselee learns to reflect on his/her experience, to use his/her resources, to solve problems and manage his/her learning process. Counselling is a communication process and conversation is the most important part of it. ... I have not studied theories, but I have worked with enthusiasm and from the bottom of my heart during the 25 years of my career. Unaware of it I have used some parts of SocioDynamic counselling although I have not acquainted myself with Peavy's ideas before the training course. It is wonderful to get tools and methods which I will be, I am sure about that, able to use in my client work as well as in my work as a manager and as a supervisor.

Life-space mapping

The idea of life-space mapping is to make the client's life as a whole visible and to enable the client to work with it. SocioDynamic counselling uses drawings, visualisations and different forms of diagrams as key counselling tools. There are various forms and variations of graphic counselling methods and counsellors are encouraged to mould them and innovate new ones themselves. Vance Peavy (1997a) describes his way of using life-space mapping as follows:

I use sheets of paper and a pencil or coloured pens to map with. After I have begun to get a word picture of the difficulty which the other is presenting to me, I say something like:

- If we drew a map of your situation, it might get clearer to both of us – does that seem like a good idea to you?
- If the other agrees, then I take a sheet of paper and ask the other to think of the whole sheet as her present life-space. I then ask her to draw a small circle somewhere on the page and label it "self".
- Then we proceed to make a map of what is going on in her life that seems to have relevance to the issue she is confronting. We sometimes trade the pencil back and forth so that we get the feeling of "working together". Other times the other does most or all of the drawing and occasionally I will do most or all of it myself. We map out experiences, events, people, relationships, needs, voices, obstacles, possibilities and information. Depending upon the propensities and skill of the other, we use drawing, images, symbols, word, and sometimes colours to indicate meanings. (Peavy, 1997b, p. 72).

The following two self-reflections describe two employment counsellors' experiences of using life-space mapping or modifications of it.

Counsellor 3: meeting with an immigrant applying for a work permit in Finland

The counsellor drew with the client a map of the work permit process that was added to by the client's own visual plan of what he was going to do after the counselling. The counsellor reflects on her experiences:

Drawing a map taught me the concreteness of visualisations. The old saying "one picture tells more than a hundred words" was confirmed. Drawing makes the client an active participant of the process and helps him to grasp new solutions. My role turned into the one of a co-traveller and a generator of new alternatives. The mapping enabled the client to make the needed further enquiries more easily. It was also easier for him to describe his career decision process to his wife.

Counsellor 4: using mapping in making a job-seeking plan

The counsellor asked the client, a 21-year-old mechanic, to make a drawing of what things and relationships with other people were affecting his plans for the future. The counsellor reflects on her experience:

Listening to the client's current plans it seemed to me that he is going to repeat solutions that do not lead him to work life. At that stage I decided to try to do the drawing task. Before the counselling session I thought that it is not a method that would suit my working style. The client used about 15 minutes for making the drawing. The themes that came out were: "work experience", "home", "driver's licence". Through the discussion about the drawing the client began to consider new labour market training options that he had not thought of before.

The client explained that drawing a map was a suitable method for him as it made it easier for him to tell someone else about his current life situation. He did not have to speak and reflect at the same time but he could take the time he needed for self-reflection and explain his ideas after that. The counsellor learned that home is a significant factor in the client's life which the counsellor would not have understood without the drawing. The client was clearly more relaxed than before he made the drawing.

Training employment counsellors to use SocioDynamic counselling tools seems to have a common story to tell as reflected in the short vignettes of the employment counsellors above. First, there is some hesitance about using the methods in real client work. The methods seem at first to be "too different" from traditional interview techniques. Second, as the employment counsellors use the methods after overcoming their initial hesitation, they are surprised to note that their clients usually welcome the methods and the untraditional and unexpected new methods arouse their curiosity. Third, using SocioDynamic methods usually identified new aspects of the client's life-world that have great impact on their road to employment. The employment counsellors often tell that they were not aware of the client's life situation before using the new methods even in cases when they have met with the clients for several years. Fourth, the new methods change the role of the employment counsellors. The common role change is towards a more equal relationship with the clients, described in various ways like "a co-traveller". The new more equal relationship with the clients leave the clients more space in the counselling process, they become real agents of the process, they are more committed to the plans they have made themselves and their service needs may be identified more easily. These are all fruitful outcomes regarding the current labour market policies that emphasise "activation" of job-seekers.

Closing remarks – SocioDynamic counselling and the "third birth" of career counselling

My mutual concern with Vance at the Lisbon conference was how to develop career counselling concepts and practices that would meet the challenges of the "postmodern turn" of working life. Vance developed his ideas through the concept of life-space while I developed my ideas about the counselling process by reframing it as a counsellor-client negotiation process (Vähämöttönen, 1998).

We both developed visualisations, mapping and metaphors (Vähämöttönen, 1998; Spangar, 2004) as key methods in the counselling process. The 1990s have witnessed several other approaches successfully tackling the challenges of post-industrial working life. The new approaches resonate well with the paradigmatic turn now taking place in the field of career counselling. Richardson (1993; 2000) has described the current paradigm change as a shift from "career ideologies" to a stance of the "location of work in people's lives". Such a shift indicates the necessity for counsellors also to move from focusing solely on work and careers to conceptualisations and practical counselling methods that empower citizens' lives through relationships more generally.

It may now be argued that we are in the middle of the "*third* birth of career counselling" (Spangar and Arnkil, 2005, pp. 28–9). The "first birth" took place at the end of the 1900s in the work of Frank Parsons (Richardson, 1993). The post-war industrial society gave career counselling its "second birth" based mainly on academic psychology and counselling professionalism. The "*third* birth" today, negotiating around the location of work in people's lives, challenges career counselling professionals and institutions to develop their concepts and practical tools in cooperation with a wide range of other professionals whose work has become more and more "counselling-like". In this context the SocioDynamic approach has proven useful as it has enabled non-professionals and non-psychologists, like employment counsellors, to adopt counselling methods. SocioDynamic concepts of career counselling as a "practice of wisdom" (Peavy, 2004b, p. 26), as a "culture of healing" (Peavy, 1996, p. 141) and the reconceptualisation of the counsellor role as a "bricoleur" (Peavy, 1997a, p. 24) – "jack of all trades" rather than a counselling expert in a one-up position to the client – have all enhanced the "*third* birth" of career counselling by building bridges between professional counsellors and the non-professionals. The emphasis on dialogue strongly present in the SocioDynamic approach is a widely welcomed orientation and method in the current societal condition. The need for dialogue extends "horizontally" amongst counsellors in different organisations and "vertically" from front-line client work to the levels of management and policy-making. It is no wonder now that the "top level" seems to be "re-inventing" career counselling (Organisation for Economic Cooperation and Development, 2004). An obvious reason for that is, as Vance states in his last book (Peavy, 2004a), that counselling is strongly related to fostering social capital by increasing trust in society.

Finally, the SocioDynamic approach encourages counsellors and researchers to openly express their individual life experience as influences in their theories and methods, both in counselling research and practice. Vance's theories of counselling reflected his often dramatic life experiences which is shown beautifully in Larsen's (2004) article on Vance's life and its connections with his ideas about counselling. The "*third* birth of career counselling" also seems to lend more space and legitimacy for the "subjectivity" of counsellors as a helping tool for their clients.

Note

1   The author's name at the time.

Acknowledgements

Special thanks go to the employment counsellors Seija Leppänen, Anja Puustinen, Maritta Manninen and Hannele Tuhkanen. They kindly allowed me to use their own client work examples to demonstrate SocioDynamic counselling practice.

References

Bakhtin, M. (1984) *Problems of Dostoevsky's Poetics*. Minneapolis, MN: University of Minneapolis Press.

Beck, U. (1992) *Risk Society*. London: Sage.

Bourdiueu, P. (2002) *Outline of a Theory of Practice*. Cambridge: Cambridge University Press.

Giddens, A. (1991) *Modernity and Self-identity. Self and Society in the Late Modern Age*. Cambridge: Polity Press.

Giddens, A. (1995) 'Living in post-traditional society', in U. Beck, A. Giddens and S. Lash (eds), *Reflexive Modernization: Politics, Tradition and Aesthetics of Modern Social Order* (pp. 56–109). Cambridge, MA: Stanford University Press.

Hage, J. and Powers, C. H. (1992) *Postindustrial lives: Roles and relationships in the 21st century*. Newbury Park, CA: Sage.

Kierkegaard, S. (1859/1952) *The Point of View for My Work as an Author*. New York: Harper Torchbooks.

Larsen, D. J. (2004) 'Daybreak: a scholarly biography of counsellor educator Dr. Vance Peavy'. *International Journal for the Advancement of Counselling*, 26(2), 177–89.

Lewin, K. (1948) *Resolving Social Conflicts*. New York: Harper and Brothers Publishers.

Organisation for Economic Cooperation and Development. (2004) *Career Guidance and Public Policy: Bridging the Gap*. Paris: OECD.

Peavy, R. V. (1992) *Visions of the Future: Worklife and Counselling*. CCTP, University of Victoria, November, Victoria, Canada.

Peavy, R. V. (1996) 'Counselling as a culture of healing'. *British Journal of Guidance and Counselling*, 24, 141–50.

Peavy, R. V. (1997a) 'A constructive framework for career counseling', in T. L. Sexton and B. L. Griffin (eds),*Constructivist Thinking in Counselling Practice, Research, and Training* (pp. 122–40). New York: Teachers College Press.

Peavy, R. V. (1997b) *SocioDynamic Counselling. A Constructivist Perspective for the Practice of Counselling in the Twenty-first Century*. Victoria, BC: Trafford.

Peavy, R. V. (2001) Elämäni työkirja. Konstruktivististen ohjausperiaatteiden soveltaminen: tehtäviä ja harjoituksia. Helsinki: Psykologien Kustannus (in Finnish). A translation of the manuscript: Composing and mapping my life; a Counsellor's Guidebook of Constructivist Principles and Guide Participation. Activities for Use in Training and Counselling. Unpublished manuscript.

Peavy, R. V. (2004a) *SocioDynamic Counselling. A Practical Approach to Meaning Making.* Chagrin Falls, OH: Taos Institute.

Peavy, R. V. (2004b) 'Sosiodynaaminen näkökulma ja ohjauksen käytäntö', in J. Onnismaa, H. Pasanen and T. Spangar (eds), *Counselling as a Profession and Subject of Research. Counselling Methods. Counselling Handbook, Part III* (pp. 16–47). PS-Kustannus: Jyväskylä (in Finnish).

Richardson, M. S. (1993) 'Work in people's lives: a location for counseling psychologists'. *Journal of Counseling Psychology,* 40, 423–33.

Richardson, M. S. (2000) 'A new perspective for counsellors: from career ideologies to empowerment through work and relationship practices', in A. Collin and R. Young (eds), *The Future of Career* (pp. 197–211). Cambridge: Cambridge University Press.

Rifkin, J. (1995) *End of Work: The Decline of the Global Labour Force and Dawn of the Post-market Era.* New York: G. P. Putnam's Sons.

Spangar, T. (2004) 'Using metaphors and ceremonies in career counselling', in J. Onnismaa, H. Pasanen and T. Spangar (eds), *Counselling as a Profession and Subject of Research. Counselling Methods. Counselling Handbook, Part III* (pp. 198–207). PS-Kustannus: Jyväskylä (in Finnish).

Spangar, T. and Arnkil, R. (2005) *The Call of Networking – Evaluation Report of the Guidance Services of the Oulu Employment Agency. Report for the Employment and Economic Development Centre for Northern Ostrobothnia.* Unpublished manuscript (in Finnish).

Vähämöttönen, T. T. E. (1998) 'Reframing career counselling in terms of counsellor-client negotiations'. University of Joensuu: *Publications in Social Sciences* 34. Joensuun yliopistopaino: Joensuu.

Vähämöttönen, T. T. E., Keskinen, P. A. and Parrila, R. K. (1994) 'A conceptual framework for developing an activity-based approach to career counselling'. *International Journal for the Advancement of Counselling,* 17, 19–34.

Vygotsky, L. (1978) *Mind in Society.* Cambridge, MA: Harvard University Press.

Chapter 12

Creativity and career counselling

A story still to be narrated

Mary McMahon

Creativity is fundamental to constructivist approaches to career counselling as evidenced by concepts such as co-construction and life design. Despite the need for individuals to be creative in their thinking and planning around career (Peiperl *et al.*, 2002) and suggestions that career counsellors be creative in their work (e.g., Amundson, 1998; McMahon and Patton, 2002; Peavy, 2001, 2004), little has been written in the career field that facilitates understanding of creativity as a concept nor its application to career counselling. Therefore in writing this chapter, I have also drawn from literature in counselling, family therapy, creative arts therapy and business.

The purpose of this chapter is not to present conclusive ideas about creativity or its many applications. Rather, it is to open a discussion on creativity in the career counselling literature. First, it will explore how the much-used term *creativity* may be understood. Second, the chapter will briefly describe creativity as it has been presented in the career counselling literature to date. Third, application of the creative arts in counselling will be described. A discussion will be developed around creativity as inherent to the career counselling process or as an application of techniques from the creative arts to career counselling. Fourth, it will propose that the meaning of creativity and its use in career counselling be explored and better understood. Finally a practical application will be described that may be used in counsellor education or professional development settings, or by career counsellors themselves, in order to begin a discussion on creativity in career counselling.

What is creativity?

There are many definitions or understandings of creativity and it is useful to examine these in order to begin to understand what creativity could mean for career counselling. Examples include:

- "any new action you take that causes a reaction" (Hurt, 1998, p. 40);
- "the arranging or rearranging of elements so that a new and productive process or product is formed" (Gladding and Henderson, 2000, p. 246);

- "activities or products that are truly original and break new ground" (Carson, 1999, p. 328);
- "associating known things or ideas into new combinations and relationships" (Lengnick-Hall and Lengnick-Hall, 1999, p. 65);
- creativity "involves both seeing and doing things in a different way. The *seeing* part is composed of the mental activity of opening up oneself to new possibilities. The *doing* part is behaving differently" (Gladding and Henderson, 2000, p. 246);
- "creativity usually results in the production of a tangible product that gives the client insight, such as a piece of writing or a painting, or a process that the clinician formulates, such as a new way of conducting counselling that leads clients to change" (Gladding, 1998, p. 2); and
- "the ability to produce work that is both novel (i.e., original or unexpected) and appropriate (i.e., useful or meets task constraints)" (Sternberg and Lubart, 1996, p. 677).

What is evident in these understandings of creativity is that there is no suggestion that it necessarily implies use of the creative arts. However, creativity in the literature is frequently associated with the creative arts directly or indirectly through techniques derived from them such as collage work.

As evidenced in these understandings, creativity may be viewed as a process emanating within individuals and through which original outcomes are produced. As far back as 1975, Frey claimed that "in its broadest sense, counselling is actually a creative enterprise within which the client and counsellor combine their resources to generate a new plan, develop a different outlook, formulate alternative behaviors, begin a new life" (p. 23). Such a process resonates with constructivist approaches to career counselling with their fundamental goal of a collaborative process of meaning-making in order to co-construct future stories for the client. Despite this, counselling has more often been described as a process related to education, helping, personal development and repair, than as a process of creation (Carson, 1999).

Frey (1975) suggests that creativity calls for counsellors to turn within themselves and to not rely solely on technical skill (or the latest gimmicks). Thus clients and counsellors are involved in a process of co-creation, or co-construction as it is termed in constructivist approaches, and both are "co-producers of both the processes and products of counselling, many of which call for creative thought and action" (Carson, 1999, p. 329). Clearly, what creativity is not is simply the application of gimmicks and techniques. Indeed, Murray and Rotter (2002) remind us that "techniques are creative strategies grounded in theory to help elicit change" (p. 204). Further, the application of gimmicks and techniques without a sound theoretical background may leave counsellors unsure of their appropriate use and application and how to proceed if they do not work, a process that could be harmful to clients. Thus the use of creative techniques or strategies warrants a process of honesty and conscious choice on the part of the counsellor that is informed by the counsellor's understanding of the needs of the client and also of the theory behind the technique or strategy. Timing and the client's comfort level with techniques are also important considerations in the use and choice of creative interventions (Murray and Rotter, 2002).

Writing about family therapy, Carson (1999) suggests that creativity may have less to do with techniques per se than with the dynamic process as it involves "a complex interaction of counsellor training and qualities, client personalities and presenting problems, structural and systemic considerations, the understanding and healthy expression of human emotions, and the circumstances under which counselling is taking place" (p. 331). Carson's suggestion, with its origins in constructivist philosophy, systemic thinking, active agency, the value of subjectivity and emotions, and the importance of the counsellor–client relationship illustrates the possible contribution of family therapy's understanding of creativity to discussion about its use in constructivist career counselling. Based on Carson's comments, it seems that becoming creative in counselling is not about accumulating an ever-increasing glad bag or sleeve full of techniques. It is much more about development of the person of the counsellor and the process of counselling. In this regard, Murray and Rotter (2002) observe that "techniques alone merely produce a technician skilled in gimmicks, not a therapist whose intention is to effect change" (p. 204).

To further understand the concept of creativity, it is useful to examine understandings about divergent thinking, as it is frequently used synonymously with creative thinking (Carson, 1999). Carson explains that divergent thinking may be viewed as more intuitive than data based, tentative and exploratory, and oriented towards possibilities and speculation rather than conclusions. Further, divergent thinkers tend to be able to tolerate ambiguity, hold contradictory ideas simultaneously, and avoid closing options through making judgement (Carson). Clearly there are parallels between the elements of divergent thinking and the process of constructivist career counselling, with its orientation towards multiple stories, possibilities, curiosity, respectful and tentative collaboration, meaning-making and co-construction.

In relation to the personal qualities of the counsellor, Carson (1999, p. 329) provides a comprehensive list of characteristics of highly creative people. Interestingly, the characteristics of "openness to 'inner' and 'outer' experiences", "sensitivity" and "empathy and superawareness of the needs of others" are reflective of Rogers' (1951) three necessary and essential conditions for relationships in counselling that sit comfortably with the constructivist worldview, specifically genuineness, unconditional positive regard and empathic understanding. In addition, Carson lists characteristics such as "tolerance of ambiguity", "often asks why?", "copes well with and appreciates novelty", "keen attention to the social and natural world", "emotional expressiveness", "enjoys the world of ideas", "fantasy proneness and richness of mental imagery", "vivid imagination, a sense of wonderment, and childlike playfulness". Such characteristics also sit well with counselling approaches informed by the constructivist worldview such as Peavy's (1998) SocioDynamic counselling and Amundson's (1998, 2003) concept of active engagement, and less well with counselling approaches informed by the logical positivist worldview.

In terms of creative environment, Carson (1999) suggests that the personal characteristics of counsellors previously described may be as important as a comfortable and aesthetically pleasing setting. For example, creativity may be enhanced by activities such as moving outside the confines of an office to a playground, or using movement-based processes, activities consistent with suggestions offered by Amundson (1998, 2003, see Chapter 7 of this book). Clients also have some responsibility towards the creation of a creative environment through their willingness to learn and grow. On a cautionary note, Carson reminds us that "increased creativity in clients or use of creative insight or techniques in therapy do not automatically result in therapeutic change" (p. 332).

Creativity in career counselling

Perhaps because of its trait and factor origins that continue to dominate practice, career counselling traditionally has not been viewed as a creative discipline. For example, even recent texts present models of counselling that are linear in orientation with assessment featured as a necessary step early in the process. Such models have dominated the profession throughout its history, and have resulted in criticism of career counselling. In relation to these dominant approaches, concerns have been expressed about how career counselling is presented in counsellor education programmes. For example, over a decade ago, Heppner *et al.* (1994) advocated the use of creativity in career counselling after research revealed that a perceived lack of creativity in career counselling had a negative impact on graduate students' interest in career counselling. In addition, the participants in this study also commented on the lack of creativity in their training. One of their complaints was that "listening to career counsellors who practice in a stereotyped, superficial manner was disappointing" (p. 78). Given that stereotyped models of career counselling are still being promoted in major texts, the situation of over a decade ago may be little different.

In regard to creativity, Peavy (2001) remarked that "Creativity is often downplayed as impractical, not efficient, and even a waste of time" (p. 3). Unlike the more traditional models of career counselling, Peavy's (1998) SocioDynamic approach places great value on creativity. "First the self is held to be an expression of creativity – the self-creation model. Second, it is by using creativity that many obstacles are overcome. Creativity enables the overcoming of limitations and paralysing habits. In the counselling process itself, counsellor and help-seeker often create solutions, futures, choices and pathways through their joint and spontaneous work together" (Peavy, 2001, p. 3).

Several authors agree that career counsellors are not adequately prepared to be creative in their work (e.g., Heppner *et al.*, 1994; Willis, 2003) as career counselling has traditionally been a linear activity based on assessment and oral expression. To this end, Pope and Minor (2000) present an edited collection of 71 experiential learning activities that may be used in the training of career counsellors. In addition, some of the activities described may be replicated or modified for use with clients. This book represents a significant attempt to promote creativity in the teaching and practice of career counselling. Many of the activities described in this book are reflective of suggestions made by Heppner *et al.* that creative activities may include the use of guided imagery, career genograms, metaphor, collage, timeline analysis and life mapping. A similar range of activities that may be used by career practitioners is presented in McMahon and Patton (2003).

Creativity in career counselling, particularly through the application of the creative arts, opens the possibility of tapping into learning styles such as visual, kinaesthetic, auditory and linguistic (Willis, 2003). However, there is limited evidence of the use of the creative arts in career counselling. For example, Pope and Minor (2000) contains only one creative arts-based activity (Willis, 2000) that is based on creative movement. Willis (2003) suggests that creative art therapy "can evoke emotion, promote relaxation, and help the client access an unconscious level for decision-making" (p. 45). In presenting a collage-based activity derived from art therapy, Adams (2003) concurs, suggesting that collage may be a "valuable tool to assist clients to express the unknown, forgotten, or unacknowledged future goals, and to discover and explore unique qualities in themselves" (p. 4). Willis (2003) recommends that career counsellors attempt to express their own career stories through the arts before attempting to use it with their clients.

Guidelines have been suggested for using the creative arts in counselling (Gladding, 1998) and career counselling (Willis, 2003). For example, Willis suggests that the introduction of creative processes into career counselling must be in the context of well-developed counselling relationships. In deciding to use creative arts in career assessment, Willis suggests that career counsellors:

- know the purpose of the assessment;
- design or select an activity to specifically address the needs and style of the client;
- combine the arts assessment with other assessments and interventions to assist the client in obtaining a full picture;

- process the experience thoroughly in order to increase understanding and to explore any possible meanings that may have been hidden to the client; and
- assist the client to understand what the results may mean (p. 45)

As many creative techniques may also be used as qualitative assessment processes, these guidelines are reflective of those suggested by McMahon and Patton (2002) for incorporating qualitative assessment into career counselling (see Chapter 13).

Creativity or the creative arts?

Murray and Rotter (2002) remind us that "traditional talk" has a place and is necessary in counselling, but suggest that in view of the diversity of clientele and issues facing counsellors, there is a need to offer more innovative and applicable approaches. Indeed, several of the creative techniques discussed in career counselling emanate out of the creative arts. However, as suggested earlier in this chapter, creativity in counselling does not automatically imply application of the creative arts.

The use of the creative arts has previously been described in counselling and family therapy but it has been given little attention in career counselling to date. Gladding (1998) provides the most comprehensive coverage of the use of the creative arts in counselling. Specifically, he addresses the use of music, dance, visual arts, play, imagery, drama and literature in counselling. In commenting on family therapy, Carson (1999) observes that creative approaches encourage clients to communicate spontaneously in a caring and non-threatening manner. Further, it has been claimed that creativity is relevant worldwide to people of all cultures who may enjoy creative arts in many ways (Gladding, 1998; Henderson and Gladding, 1998). Thus it is important to select creative arts that are amenable to clients' backgrounds and interests. In so doing, client counsellor rapport and client outcomes may be enhanced.

Gladding (1998) proposes a number of advantages and limitations of using the creative arts in counselling. He suggests that advantages include playfulness, a collegial relationship, the promotion of communication, recognition of the multiple natures of individuals and the world, the fostering of expression in non-verbal clients, and a tool to promote diagnosis, understanding and dialogue. Possible limitations include its application in non-therapeutic and non-scientific ways, and fears that clients may become too introspective, passive, critical or over-involved. In addition, Gladding expresses a concern that including the arts into a counsellor's repertoire may become "arts and crafts, which is much more mechanical and structured activity than would be used in the creative arts" (p. 10). Henderson and Gladding (1998) remark that "the creative arts can offer an approach to counsellors who become skilled in their usage" (p.183), once again raising the issue of the use of techniques without a sound understanding of the theory behind them.

Where to from here – a conversation on creativity?

From the discussion in this chapter, it seems that a dominant theme is that creativity does not necessarily imply the use of techniques. Techniques, if used repetitively and mechanistically, if not client driven and focused, if not processed or debriefed carefully and respectfully with clients to elicit meaning and learning, may lack creativity. Alternatively, dialogues involving nothing more than (on the surface) a respectful, reflective collaborative process may be highly creative. Thus the issue becomes more one of how we tap the innate creativity of individuals – clients and counsellors. It seems that having an array of techniques, while helpful in some situations if selected wisely, is not necessarily the answer.

Career counselling has traditionally been about the collection of facts about individuals that formed a basis for matching them to occupations. There is nothing inherently creative about facts and matching. However, there is something inherently creative about how "the facts" are interpreted or the meaning they are ascribed by individuals. For example, let's think about some possible meanings of being a gifted musician. The musician may be passionate about their playing and want nothing more than opportunities to keep playing as much and as often as they can, hopefully in paid employment. Alternatively, he/she may resent the hours practising under parental and music teacher supervision and want nothing more than to "get a life" beyond music. A further meaning could be that he/she is passionate about his/her music but has concerns about the security of a future occupation in music and thus be viewing music as a leisure option rather than a paid employment experience. As evidenced in these examples, creativity does not lie with the facts but rather with the meaning derived from them. Each set of meanings reveals some more facts, which can then be elaborated further. Thus two challenges seem to emerge from the literature on creativity. First is the need for creativity to be better understood in career counselling. Second is the challenge of preparing career counsellors who can be creative in their work regardless of technique. Indeed, creativity and its application in career counselling present as a real challenge as the profession strives to deal with increasing complexity.

Practical application

In presenting this practical application, I first toyed with the idea of presenting a technique that could be used in a group training setting or in career counselling. However, one of the central themes of this chapter is that creativity in career counselling is about more than techniques. Thus, the process described below is one of guided reflection that may be undertaken by individual counsellors

Title/topic: Reflection on creativity.

Aims/learning objectives
This process is designed to provide an opportunity for participants to reflect on creativity in their work. By the end of the session it is hoped that participants will be able to:

- understand the role they play in constructing creativity in career counselling;
- identify what they do that facilitates and inhibits creativity;
- set goals to enhance the creativity of their work.

Client group with whom you use it
Counsellor education students; career counsellors.

Work setting recommendations
This activity could be used in a classroom setting in a counsellor education programme or in a professional development workshop. Alternatively, career counsellors could undertake it themselves by arranging a quiet time for reflection.

Recommended time
1 hour.

Materials/equipment needed
No equipment is needed. However, reflection may be facilitated more easily if participants are comfortable. Some may like to lie on the floor. Some may like to close their eyes.

Step-by-step outline of the process or programme

1   Participants think about their career counselling work over the previous week until one case or client stands out for them more than any other. They then focus on that client or case and their career counselling interaction for the rest of the reflection. Counsellor educators may like to read the following stimulus questions slowly to students to guide their reflection. Career counsellors working alone may like to consider each question in turn.
    a. What theoretical standpoint informs your approach to career counselling, and what are the central tenets of it that you apply in your work?

b. What ideas did you bring into counselling about your client, their issue, or your work?

c. What were the environmental conditions in which the career counselling took place? For example, what was the nature of the service and its operation? How was the counselling room set up?

d. What aspects of the interview would you describe as creative and why?

e. What things did you say or do in the counselling session that you hadn't planned?

f. What things did the client say or do that surprised you?

g. What elements of the outcome of the session were unexpected for you?

h. What was it about you that may have facilitated creativity in the session?

i. What was it about the environment that may have facilitated creativity?

j. What was it about the client that may have facilitated creativity?

k. What was it about you that may have inhibited creativity?

l. What was it about the environment that may have inhibited creativity?

m. What was it about the client what may have inhibited creativity?

n. What would you do in a future session with that client to facilitate creativity?

2 Debrief the reflection activity. This could be done individually or in pairs and be followed by a whole group discussion. The following questions could be used as a guide.

a. What did you learn or realise about your career counselling work during the reflection process?

b. Based on your reflection, how do you understand creativity in relation to your own career counselling work?

c. What points would you like to raise in a conversation with a colleague about creativity and career counselling?

or with groups in training or professional development workshop settings. Hopefully, the reflection process may generate discussions on creativity and further exploration of this fascinating topic.

Conclusion

The dearth of career counselling literature on creativity may suggest that it is intrinsically understood by career counsellors. Alternatively, it may suggest that it is an overlooked or still to be attended to area in the career counselling literature. It is in the context of this latter meaning that this chapter has been written to open discussion on creativity and explore its meaning and possible contribution to career counselling. In an era where the need for career counselling for a diverse client group is becoming more apparent, a corresponding need for creativity in career counselling is emerging. However, creativity is not yet well understood in career counselling, and there is a risk of the adoption of creative techniques without a theoretical understanding of creativity to inform it. Thus it is hoped that this chapter will serve as a springboard for discussion.

References

Adams, M. (2003) 'Creating a personal collage to assist with career development', in McMahon, M. and Patton, W. (eds), *Ideas for Career Practitioners: Celebrating Excellence in Australian Career Practice* (pp. 4–7). Brisbane, Australia: Australian Academic Press.

Amundson, N. E. (1998) *Active Engagement: Enhancing the Career Counselling Process*. Richmond, Canada: Ergon Communications.

Amundson, N. E. (2003) *Active Engagement* (2nd edn). Richmond, Canada: Ergon Communications.

Carson, D. K. (1999) 'The importance of creativity in family therapy: a preliminary consideration'. *The Family Journal: Counseling and Therapy for Couples and Families*, 7, 326–34.

Frey, D. H. (1975) 'The anatomy of an idea: creativity in counselling'. *Personnel and Guidance Journal*, 54(1), 22–7.

Gladding, S. T. (1998) *Counseling as an Art: The Creative Arts in Counseling* (2nd edn). Alexandria, VA: American Counseling Association.

Gladding, S. T. and Henderson, D. A. (2000) 'Creativity and family counseling: the SCAMPER model as a template for promoting creative processes'. *The Family Journal: Counseling and Therapy for Couples and Families*, 8, 245–9.

Henderson, D. A. and Gladding, S. T. (1998) 'The creative arts in counseling: a multicultural perspective'. *The Arts in Psychotherapy*, 25, 183–7.

Heppner, M. J., O'Brien, K. M., Hinkelman, J. M. and Humphrey, C. F. (1994) 'Shifting the paradigm: the use of creativity in career counselling'. *Journal of Career Development*, 21(2), 77–86.

Hurt, F. (1998) 'Achieving creativity: four critical steps'. *Direct Marketing*, 60(10), 40–4.

Lengnick-Hall, M. L. and Lengnick-Hall, C. A. (1999) 'Leadership jazz: an exercise in creativity'. *Journal of Management Education*, 23(1), 65–71.

McMahon, M. and Patton, W. (2002) 'Using qualitative assessment in career counselling'. *International Journal of Educational and Vocational Guidance*, 2(1), 51–66.

McMahon, M. and Patton, W. (eds) (2003) *Ideas for Career Practitioners: Celebrating Excellence in Australian Career Practice*. Brisbane, Australia: Australian Academic Press.

Murray, P. E. and Rotter, J. C. (2002) 'Creative counselling techniques for family therapists'. *The Family Journal: Counseling and Therapy for Couples and Families*, 10(2), 203–6.

Peavy, R. V. (1998) *SocioDynamic Counselling: A Constructivist Perspective*. Victoria, Canada: Trafford.

Peavy, R. V. (2001) Part 1: *A Brief Outline of SocioDynamic Counselling: A Constructivist Approach on Helping*. Retrieved 15 March 2005, from http:// www.sociodynamic-constructivist-counselling.com/brief_outline.pdf.

Peavy, R. V. (2004) *SocioDynamic Counselling: A Practical Approach to Meaning Making*. Chagrin Falls, OH: Taos Institute.

Peiperl, M., Arthur, M. and Anand, N. (eds) (2002) *Career Creativity: Explorations in the Remaking of Work*. Oxford: Oxford University Press.

Pope, M. and Minor, C. W. (eds) (2000) *Experiential Activities for Teaching Career Counseling Classes and for Facilitating Career Groups*. Columbus, OH: National Career Development Association.

Rogers, C. (1951) *Client-centered Therapy*. Boston, MA: Houghton Mifflin.

Willis, C. J. (2000) 'Creative movement and the career decision process', in M. Pope and C. W. Minor (eds), *Experiential Activities for Teaching Career Counseling Classes and for Facilitating Career Groups* (pp. 87–90). Columbus, OH: National Career Development Association.

Sternberg, R. J. and Lubart, T. I. (1996) 'Investing in creativity'. *Arts in Psychotherapy*, 24, 677–88.

Willis, C. J. (2003) 'Using creative arts in the career assessment process, in *Global Realities: Celebrating our Differences, Honouring our Connections*, pp. 43–8. (ERIC Document Reproduction Service No. ED480502).

Part IV

Constructivist career assessment

Chapter 13

Qualitative career assessment

Mary McMahon and Wendy Patton

Assessment has been integral to the work of career counsellors since the profession originated in the early 1900s with the work of Parsons (1909). Since that time, the type of assessment has largely determined the structure of the counselling process and the roles assumed by counsellors and clients. Most of the emphasis on career assessment has focused on quantitative assessment and career counsellors have been slow to move from this traditional position (Brown and Brooks, 1996).

Quantitative assessment sits comfortably with the logical-positivist worldview with its emphasis on objective, value-free knowledge. Thus career counselling has traditionally been depicted as a linear process with strong emphasis on assessment (Brown and Brooks, 1991; Subich and Simonson, 2001). More recently, the constructivist worldview with its emphasis on meaning-making, active agency and holism has been influential in advances in career theory and practice. Corresponding with this worldview shift there has been renewed interest in the use of qualitative career assessment.

This chapter first explores a history of qualitative career assessment as a story that may have been largely silenced or overshadowed for many years. Second, it examines the advantages of qualitative career assessment and considerations for its use in career counselling. Finally, the chapter outlines a practical application of qualitative career assessment that could be used by counsellor educators or practitioners.

Starting at the very beginning

Frank Parsons, founder of the Vocations Bureau in Boston, is "… credited with founding the career counseling specialization of modern day professional counseling and the related fields of vocational psychology and counseling psychology" (Pope and Sveinsdottir, 2005, p. 105). In essence, Parsons identified three elements of career decision making that have pervaded career counselling and career assessment to the present day. Further, he pioneered a process, predicated on assessment, that has also had a lasting legacy, specifically that choosing a vocation is based on self-understanding, world of work knowledge and "true reasoning on the relations of these two groups of facts" (Parsons, 1909, p. 5).

The matching process promoted by Parsons has dominated career practice to the present day as it spawned what has come to be known as trait and factor approaches and more recently person-environment fit approaches to career theory and practice. Indeed, it has been the dominant story in career assessment with Borgen (1991) suggesting that "Parsons' paradigm is a taproot that still invigorates vocational psychology" (p. 265), a situation that remains unchanged today. The trait and factor and person-environment fit approaches emanate out of the logical-positivist worldview that relies on measurement and objective data that is interpreted by an expert who, on that basis, also makes predictions. Indeed, it is this legacy for which Parsons is best known even though McDaniels (1994) claims that "he would be very unhappy when he learned about the career counselor's extensive overuse of standardized tests and inventories" (p. 328).

What is less well known about Parsons' work is his emphasis on the involvement of the client in the career assessment process. For example, clients were required to complete a 100-item questionnaire prior to their career counselling interview. In addition, those who were not yet at a stage where they could make a decision were encouraged by Parsons to gather occupational information by various methods including reading, work observation and work experience before returning for another interview. Further, Parsons (1909) advocated personal analysis to facilitate self-understanding and provided a comprehensive "personal record and self-analysis" questionnaire (p. 27) for clients to complete in private with help where necessary from family, friends, employers or teachers.

Thus, in these suggestions, Parsons advocated an active role for the client, a role consistent with constructivist notions of active agency. However, Zytowski and Swanson (1994) claim that vocational psychology has always struggled with the issue of self-assessment and how much confidence to place in it despite evidence that attests to its validity. This struggle was apparent as early as 1913 when Munsterberg (as cited in Zytowski and Swanson) claimed that Parsons' Vocations Bureau must "emancipate itself from the methods of self-observation, and replace them with objective experiment in the psychological laboratory" (p. 307). This move away from self-assessment is reflected today in widespread use of quantitative counsellor administered processes.

The notion of self-assessment is reflective of the constructivist concept of active agency. Jones (1994) suggests that Parsons' concept of self-assessment and the written tasks his clients completed are reflective of self-assessment techniques that are used today such as genograms, written exercises such as lifeline exercises and occupational card sorts. Such techniques constitute qualitative career assessment processes and promote individual agency. Active agency is also promoted by Parsons in his concept of true reasoning, where he promoted the development of analytic powers in his clients to integrate the information they gathered. McDaniels (1994) claims that Parsons recognised that self-understanding is a process rather than a product, that it is best fostered by the active participation by individuals in "multifaceted investigations and inquiries" (p. 328), and that it goes beyond choosing occupations to self-assessment across the lifespan. Further, Parsons (1909) recommended that a client "come to wise decisions himself" (p. 4) because no-one may decide what occupation another person should choose. Such thinking is clearly tinged with "a constructivist flavor" (Spokane and Glickman, 1994, p. 303) that is suggestive of clients designing and building their own careers.

What is also not well known about the work of Parsons is his acknowledgement of contextual influences in the career decision making process. In suggesting that the young people with whom he worked invited the opinion of family, friends, employers and teachers, Parsons (1909) was encouraging clients to involve influential people from their social systems. In addition to gathering information on abilities and interests, he also encouraged reflection on other contextual influences such as family, health, resources such as financial status, lifestyle and mobility. While he has been criticised for not placing enough emphasis on the influence of family and culture (Spokane and Glickman, 1994), his reference to influences such as those mentioned previously is reflective of the more holistic view of career decision-making that accords with the constructivist worldview.

As mentioned previously, the work of Parsons is most commonly associated with the logical-positivist worldview. However, closer examination of his work emphasises the importance he placed on intrapersonal and interpersonal concerns in career decision-making processes (O'Brien, 2001). His acknowledgement of a broader context and the active role of the client in their own career decision making do not sit comfortably under the logical-positivist worldview and, in fact, sit more comfortably with the constructivist worldview. Indeed, it has been suggested that "Parsons presaged the constructivist position" (Spokane and Glickman, 1994, p. 298). It may be that just as our lives are multi-storied, so too was the work of Frank Parsons, but that the power of the dominant story silenced or overshadowed a possible alternative story. That stories are culturally located may also warrant some consideration in this regard, as the dominant story on career assessment is culturally located in what has been described as "a multi-million dollar industry" (Zytowski and Swanson, 1994, p. 308). The dominance of this story is still evidenced in consecutive annual reviews of practice and research in career counselling and development published in the journal *The Career Development Quarterly* (e.g., Arbona, 2000; Dagley and Salter, 2004; Flores *et al.*, 2003; Luzzo and MacGregor, 2001; Whiston and Brecheisen, 2002; Young and Chen, 1999), where qualitative career assessment is seldom, if at all, mentioned and then only briefly.

Qualitative career assessment: what's in it for career counsellors?

Given the dominant quantitative career assessment story that has served the profession well for many years and which is still pervasive, as well as the paucity of literature available on qualitative career assessment, it may not be unreasonable for career counsellors to doubt its usefulness and to wonder "what's in it for me". However, there is no doubt that the nature of society and the workforce has changed and that career counsellors are dealing with a broader range of client groups on a complex array of career issues. Thus there have been calls for career counselling to reform itself into an interpretive discipline (Savickas, 1993) and for career assessment practices to keep pace with societal and workforce changes (Subich, 1996). In particular, quantitative career assessment's inability to respond to issues of diversity, lack of attention to contextual influences and continued reliance on a "counsellor as expert" model have resulted in criticism of this traditional approach. Goldman (1994) reflected that quantitative career assessment instruments are not well used by most career counsellors and suggested that "the marriage is over" (p. 217) between counselling and standardised assessment. Bradley (1994) concurs, claiming that "tests reflect old science" (p. 224) and wondering how counselling and tests ever became partners.

It has been suggested that qualitative career assessment has the potential to address some of these shortcomings (Goldman, 1990, 1992, 1994; Subich, 1996). Probably the most comprehensive outline of the advantages of qualitative assessment, even though over a decade old, is that provided by Goldman (1990, 1992). Specifically, the advantages that Goldman suggests are that qualitative assessment:

- fosters an active role for the client who is actively involved in collecting information and elaborating meaning;
- tends to be more holistic and integrative;
- emphasises learning about oneself within a developmental framework;
- promotes a more collaborative relationship between client and counsellor;
- may be used effectively in groups because they foster learning and growth; and
- is flexible and adaptable and therefore valuable for use with clients from diverse backgrounds.

In addition, Okocha (1998) claims that qualitative career assessment processes may enliven career counselling, and that it may be beneficial for those who are visual, kinaesthetic or tactile learners. Further qualitative assessment processes accommodate subjective and affective client processes as well as cognitive processes, and value client interpretation and meaning (Brott, 2004; McMahon and Patton, 2002b). Through accessing a range of contextual data, qualitative career assessment paints holistic pictures of career issues (McMahon and Patton, 2002b).

Despite these obvious advantages, qualitative career assessment is not without its critics who have suggested that it may be time-consuming and labour intensive, have questionable reliability and validity, be too informal and lack scientific rigour (Okocha, 1998). However, McMahon, Watson and Patton (in press) counter this criticism by describing the rigour involved in the development of a qualitative career assessment process. Also in defence of qualitative assessment, Richardson (1996) claims that "qualitative research should not be evaluated in terms of the canons of validity that have evolved for the assessment of quantitative research, since these have different epistemological priorities and commitments" (pp. 191–2). For example, the criteria for adequacy of assessment developed under the constructivist worldview are "primarily interpretative and phenomenological" whereas under the logical-positivist worldview they are "normative and statistical" (Niemeyer and Niemeyer, 1993, p. 23).

What exactly is it and how do I use it?

So, what exactly is qualitative career assessment, and how might it be applied in career counselling practice? Okocha (1998) describes qualitative assessment as "informal forms of assessment" (pp. 151–2) that offer counsellors "methods of helping clients to know and understand themselves better – methods that are flexible, open-ended, holistic, and nonstatistical" (Goldman, 1992, p. 616). Qualitative career assessment accords with the philosophy of the constructivist worldview in its promotion in counselling of active agency, meaning-making, holism and collaborative relationships. Therefore, from a constructivist perspective, terms such as diagnosis and assessment fit less well (Peavy, 1998). In addition, even the terms assessment and instrument have an uncomfortable fit. In this regard, some authors (e.g., McMahon and Patton, 2002a, 2002b; McMahon, Patton and Watson, 2003; McMahon, Watson and Patton, in press) prefer to use the term qualitative assessment *process* rather than instrument or measure to reflect its dynamic, constructive and relational nature.

Consistent with the constructivist philosophy, Brott (2004) suggests that constructivist approaches to career counselling promote a shift in the purpose of career assessment to emphasise assessment that may provide information that may "be woven into the client's story to form a more holistic and integrative picture of the client" (p. 190). In this regard, Peavy (1998) proposes that the aim of assessment is to "open up avenues of movement, promote empowerment, support transitions, and assist the client to gain eligibility for more participation" in their preferred future (p. 180). Such an aim is reflective of what has been described as a fundamental goal of constructivist counselling: "understanding personal patterns of meaning – that is, the way a client organizes and makes sense of his or her experience over time" (Lyddon and Alford, 1993, p. 52). Thus, qualitative assessment processes narrow the gap between assessment and counselling, and result in a seamless process that is collaborative between client and counsellor and facilitative of meaning-making, "client empowerment, and the awareness of contextual issues" (Subich, 1996, p. 286). In so doing, qualitative career assessment may also help facilitate attention to individual diversity (Subich).

Qualitative methods may assess "traditional vocational variables such as interests, values, and abilities as well as less traditional variables such as socialization, barriers, and cultural orientation" (Subich, 1996, p. 285). Zunker and Norris (1998) suggest that qualitative assessment processes may supplement or raise questions about information obtained in other ways such as more traditional forms of assessment, thus reducing reliance on any one particular source of information. Goldman (1992) suggests that qualitative career assessment processes include "simulations, exercises and games that stimulate people to respond, cognitively and affectively, as they might in comparable life situations" (p. 616). The most common forms of qualitative career assessment are genograms, timelines or lifelines, card sorts and early recollections. In addition, some theorists have developed qualitative assessment processes that complement their theoretical viewpoint. For example, Peavy (1998) advocates the use of life-space mapping, Amundson (1998) developed a pattern identification exercise and Patton and McMahon (1999) advocate the use of their Systems Theory Framework that underpins the development of the My System of Career Influences reflection process (MSCI) (McMahon, Patton and Watson, 2005).

Incorporating qualitative career assessment into career counselling suggests a different process from the traditional linear counselling processes that were predicated on psychometric assessment. Constructivist career counselling is less reliant on assessment and more focused on story and meaning-making in whatever form that takes. Thus the process of constructivist career counselling is less easy to describe as it needs to accommodate the flexibility of a process in which the client has a much greater involvement and assessment may or may not be used.

McMahon and Patton (2002a) suggested a process (see Figure 13.1) that reflects the new location of career assessment within career counselling and also accommodates constructivist career counselling's emphasis on relationship, client agency, story and meaning-making. In essence, this process illustrates the centrality of story and meaning-making within the life-space of the client in order that the next chapter of their career story continue and a possible future is co-constructed. As depicted in Figure 13.1, the need for assessment of any form will evolve as the client-counsellor interaction unfolds. McMahon and Patton suggest that this process may be applicable to the use of traditional quantitative or qualitative assessment, but that its use will be determined through the client–counsellor dialogue on the basis of client needs, and that clients will have greater input into its selection and interpretation. This process also takes into account assessment that may have been done by clients prior to their entering a counselling relationship. For example, they may have undertaken self-assessment of their work values based on their previous employment and life/career priorities. Alternatively, they may have undertaken web-based career assessment processes. Such personal assessment may be sufficient to elaborate such meaning that the next chapter of their career story is co-constructed without recourse to further assessment. Unlike counselling processes emanating out of the logical-positivist worldview, this process is flexible, collaborative and recognises the agency of clients.

The career counselling process described above may be complemented by guidelines proposed by McMahon and Patton (2002b) for the inclusion of assessment into the career counselling process. These guidelines include:

- *Individualise the process for the client*
  Recognise the uniqueness of each client in the selection and use of assessment processes.
- *Map the qualitative assessment onto the story previously told by the client*
  Assessment that relates to or emanates out of the story told by the client is likely to be more meaningful.
- *Make the qualitative assessment fit for the client not the client fit the assessment*
  Be flexible in the use of qualitative career assessment to ensure that it is meaningful for the client.
- *Broach the subject of using a qualitative assessment device tentatively, respectfully and informatively*
  Invite the client to participate in assessment processes after careful explanation of their usefulness.
- *Acknowledge that it is the client's prerogative to engage in the activity*
  It is the client's right to participate or not participate, or to discontinue with an assessment process.
- *Work with and support the client through the process of the assessment using counselling skills*
  The career counsellor's role in the process is as a guide and supporter, or that of "nurturer" (Parker, 2002, p. 84).
- *Debrief/process the activity*
  Debriefing at the end of the process encourages clients to elicit meaning and learning and to identify ways of applying it in the construction of the new chapter of their career story.
- *Invite feedback on qualitative assessment processes*
  Counsellors may learn from the process by inviting client feedback and in so doing valuing the client's contribution.
- *Be creative*
  Career counsellors' courage to be creative and to vary qualitative career assessment processes in collaboration with clients may foster a meaningful process.

Starting point

Outcomes

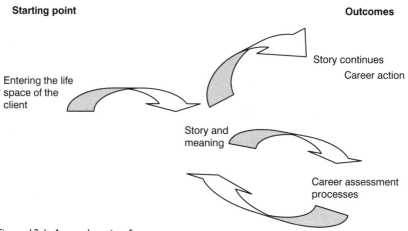

Entering the life
space of the
client

Story continues

Career action

Story and
meaning

Career assessment
processes

Figure 13.1 A new location for career assessment

Practical application

The process and guidelines outlined by McMahon and Patton (2002a, 2002b)
provide some much needed guidance for career counsellors in the use of
qualitative career assessment. The following activity provides an opportunity
to reflect on the application of this process and guidelines in a career
counselling session. While the activity is initially described for students and
counsellors in formal settings, an optional activity is described for counsellors
working independently.

Title/topic: Reflection on a counsellor at work

Aims/learning objectives
It is hoped that by undertaking this activity, participants will be able
to:
- understand how to incorporate qualitative career assessment into
  their work;
- recognise strategies that facilitate the successful and appropriate
  use of qualitative career assessment; and
- identify strategies that they could apply in their own work.

Client group with whom you use it
Counsellor education students; career counsellors.

Work setting recommendations
This activity could be used in a classroom setting in a counsellor
education programme or in a professional development workshop.

Recommended time
90 minutes.

Materials/equipment needed
- Either a video or DVD of a professional counsellor facilitating a qualitative career assessment process (e.g., Peavy, 1995), or
- a video or DVD of a student facilitating a qualitative career assessment process, or
- a live demonstration of the instructor or a student facilitating a qualitative career assessment process.
- Participants will each need a copy of guidelines for including assessment into career counselling (See Figure 13.2) based on those developed by McMahon and Patton (2002b) on which they may make notes.

(Note: Depending on the facilities available, if there are multiple video or DVD players and observation points, students may each present a recording of their work and engage in the following process with their peers.)

Step-by-step outline of the process or programme
1 Participants watch either the video or live demonstration of career counselling, and as they do so, they make notes on the guidelines for incorporating qualitative career assessment into career counselling using Figure 13.2.
2 In either small groups or with the whole group, students discuss their observations.
3 Following the discussion, participants make notes related to what they believe they already do in their own work, and set goals about what they would like to incorporate into their work in future.

Optional activity for career counsellors

Career counsellors may invite feedback from a client on their work according to the guidelines outlined by McMahon and Patton (2002b). Alternatively, they may invite a colleague, with the permission of the client, to observe a career counselling session in which they incorporate a qualitative career assessment process. During the session the colleague observes the process for evidence of the guidelines presented by McMahon and Patton. After the session, both the counsellor and their colleague discuss the observations, following which the counsellor sets themselves some goals for the future. Such process could be incorporated into counsellor supervision.

• Individualise the process for the client	• Map the qualitative assessment onto the story previously told by the client	• Make the qualitative assessment fit for the client not the client fit the assessment	• Broach the subject of using a qualitative assessment tentatively, respectfully and informatively	• Acknowledge that it is the client's prerogative to engage in the activity	• Work with and support the client through the process of the assessment using counselling skills	• Debrief/process the activity	• Invite feedback on qualitative assessment processes	• Be creative

Figure 13.2 Guidelines for including assessment into the career counselling process (based on McMahon and Patton, 2002b)

Conclusion

As evidenced throughout this chapter, qualitative career assessment may not be the relative newcomer to career counselling that we may have been led to believe. Indeed, it may be a story that has been overshadowed throughout the history of the profession until the relatively recent influence of constructivism. Consequently, to date it is not well documented despite the richness that it offers counsellors and clients in their meaning-making endeavours. This chapter in no way suggests that qualitative assessment should replace traditional forms of assessment, but rather that they may co-exist in complementary ways. Indeed, the process and guidelines outlined in this chapter may be applied to both forms of assessment. The potential of qualitative career assessment to aid the work of career counsellors is gradually being realised, and we hope that this chapter will encourage more practitioners to incorporate it into their own work.

References

Amundson, N. E. (1998) *Active Engagement Enhancing the Career Counselling Process*. Richmond, Canada: Ergon Communications.

Arbona, C. (2000) 'Practice and research in career counseling and development – 1999'. *The Career Development Quarterly*, 49, 98–134.

Borgen, F. H. (1991) 'Megatrends and milestones in vocational behavior: a 20 year counseling psychology retrospective'. *Journal of Vocational Behavior*, 39, 263–90.

Bradley, R. W. (1994) 'Tests and counseling: how did we ever become partners'. *Measurement and Evaluation in Counseling and Development*, 26, 224–6.

Brott, P. E. (2004) 'Constructivist assessment in career counseling'. *Journal of Career Development*, 30, 189–200.

Brown, D. and Brooks, L. (1991) *Career Counseling Techniques*. Needham Heights, MA: Allyn and Bacon.

Brown, D. and Brooks, L. (1996) 'Introduction to theories of career development and choice', in D. Brown and L. Brooks (eds), *Career Choice and Development* (3rd edn, pp. 1–30). San Francisco, CA: Jossey-Bass.

Dagley, J. C. and Salter, S. K. (2004) 'Practice and research in career counseling and development – 2003'. *The Career Development Quarterly*, 53, 98–157.

Flores, L. Y., Scott, A. B., Wang, Y., Yakushko, O., McCloskey, C. M., Spencer, K. G., et al. (2003) 'Practice and research in career counseling and development – 2002'. *The Career Development Quarterly*, 52, 98–131.

Goldman, L. (1990) 'Qualitative assessment'. *The Counseling Psychologist*, 18, 205–13.

Goldman, L. (1992) 'Qualitative assessment: an approach for counselors'. *Journal of Counseling and Development*, 70, 616–21.

Goldman, L. (1994) 'The marriage is over … for most of us'. *Measurement and Evaluation in Counseling and Development*, 26, 217–18.

Jones, L. K. (1994) 'Frank Parsons' contribution to career counseling'. *Journal of Career Development*, 20, 287–294.

Luzzo, D. A. and MacGregor, M. W. (2001) 'Practice and research in career development – 2000'. *The Career Development Quarterly*, 50, 98–139.

Lyddon, W. J. and Alford, D. J. (1993) 'Constructivist assessment: a developmental-epistemic perspective', in G. J. Neimeyer (ed.), *Constructivist Assessment: A Casebook* (pp. 31–57). Newbury Park, CA: Sage.

McDaniels, C. (1994) 'Frank Parsons: his heritage leads us into the twenty-first century'. *Journal of Career Development*, 20, 327–32.

McMahon, M. and Patton, W. (2002a) 'Assessment: a continuum of practice and a new location in career counselling'. *International Careers Journal*, 3(4), (The Global Careers-Work Café). Available: http://www.careers-cafe.com.

McMahon, M. and Patton, W. (2002b) 'Using qualitative assessment in career counselling'. *International Journal of Educational and Vocational Guidance*, 2(1), 51–66.

McMahon, M. Patton, W. and Watson, M. (2003) 'Developing qualitative career assessment processes'. *The Career Development Quarterly*, 51(3), 194–202.

McMahon, M. Patton, W. and Watson, M. (2005) *My System of Career Influences.* Camberwell: ACER Press.

McMahon, M. Watson, M. and Patton, W. (in press) 'Developing a qualitative career assessment process: the My System of Career Influences reflection activity'. *Journal of Career Assessment*.

Niemeyer, G. J. and Niemeyer, R. A. (1993) 'Defining the boundaries of constructivist assessment', in G. J. Niemeyer (ed.), *Constructivist Assessment: A Casebook* (pp. 1–30). Newbury Park, CA: Sage.

O'Brien, K. M. (2001) 'The legacy of Parsons: career counselors and vocational psychologists as agents of social change'. *The Career Development Quarterly*, 50(1), 66–76.

Okocha, A. A. G. (1998) 'Using qualitative appraisal strategies in career counseling'. *Journal of Employment Counseling*, 35, 151–9.

Parker, P. (2002) 'Working with the intelligent career model'. *Journal of Employment Counseling*, 39, 83–96.

Parsons, F. (1909) *Choosing a Vocation.* Boston, MA: Houghton Mifflin.

Patton, W. and McMahon, M. (1999) *Career Development and Systems Theory: A New Relationship.* Pacific Grove, CA: Brooks/Cole.

Peavy, R. V. (1995) *Helping Relationships: Constructivist Counselling and Therapy* (video). Victoria, Canada: University of Victoria Division of Continuing Studies and the Faculty of Education.

Peavy, R. V. (1998) *Sociodynamic Counselling: A Constructivist Perspective.* Victoria, Canada: Trafford.

Pope, M. and Sveinsdottir, M. (2005) 'Frank, we hardly knew ye: the very personal side of Frank Parsons'. *Journal of Counseling and Development*, 83, 105–15.

Richardson, J. T. E. (1996) *Handbook of Qualitative Research Methods for Psychology and the Social Sciences.* Leicester: BPS Books.

Savickas, M. L. (1993) 'Career counseling in the postmodern era'. *Journal of Cognitive Psychotherapy: An International Quarterly*, 7, 205–15.

Spokane, A. R. and Glickman, I. T. (1994) 'Light, information, inspiration, cooperation: origins of the clinical science of career intervention'. *Journal of Career Development*, 20, 295–304.

Subich, L. M. (1996) 'Addressing diversity in the process of career assessment', in M. L. Savickas and W. B. Walsh (eds), *Handbook of Career Counseling Theory and Practice* (pp. 277–89). Palo Alto, CA: Davies-Black.

Subich, L. M. and Simonson, K. (2001) 'Career counselling: the evolution of theory', in F. T. L. Leong and A. Barak (eds), *Contemporary Models in Vocational Psychology* (pp. 257–78). Mahwah, NJ: Erlbaum.

Whiston, S. C. and Brecheisen, B. K. (2002) 'Practice and research in career counseling and development – 2001'. *The Career Development Quarterly*, 51, 98–154.

Young, R. A. and Chen, C. P. (1999) 'Practice and research in career counseling and development – 1998'. *The Career Development Quarterly*, 48, 98–141.

Zunker, V. G. and Norris, D. S. (1998) *Using Assessment Results for Career Development* (5th edn). Pacific Grove, CA: Brooks/Cole.

Zytowski, D. G. and Swanson, J. L. (1994) 'Parsons' contribution to career assessment'. *Journal of Career Development*, 20, 305–10.

Chapter 14

Card sorts

Constructivist assessment tools

Polly Parker

How can you have a constructivist assessment tool? At first glance this term sounds like an oxymoron. Assessment smacks of traditional approaches that classify people against normative samples of comparative data. These approaches emphasise what is objective and statistically measurable. They favour reductionist thinking over the individual's unique world view and search for meaning (Oxenford, 2001). By contrast, constructivism is grounded in the generation of meaning relevant to the uniqueness of an individual life (Peavy, 1998). Users of "assessment tools" are thus called on to question their own assumptions behind the processes and methods that they use.

The most common form of constructivist assessment is card sorts. A wide range of card sorts is available in career counselling practice, including values sorts (Knowdell and Chapman, 1993), skills sorts, interest sorts (Athanasou, 1998) vocational sorts (Takai and Holland, 1979), occupational choice sorts (Peterson, 1998), transferable skill sorts and retirement activities sorts (Millington and Reed, 1997). The general approach across all of these card sorts is similar – to have the client select particular items and talk with the counsellor about their implications. However, the labels of the card sorts indicate a more restrictive purpose. The typical card sort is based on an underlying theory of values, or interests, and its implications. Client choices are meant to predict their suitability for certain kinds of work or activity. The counsellor is participating in a traditional, classification-based approach.

Card sorts have many positive features that make them valuable in career counselling (Goldman 1992; Slaney and MacKinnon-Slaney, 1990). So, how can sorting cards serve to create meaning rather than to classify and box people in? How can they be used to generate narratives that are unique representations of a person's life story? How can they offer a different approach from traditional matching of people to occupations, and instead guide thoughts, beliefs and activity in a manner that is congruent with constructivist principles? Addressing these challenges is the focus of this chapter.

Some background on card sorts

Card sorts are ubiquitous. They have been used to elicit information about, for example, food and activity preferences (Sherwood *et al*., 2003), ecological knowledge of indigenous communities (Butler, 2004), educational needs of patients with heart failure (Luniewski *et al*., 1999), coping behaviour in health and disease (Schwartz *et al*., 1998), rehabilitation (Millington and Reed, 1997) and line managers' responsibility in HR (Thornhill and Saunders, 1998).

The tactile aspect of physically sorting the cards (or of being in control of a computer based, on-line card sort) is particularly favourable for people who have a kinaesthetic learning style. Card sorts can stimulate memories and promote understanding about how people classify information (Ellen, 1992). They can provide for a more concrete procedure and in turn greater satisfaction of clients (Amundson, 1998). They can provide greater stimulation for clients than any direct instruction to write a career history or keep a personal diary (Parker, 2000). The non-verbal medium allows for open-ended investigation of abstract relationships (Butler, 2004),

However, as already noted, many card sorts – and many of those used in career counselling – are grounded in theories of classification. They are usually supported by extensive statistical documentation about the effectiveness of the card sort in distinguishing between classifications. What is less well documented is what such classification may mean for the client, and what assumptions are being made in the subsequent counselling process (Ellen, 1992). These issues are important if we are to confront the oxymoron suggested in the title to this chapter. The context in which cards are sorted, the instructions given and the relationship between the client and the assessor/ counsellor are all fundamental in differentiating between usage that is or is not constructivist in approach.

The constructivist approach

While there is no single agreed upon definition of the term constructivism, in typical social science usage it indicates an emphasis on persons as active agents in their ongoing development (Peavy, 1994). This is congruent with calls for people to be more active in pursuing their personal career agendas in the emerging knowledge economy, and to maintain employability in changing times. With fewer signposts to show the "right way forward" individuals must continuously confront ambiguity and uncertainty as they navigate paths through both career and life. In a "boundaryless" career world, it is the internally generated subjective career, rather than the externally directed objective career, that can best guide the individual (Arthur and Rousseau, 1996; Parker, 2002).

Contemporary careers provide more opportunities to express oneself and to elicit personal meaning from one's work, but they also contribute to mounting pressure to ensure psychological success (Mirvis and Hall, 1994). The "balancing act" to ensure success in a twenty-first century career is not easy (Pelsma and Arnett, 2002). Career counsellors have a significant contribution to assist career actors in this balancing act. Acting as change agents they may help clients "to achieve more holistic lives and to be agents for positive change in society through the choices and decisions they make" (Hansen, 2001, p. 266). Careers are inseparable from psychological aspects of life and supporting people's personal growth becomes key (Heron, 1990).

Career counselling therefore calls for similar psychological processes to personal counselling (Gysbers, Heppner and Johnston, 1998; Subich, 1993). Furthermore, integrated rather than restricted approaches better enable important and largely overlooked emotional factors to be addressed (Kidd, 2004). Constructivist approaches can help by introducing a shift away from reductionist thinking towards an holistic self-organising approach towards meaning-making and the exploration of new possibilities. That is, they offer a philosophical framework that permits the counsellor to turn away from the "psychometric self" towards the "storied self" (Peavy, 1994).

Operating from a constructivist epistemology, counsellors emphasise the interactive role they have with clients, acting as allies and collaborators in a shared process (Fried, 2001). The counsellor is an expert in the process and the client is the expert in his/her own life. The success of the counsellor and client working together on the client's life depends on establishing a positive climate that is conducive to learning and openness to experience. People thrive when they believe they *matter* (Schlossberg *et al.*, 1989).

Thus establishing a mattering climate is a pre-requisite for constructivist counsellors. They need to create and sustain a "low threat" environment in which clients can feel safe yet open to being challenged, and can freely express and try out new ideas (Oxenford, 2001). Counsellors need to be receptive to the client and to his or her situation (Emmett 2001; Peavy, 1994), an approach that may be pursued through "active engagement", a collaborative process whereby the counsellor's understanding of process facilitates the client's expression of his or her unique career narrative (Amundson, 2003).

Client–counsellor interaction

Having established the appropriate climate, the client and counsellor may then work directly with the personal experience of the client, a tenet of both constructivism and adult development (Brookfield, 1994; Lee and Johnston, 2001). Identifying the purpose of the session is a pre-requisite for the sorting of cards to produce primary data. The act of sorting the cards is itself a precursor to a process through which clients can clarify, reflect upon and evaluate their current career situation to arrive at new understandings.

Eliciting personal meaning, a central aspect of constructivism, comes through a process of critical reflection on an individual's situation. This process develops "mindfulness" (Peavy, 1994), a desirable goal in its own right. Mindfulness involves the emergence of self-awareness and understanding, and the development of a life-career story after reflecting on experiences and examining assumptions and biases that have developed over time (Langer and Moldoveanu, 2000). Through the interpretations they make and the actions they take, clients actively organise their own world. Contemplation on the relative significance of particular experiences enables clients to organise patterns of meaning and thereby create a "self" (Peavy, 1994, p. 32).

Thus, counsellors empower clients to be proactive in examining their own stories. Increasingly, social conditions call for individuals to be both proactive and reflective, capable of agency and creativity while remaining aware of the contexts in which they live and work. A variety of techniques may be used for this including journal writing, visualisations, relationship mapping and identifying objects that give particular meaning. Subsequent discussion of each of these with the counsellor facilitate retrospective sense-making (Weick, 1995).

Mindfulness and personal meaning comes from the subjective career. The *subjective* career (in contrast to the *objective* career) suggests that people can pursue their own career agenda. The subjective career is the internally ascribed criteria for success and is under personal control as individuals interpret the meaning of all aspects of their career. Thus, when priority is attributed to the subjective rather than on the objective career, success comes from achieving goals that are personally significant rather than those set by other people. It is through subjective criteria that people enact their values, beliefs and authenticity, and integrate multiple roles into an holistic view of their life.

It is particularly timely to reassert the value of the subjective career in the search for appropriate guides and interventions for the twenty-first century. However, the subjective career is difficult to measure with any precision, a concern that has resulted in questions about the concept's utility, even by its proponents (Stebbins, 1970). Researchers have shied away from interpreting and explaining the world as experienced by other people. By contrast, constructivists are more interested in eliciting personal meaning that has "face validity" rather than statistical significance. The emphasis is on trustworthiness and the underlying conceptual approach (Oxenford, 2001).

An illustrative approach: the Intelligent Career Card Sort (ICCS®)

While most card sorts are based on one particular aspect of the career – such as personal values or vocational choice – the underlying model of the "intelligent career" is holistic (Arthur *et al.*, 1995). The model first emerged in response to the notion of "intelligent enterprise", that is of the way organisations function in the emerging knowledge economy (Quinn, 1992). In Quinn's and other writers' views, the knowledge-driven organisation described the functioning through three interdependent areas of competency:

the organisation's culture, know-how and networks. The intelligent career provides a way for individuals to align their participation in the knowledge economy through three complementary ways of knowing: knowing-why (reflecting an individual's motivation and identity), knowing-how (reflecting an individual's skills and expertise) and knowing-whom (reflecting an individual's relationships and reputation).

These three ways of knowing offer an holistic approach in which self-awareness is fundamental. Personal values and interests, the motivation to work, family circumstances, skills and knowledge, tacit knowledge, foci for new learning, and the breadth of relationships that provide support for the career actor are all integral aspects of the intelligent career concept. The underlying model also points to the continuing interdependence of these three ways of knowing – and so, for example, between individual motivation, skill development and peer group support – as careers unfold. The intelligent career framework may be used effectively by career counsellors to integrate career development activities and to facilitate clients' sense-making of seemingly diverse career development inputs (Parker *et al.*, 2004). Exercises may be conducted within each of the three ways of knowing using constructivist approaches outlined above.

This model was used to underpin the design of the Intelligent Career Card Sort® (ICCS®) (Parker, 1996). In its current form, the ICCS® consists of three sets of cards, each reflecting to one of the three ways of knowing – *knowing-why, knowing-how* and *knowing-whom* – previously described. There are a total of 112 cards, 40 in knowing-why, 36 in knowing-how and 36 in knowing-whom, from which clients select what they see as the most important items. For example, an item on one of the knowing-why cards is "I enjoy helping other people". The ICCS® was developed to enable clients to critically examine their own experience, a key feature of the constructivist paradigm.

The process of narrative generation

The general approach in the use of card sorts is for clients to physically sort, select and react to text on particular cards that are relevant to the client's career. However, the narrative that follows will be influenced by the underlying theory, for example of occupational choice or personal values, from which any card sort is derived. For the ICCS® the sorting process is identical for each of the three sets of cards. The client begins with one set of cards and quickly sorts them into two piles according to their immediate appeal: "this applies to me", or "this doesn't apply to me". The second step is to take the cards the client identifies with and divide them into two piles: "These are more important" and "these are less important". From the "more important" cards, the client selects seven and finally places those in rank order. The final selections are then printed off for the client and provide input for the next stage of the process.

All ICCS® clients initially select items according to the text on the card. However, the personal meaning of the item only emerges from deeper individual analysis of personal career situations. At this point of the process, there is a range of ways in which the counsellor may proceed. This may depend on the purpose identified by client and counsellor at the beginning of the session.

One option is to work on a one-to-one basis, while another is to process the data in a small group or team situation. Group situations allow for each member to tell their story (Brott, 2001). Each other member acts as an "interested, curious, and tentative inquirer, respectful listener and tentative observer" (McMahon and Patton, 2002, p. 59). The best results are achieved when group members each work within one way of knowing and subsequently work together in the two other ways. Using this process the interdependencies among the three ways of knowing become clearer. However, it is essential to remember that the group process is not a discussion but a mutual process of active support of one another in turn.

Another factor is the time available. Individual counselling sessions may last for an hour per week and extend over several weeks, while a group session may be completed in three to six hours. Workshops can be tailored to suit the times available and range from one to several hours. In each of the above options, clients may choose to incorporate journal writing, or to focus on paired or group listening activities, according to time, preferences and abilities.

Using narratives in career counselling is a relatively new phenomenon yet one that is likely to become increasingly important (Savickas, 1993). A narrative is a story about career that connects the past to the present and enables a range of possible futures (see Chapter 9 of this book). Narratives enable clients to use their personal story as a way forward. The client is both the author and the main character in their story which helps them to understand themselves (Christensen and Johnston, 2003). The counsellor supports and in the process becomes a co-author. However, the client may also reconstruct their stories and tell them as they would like them to be (Cochran, 1997).

As the story is generated, a new kind of self-knowledge emerges that is grounded in a unique life experience and integrates values, knowledge, skills and attitudes into a renewed focus within a person. The construction of the whole demands that many parts are brought together. The process is inherently constructivist and reveals patterns that give meaning to life stories and integrates a variety of previous experiences into a coherent whole.

A case study example

Marina was a single, 30-year-old woman who worked in education. She had just ended a long-term relationship and was considering her future in relation to work and her life. The ICCS® was completed in a face-to-face situation after an initial discussion. Marina had subsequently spent two weeks of personal journal writing to expand on the meaning of each item she had selected. She was asked to think of specific examples from her own experience to describe her point of view on each item. In this way a narrative was generated that illustrated both a process and a product (Bujold, 2002).

The second session with the counsellor began with a reflection on the creative process of writing. Marina could then articulate parts of her narrative that were uppermost in her mind. She began by commenting on how the process had enabled her to think more broadly about the selection of items as a group, as well as delving deeply into each individual item. The most important item for Marina under knowing-why was maintaining stability in her present location. She realised that this was not negotiable and that after much recent change in her life, she needed some certainty and familiarity. The educational environment was one she knew and could use as a broad base for her to connect with others, particularly those with special needs (whom she taught) and thus promote their success.

Marina recognised that this type of work provided her with a challenge and a sense of achievement that was an important career driver for her. She loved her work yet also knew that when off work, she really wanted to be off. Her independent streak underpinned her particular lifestyle needs that required her to have autonomy and enable her to be flexible in scheduling. Her work-life balance was prominent in her mind and although "work is a small part of my life, it is important". This came up as she accepted that money was only part of the story and her work gave an avenue to make an active contribution to society, which accorded with her values.

The most important *knowing-how* item was *I seek to improve my interpersonal skills*. Through her journaling, Marina had written about the value she placed on good quality relationships. In identifying specific relationships as she had been asked to do, Marina realised that there were examples where her own inter-personal skills had created some difficulties for her. She decided that this was an area on which to focus and suggested some specific ways to do so. She was consciously aware of a developmental process occurring at the same time as she applied her knowledge to her current environment. This encouraged her to see that she was indeed *becoming a more strategic thinker*, which was affirming for her.

Marina's ability to see the big picture and also focus on the details of the moment emerged in discussion about *pursuing skills and knowledge specific to her occupation*. She valued building her CV by doing different things as she leveraged her current knowledge to grow in new areas. She saw herself *learning at the forefront of her adopted field* by studying, learning and then reflecting on what she was doing. Much of this was applied in project work that also enabled her to balance her lifestyle needs.

The third way of knowing, *knowing-whom*, began with *I develop relationships with family*. Marina described some recent difficulties that her brother had experienced and how she and other family members had provided support. She saw this as a reciprocal benefit as her family had been there for her in her recent break up. The regular communication was fun for her and also extremely important to her for practical support. She also *maintained relationships with school or college friends* in a similar manner. This did not necessarily mean frequent contact but reflected a conscious effort to keep in touch to share feelings, provide support and maintain trust.

Another key aspect of Marina's story was the way she *actively cultivated relationships to make new friends.* As a woman with a preference for introversion, making real friendships with new people was challenging compared to maintaining relationships with those she had known for some time. However, during her writing she had described the breadth and depth of her relationships, and she could see the benefits of a wide circle of friends. Being able to identify groups of people with whom she felt very safe and supported enabled her to consider other groups where more focus and attention could build trust as a strong underpinning of new relationships.

After a week's break for further reflection and consideration of themes and patterns that were evident from her journaling and subsequent discussions, Marina met again with the counsellor. Together they looked first at the themes Marina had identified, which included contributing to society, independence and a linked sense of achievement and challenge (knowing-why). Knowing-how themes included having short-term foci like projects, consciously developing skills to add value in her current setting, as well as leveraging those skills for future advantage. Knowing-whom themes concentrated on maintaining the excellent relationships she had with family and old friends. Another theme, however, was the developing of new relationships with people to broaden her base of support.

The interdependence of the themes in the different ways of knowing contributed to a larger picture for Marina of the complexity of her career and at the same time, the ease with which she could identify what was important to her and which areas to pin point for her future development. Marina reported this as an immense sense of relief. She could identify multiple dimensions in her story, and could draw on her previous experience to know – really know – that she could deal with whatever obstacles came up as she moved forward. Given that she had presented in a "stuck" position, such a revelation to herself had a profound impact on her attitude and self-belief to organise her life in the present and in the future.

The case described above demonstrates many of the inherent aspects of constructivism in a way that listing them out could not do justice to. First the trusting relationship Marina had with the counsellor paved the way for some deeper analysis and raised self-awareness of her situation (McMahon *et al.*, 2003). She was able to recognise different aspects that sometimes appeared to be contradictory and yet she managed to handle the ambiguity in a constructive way.

The card sorting was the beginning of a constructivist process for Marina. The deep work began when the sorting process ended and the reflection on the personal meaning began, grounding each item in her personal experience, to reveal patterns and themes. In this process she formed a subjective narrative that did not necessarily correspond to factual truth (Bujold, 2002). However, it was a critical process in reaffirming Marina's construction of herself as an able person who could cope with her recent loss (as well as others) and see not only the meaning that she bestowed on important events, but also the way that had influenced her subsequent attitudes and behaviours.

Conclusion

The use of card sorts is a quintessentially constructivist approach when the process is a facilitative intervention that seeks to elicit self-discovery and self-directed learning. Developing a mutually respectful relationship with clients enables the careers counsellor or educator to support and empower that person to assume responsibility for themselves in their career awareness and decision-making. Working with real examples from the client's experience provides a platform from which to affirm the worth and value of qualities and attitudes that are located in the person's soul and deeply affect all aspects of career. Multiple perspectives are integrated into a cognitive, affective and spiritual whole.

Moreover, the changed role of the careers counsellor described above highlights a need for greater diversity in the approaches counsellors use in assessment and process. Supporting the emergence of a career narrative blends theoretical perspectives with lived experience. Living and learning come together in a way that may have life-changing outcomes for clients.

References

Amundson, N. E. (1998) *Active Engagement. Enhancing the Career Counselling Process*. Richmond, Canada: Ergon Communications.

Amundson, N. E. (2003) *Active Engagement* (2nd edn). Richmond, Canada: Ergon Communications.

Arthur, M. B. Claman, P. H. and DeFillippi, R. J. (1995) 'Intelligent enterprise, intelligent career'. *Academy of Management Executive*, 9(4), 7–20.

Arthur, M. B. and Rousseau, D. M. (eds) (1996) *The Boundaryless Career. A New Employment Principle for a New Organisational Era*. New York: Oxford University Press.

Athanasou, J. A. (1998) *Career Interest Test*. Sydney, Australia: Hobsons Press.

Brookfield, S. (1994) 'Tales from the dark side: a phenomenography of adult critical reflection'. *International Journal of Lifelong Education*, 13(3), 203–16.

Brott, P. E. (2001) 'The storied approach: a postmodern perspective for career counseling'. *The Career Development Quarterly*, 49, 304–13.

Bujold, C. (2002) 'Constructing career through narrative'. *Journal of Vocational Behavior*, 64, 470–84.

Butler, C. (2004) 'Researching traditional ecological knowledge for multiple uses'. *Canadian Journal of Native Education*, 28(1), 33–49.

Christensen, T. C. and Johnston, J. A. (2003) 'Incorporating the narrative in career planning'. *Journal of Career Development*, 29(3), 149–60.

Cochran, L. (1997) *Career Counseling: A Narrative Approach.* Thousand Oaks, CA: Sage.

Ellen, R. (1992) *The Cultural Relations of Classification: An Analysis of Nuaulu Animal Categories from Central Seram.* Cambridge: Cambridge University Press.

Emmett, J. (2001) 'A constructivist approach to the teaching of career counseling', in K. Eriksen and G. McAuliffe (eds), *Teaching Counselors and Therapists: Constructivist and Developmental Course Design* (pp. 139–67). Westport, CT: Bergin and Garvey.

Fried, J. (2001) 'Student development education as the practice of liberation: a constructivist approach, in K. Eriksen and G. McAuliffe (eds), *Teaching Counselors and Therapists: Constructivist and Developmental Course Design* (pp. 293–319). Westport, CT: Bergin and Garvey.

Goldman, L. (1992) 'Qualitative assessment: an approach for counselors'. *Journal of Counseling and Development*, 70, 616–21.

Gysbers, N. C., Heppner, M. J. and Johnston, J. A. (1998) *Career Counseling: Process, Issues and Techniques.* Needham Heights, MA: Allyn and Bacon.

Hansen, L. S. (2001) 'Integrating work, family, and community through holistic life planning'. *The Career Development Quarterly*, 49(3), 261–74.

Heron, J. (1990) *Helping the Client A Creative Practical Guide.* London: Sage.

Kidd, J. M. (2004) 'Emotion in career contexts: challenges for theory and research'. *Journal of Vocational Behavior*, 64, 441–54.

Knowdell, R. and Chapman, E. N. (1993) *Personal Counseling: Helping Others Help Themselves.* Merlo Park, CA: Course Technology Crisp.

Langer, E. J. and Moldoveanu, M. (2000) The Construct of Mindfulness. *Journal of Social Issues*, 56(1), 1–9.

Lee, F. K. and Johnston, J. A. (2001) 'Innovations in career counseling'. *Journal of Career Development*, 27(3), 177–85.

Luniewski, M., Reigle, J. and White, B. (1999) 'Card sort: an assessment tool for the educational needs of patients with heart failure'. *American Journal of Critical Care*, 8(5), 297–303.

McMahon, M. and Patton, W. (2002) 'Using qualitative assessment in career counselling'. *International Journal for Educational and Vocational Guidance*, 2, 51–66.

McMahon, M., Patton, W. and Watson, M. (2003) 'Developing qualitative career assessment processes'. *The Career Development Quarterly*, 51(3), 194–202.

Millington, M. J. and Reed, C. A. (1997) Employment expectations in rehabilitation counseling: factors of employment selection. *Rehabilitation Counseling Bulletin*, 40(3), 215–28.

Mirvis, P. and Hall, D. (1994) 'Psychological success and the boundaryless career'. *Journal of Organisational Behaviour*, 15, 365–80.

Oxenford, C. (2001) 'Discovering assessment', in K. Eriksen and G. McAuliffe (eds), *Teaching Counselors and Therapists: Constructivist and Developmental Course Design* (pp. 93–112). Westport, CT: Bergin & Garvey.

Parker, H. L. P. (1996) *The New Career Paradigm: An Exploration of 'Intelligent Career' Behaviour among MBA Graduates and Students*. Unpublished master's thesis. Auckland: The University of Auckland.

Parker, H. L. P. (2000) *Career Communities*. Unpublished doctoral thesis. Auckland: The University of Auckland.

Parker, P. (2002) 'Working with the intelligent career model'. *Journal of Employment Counseling*, 39(2), 83–96.

Parker, P., Arthur, M. B. and Inkson, K. (2004) 'Career communities: a preliminary exploration of member-defined career support structures'. *Journal of Organisational Behavior*, 25, 489–514.

Peavy, R. V. (1994) 'A constructivist perspective for counselling'. *Educational and Vocational Guidance*, 55, 31–7.

Peavy, R. V. (1998) *SocioDynamic Counselling: A Constructivist Perspective*. Victoria, Canada: Trafford Publishing.

Pelsma, D. and Arnett, R. (2002) 'Helping clients cope with change in the twenty-first century: a balancing act'. *Journal of Career Development*, 28(3), 169–79.

Peterson, G. W. (1998) 'Using a vocational card sort as an assessment of occupational knowledge'. *Journal of Career Assessment*, 6(1), 49–67.

Quinn, J. B. (1992) *Intelligent Enterprise: A Knowledge and Service Based Paradigm for Industry*. New York: The Free Press.

Savickas, M. L. (1993) 'Career counseling in the post modern era'. *Journal of Cognitive Psychotherapy: An International Quarterly*, 7, 205–15.

Schlossberg, N., Lynch, A. and Chickering, A. (1989) *Improving Higher Education Environments for Adults*. San Francisco, CA: Jossey-Bass.

Schwartz, C. E., Chung-Kang, P., Lester, N., Daltroy, L. H. and Goldberger, A. L. (1998) 'Self-reported coping behaviour in health and disease: assessment with a card sort game'. *Behavioural Medicine*, 24(1), 41–5.

Sherwood, N. E., Story, M. and Neumark-Sztainer, D. (2003) 'A visual card-sorting technique for assessing food and activity preferences'. *Nutrition Research Newsletter*, 22(1), 2–3.

Slaney, R. B. and MacKinnon-Slaney, F. (1990) 'The use of vocational card sorts in career counseling', in C. E. Watkins and V. L. Campbell (eds), *Testing in Counseling Practice* (pp. 317-71). Hillsdale, NJ: Erlbaum.

Stebbins, R. A. (1970) 'Career: the subjective approach'. *Sociology Quarterly*, 11, 32–49.

Subich, L. M. (1993) 'How personal is career counseling?' *The Career Development Quarterly*, 42, 129–31.

Takai, R. and Holland, J. L. (1979) 'Comparison of the vocational card sort, the SDS, and the vocational exploration insight kit'. *The Vocational Guidance Quarterly*, 27, 312–18.

Thornhill, A. and Saunders, M. N. K. (1998) 'What if line managers don't realize they're responsible for HR?' *Personnel Review*, 27(6), 460–6.

Weick, K. E. (1995) *Sensemaking in Organisations*. Thousand Oaks, CA: Sage.

Chapter 15

Constructivist career tools on the internet

Challenge and potentials

Heidi Viljamaa, Wendy Patton and Mary McMahon

Career development is an exciting field to be working in at the beginning of the twenty-first century. Expertise that benefited few in the past, is rapidly becoming available to all who can access the internet. Systematic approaches to career development are becoming a key part of both individual and organisational life. Career development professionals are becoming increasingly important contributors to the world's future; we are in a position to empower individuals to aspire to live the best life they can. In turn, these individuals create the worlds about them, both within work and outside. It is no surprise that many new professionals have chosen career development as their field over the last few years. What is making our role so important is related to the huge changes which are impacting on individuals' life, learning and work, and therefore on lifelong career decision making. One of these changes is in practices of communication, in particular the development of the internet, and this change inevitably has implications for all aspects of individuals' lives, and for the practice of career development.

The internet now provides instantaneous communication to millions of people around the world, and the number of people relying on its capacities is increasing exponentially. In this chapter we wish first to focus on the challenges of the internet to career development specialists. After describing the central challenges of quantity and quality, we will explore ways in which we can positively incorporate the internet into effective career practice. We will then consider the importance of a constructivist perspective in ensuring that individuals' engagement with the internet in career development is supported appropriately by career development facilitators. Finally, using this perspective, we will provide a case study in the use of web-based career tools, based on the work of the first author in developing the CareerStorm Navigator.

Challenges for the twenty-first-century career professional

Perhaps the primary challenge to our profession at the turn of the century is the *challenge of quantity* brought about through the many issues in life, learning and work which individuals need to navigate at multiple times throughout their lives (Jarvis, 2002; McMahon *et al.*, 2003). The features of the changing world and its accelerating complexity and non-linearity have been well documented (Arthur *et al.*, 1999; Herr, 1997; Patton and McMahon, 1999; Poehnell and Amundson, 2002). Competencies acquired for one job may not serve for any period of time, work is no longer charact-erised by a set of tasks, which are mastered once, and a career is no longer characterised by a vertical process of advancement within the one organisation. Increasingly, work can be characterised as a series of periods within and outside paid employment, linked by experiences of learning and retraining. Choices expand, jobs are unstable, institutions are in flux, and making choices is increasingly more difficult. More individuals need support to navigate changing career and life circumstances more often throughout their lives.

For our profession, there is secondly the *challenge of quality*. The nature of individual's need has changed from one time "career choice" to a life-long need to proactively manage one's career. Ready-made career paths are few. No one else manages an individual's career on his or her behalf. With the increasing number of decisions to be made in a lifetime, the uncertainty of how we make good decisions has also increased. This change in circumstances requires a new approach. A one-time intervention focusing on career choice with the help of a test is insufficient. Individuals must be prepared to navigate their careers and lives over time. Career professionals around the world are faced with the unrealistic expectation: "you're the expert, please tell me how to live my life". One of the key challenges is to help individuals shift their expectations from "expecting solutions" to thinking through what unique solutions they can provide. Under the changing and uncertain circumstances of early twenty-first century, individuals need to become more pro-active in navigating their career. In order to meet this changing expectation, the quality of the career counselling process, interventions and tools needs to accommodate to this change. The OECD review of career guidance in 14 countries acknowledged that policy decisions need to "develop systems that develop career self-management skills that match levels of personal help, from brief to extensive, to personal needs and circumstances, rather than assuming that everybody needs intensive and personal career guidance" (2004, p. 14).

How is this best done to ensure the individual is actively engaged and supported in the development of career self-management skills? These developments and related developments in education and the world of work imply a greatly increased role for information, guidance and counselling services. Mastery of appropriate career management skills cannot be left to chance, nor is it sufficient that they be available to a select few who have particular access. Grubb (2002) draws attention to the creation of web accessible information resources, what he refers to as a "self-service" approach to career information and guidance that has been undertaken by many countries. Such approaches assume that all individuals have access (availability and skills) and processing skills. Learning to self-manage career development requires investing in personal and information-related skills to ensure that individuals are able to become actively involved in their careers in uncertain times – human support in the learning process is essential. While the aim of career management is to equip people to be self-reliant, individuals need skills and support in developing and maintaining this life skill. Providing individuals with information on a website is not sufficient. It is to expand our discussion on this first challenge that we will now turn.

Responding to the challenge of quantity

There is no doubt that an expanded use of information and communication technologies is an important component in the creation of life-long career guidance systems. A number of authors have acknowledged the transforming role of the internet in career information and guidance practice (O'Halloran *et al.*, 2002; Watts, 2002; OECD, 2004), with Watts identifying the potential of ICT to significantly increase access to guidance services, "freeing it from constraints of time and space" (p. 144). In doing so he also acknowledges the restrictions in terms of access to the internet, and possession of skills to effectively use the internet and related resources. While this view is shared by many, it is clear that inclusion of ICT alone into career guidance practice is not sufficient. Watts (2002) describes integrative processes whereby a varied range of interventions (e.g., ICT, group work, curriculum interventions) are employed, with the integration being undertaken by the individual, with support from a guidance counsellor.

O'Halloran and her colleagues (2002) stress the importance of clients being supported in accessing and evaluating the appropriateness and credibility of websites, and also "question the appropriateness of having clients take online assessments outside the counselor's office, without the appropriate monitoring support" (p. 375). Sampson (2002) adds that, in some locations, there may not be sufficient auditory and visual privacy for clients in using the computer or telephone for distance counselling. These questions have driven the challenge of provision of appropriate use of ICT, and the new challenges of training users and practitioners in this use. This appropriate use also emphasises adherence to ethical considerations (O'Halloran *et al.*, Sampson, 2002).

The effective use of internet resources will require both recognising the new face of the client population, and redefining our role as professionals. In terms of the client population, we must be open to the possibility that our users will not typically be from the upper economic sectors, but will be attempting to use whatever low-cost resources are available to make good decisions. If there are resources available on the internet, they will make use of them to reach their own decisions. Peter Plant has termed this "kitchen table counselling" (personal communication, 1 December 1996) meaning that career decisions are made to a greater extent in people's homes, often without an expert, but employing whatever information can be located on the internet.

In terms of the role of the career development professional, we must be open to shifting away from being a gatekeeper for information, an expert on how others should make a career choice or an evaluator of how realistic their plans may be. Rather, we should move towards helping people find the good and best sources for information, supporting life-long career skills development and facilitating people's movement in the direction they desire to move. In doing so, they will discover to what extent their plan is realistic. The shift in our position is from being an expert, who delivers answers, to being a "negotiating partner", who helps the individual through sensitive dialogue to make meaning of their career and life (Onnismaa, 2003). If we are ready to adopt this new role, then we must deliberate creatively on our ways of working, our conception of our clients and our sense of the fluidity of the self.

It is the career guidance professional who can emphasise that career management skills are complex people skills that require an intense interaction between learner and facilitator.

> The paradox of the information age is that we are awash in information … through systematic efforts to construct "self-service" approaches to career information, and through one-stop information centres. But more information is not necessarily better than less information if people have no idea how to use it, and so something different may be necessary to prepare the new workers and citizens of the Information Society.
>
> (Grubb, 2002, p. 5)

However, it is clear that information on its own, while necessary, is not sufficient for reasons of differential equity of access, difficulties in locating the right information, and the need to process the information with a trained professional. It is only then that information can be converted to action.

While the technology affords the promise of greater availability of web-based career information and career guidance, much more research is required to validate its effectiveness over time and cost considerations. Gati *et al.* (2003) evaluated an internet-based career development intervention and noted that the benefit of the programme was highest for those who already had a high degree of career decidedness. Harris-Bowlsbey (2003) reminds us that we need to compare the effectiveness of personal face-to-face facilitative counselling relationships with those which are developed though technology enhancement, such as via email or camera-assisted connections.

With this discussion of the challenge of quantity in place, we are now ready to address the problem of quality in the counselling relationship.

Constructivist theory and the challenge of quality

While there has been exponential growth in the quantity of career information and career assessment material on the internet, the growth of material that is more reflective of the constructivist worldview is less evident. Constructivist approaches to career counselling with their relational and holistic nature, lend themselves less easily to the design of web-based tools. That said, it is not impossible as the description of CareerStorm Navigator later in this chapter demonstrates. Constructivism recognises that information is received, interpreted and acted upon by individuals in different ways (Patton and McMahon, 1999). It emphasises that in order to be useful in decision-making, information, in this context career information, must be appropriately interpreted and the capacity to do so does not come along with what Grubb (2002, p. 9) refers to as a simple "information dump". What is most important is that the capacity to effectively process information is developed in individuals. Constructivist approaches aim to develop deeper and more integrated understandings or constructs of how the world works, and encourage increasing self-reliance on the part of the learner. It is only through such approaches that the aim of facilitating individuals to construct their own identities, their careers and the relationship between learning and work in their lives which also include family, community and other sources of fulfilment and commitment can be adequately attained.

Thus it seems that reaching larger numbers of people may well be the easier of the two impending challenges, quantity and quality. More difficult is the question of quality: how to provide individually relevant tools for career planning. We confront vast differences within the population of potential users on the internet: however "one size fits all" is not a responsible option. At the same time, one-on-one interviewing is impracticable. Constructivist theory can be of substantial help to us working within the context of the internet to transform the quality of our helping relationships. Addressing the issue of quality necessitates that consideration is given to complex questions related to issues such as the uniqueness of individuals, the shift from test and tell approaches to narrative approaches, a learning perspective, giving up our expertise, holistic approaches and the emergence of intimacy, and what is possible in relation to change. Each will now be briefly described.

A focus on individuals as unique

In constructivist theory, emphasis is placed on the individual's unique orientation to the world. The theory recognises that every individual may understand the world in a different way, and will thus possess a unique array of values and motives. It invites us first and foremost to be sensitive to the individual variations in orientation to the world. As career specialists have come to adopt constructivist ideas there have already been important changes in approaches to career counselling. We realise for one that the positivist forms of career assessment, in which the professional determines the dimensions, traits and motives of importance are products of our own conceptual orientation. As a result, they may be insensitive to the particularities of those we try to help (McMahon and Patton, 2002). We have also come to realise that we cannot offer ourselves as experts on career choices. We can offer resources for individual deliberation, but there is no knowledge sound enough to speak adequately across the vast range of differences. In this regard, the applicability of theory and practice across cultures has been questioned (see Chapter 4 of this book). As a result of constructivist theory, we have also been encouraged to consider shifting our focus from one-to-one relations with clients to working with groups. Exchanges within groups can generate multiple insights, and reduce the expectation that a single person is "the expert".

Moving beyond test and tell to narrative

More recent constructivist theory, influenced by a range of postmodern and constructionist scholarship, has come to place a strong emphasis on individual narrative. Peavy (1998) regards this as a move from the logical-positivist *psychometric self* to the constructivist *narrated self*, and he encourages career counsellors to move from a "self-as-trait" view of clients to a "self-as-narrative" view (Peavy, 1995, p. 2). As career counsellors, we are invited not only to be sensitive to the individual's unique manner of conceptualising self and world, but also to his or her story of self. Story represents an attempt by individuals to make meaning of and actively construct their lives (Patton and McMahon, 1999), and because of the complexity of life no single story is adequate. Therefore the lives of people are multi-storied. When individuals seek career guidance, where do they place themselves in the unfolding story of self? Their approach to their career choices will be significantly influenced by their self-narrative or self-story. As we have come to appreciate this possibility, so have we become increasingly doubtful about measuring or evaluating the person one time only for life. Increasingly, it has been recognised that people will transition between learning and work several times in a lifetime and have many life/career decisions to make. In this sense constructivist theory is aligned with the widely promoted concepts of life-long learning and life-long guidance (OECD, 2004) and emphasis on career skills development (Jarvis, 2002).

A learning perspective

Life-long learning is viewed as a critical component of the knowledge economy. It provides a mechanism for maintaining a flexible and adaptable workforce capable of keeping pace with the challenges of global competition and rapid technological and organisational change (Guridi *et al.*, 2003). In the knowledge economy, individuals are expected to proactively shape their careers as they move in and out of work and learning across their lives. It is in this context that career guidance is being seen as "an important part of a national strategy for lifelong learning and sustained employability, driven by individuals themselves" (Watts and Fretwell, 2004, p. 8), and that career guidance practitioners are being urged to develop services that are responsive to this different context and to this different understanding of the needs of individuals. This emerging view has significant implications for how we view the challenge of career guidance. It calls attention once again to a shift in our practice from offering answers to resources. As Herminia Ibarra (2003) has put it, "There is no one perfect career waiting to be discovered. Instead, there are many possible selves we might become – and finding the one that fits is the result of doing and experimenting – trying on possibilities through a process of trial and error" (p. 30). We shift, then, from offering fish to the needy to teaching the art of fishing. Clients are increasingly enabled to manage their careers and lives under continuously changing circumstances.

Giving up our expertise

A constructivist orientation to quality resources also confronts us with difficult challenges. Foremost, perhaps, is the challenge of giving up our expertise: do we make ourselves redundant as we teach our clients our skills and give away our resources? Indeed, this question may be asked of all constructivist-based approaches whether web-based or not. One of the most striking differences between the traditional objectivist test-and-tell approaches and constructivist approaches is the shift of the counsellor role from one of expert to one of facilitator (Patton and McMahon, 1999), described by Savickas (1992) as a shift to "biographers who interpret lives in progress rather than as actuaries who count interests and abilities" (p. 338). We run the risk of disappointing individuals when we tell them we cannot be the experts and that they must find a way to navigate their way through life. Do we confront our clients with too much ambiguity, when all they want is a clear start in a new direction? Career/life navigation can be time-consuming and difficult, because ultimately it is a process of deciding how we live our lives and who we want to become. Experts can surely inform us; family, lovers and friends will certainly be happy to offer advice. Ultimately, it is the individual who must make decisions, and the issues will inevitably be complex. We must locate ways to help our clients appreciate the significance of managing their own lives albeit within a facilitative framework.

The move to holistic approaches and intimacy

A further challenge we confront is that of intimacy. The resources we offer are often confined to issues of professional life, and many are occupationally focused. However, our professions are inevitably intertwined with the remainder of our lives. For example, Savickas (1993) claims "career is personal" (p. 212). In this regard, debate has ensued in the career counselling literature about the fusion of career and personal counselling (e.g., Manuele-Adkins, 1992; Subich, 1993) and Richardson (1993, 1996) has urged theorists and practitioners to consider the location of work in people's lives. When career and life mix, we move into discussions about love, relationships, children, health, spiritual values or beliefs. How, then, can we broaden our professional practices to consider the big question: "how do you want to live your life?". This level of dialogue can be highly personal and may seem alien to our traditional career practices. Further, intimate issues such as this can also create discomfort, for the client and also for the professional. Both are vulnerable.

The possible

Related to the question about counsellor expertise, is the difficult issue of the possible. For instance, what is under our power to change for the better, and how much time will be required to bring about change? In spite of our providing resources for deliberating about one's desires and values, neither we nor our clients can see with clarity whether change can be brought about. We may be able to open other people's minds to think about the possible selves they could become. But how can they achieve these dreams in a complex, resistant and sometimes hostile world? And will the change be visible and external, or take place within an invisible world of the interior?

These are complex questions of quality career guidance, and deserve our continuing attention. We cannot answer all these questions in the space given. The first author and her colleagues have endeavoured to take positive steps in promising directions. They have tried to deconstruct old ways and reconstruct new ways of functioning in the context of internet communication. These attempts will become clearer in the following section.

CareerStorm navigator: a web-based constructivist career tool

These challenges and visions have been central to the work of the developers (Viljamaa and colleagues) of CareerStorm Navigator for almost 10 years. The developers have taken as their major mission the creation of qualitatively sensitive, web-based career planning tools. The process has been deeply affirming, and at the same time one of continuous learning and readjustment. To illustrate the preceding discussion, this section describes this work, what it offers and how it is used. It also illustrates the influence of constructivism in the design of these resources. Finally, we can look at emerging visions of the future this web-based tool invites.

CareerStorm Navigator is a web-based set of resources that enables individuals to reflect upon their work and life experiences from multiple perspectives. At the time of writing this chapter, CareerStorm Navigator includes seven career tools: Position, Destination, Interests, Skills, Values, Style and Compare.

Before gaining access to the resource, the individual needs to connect with a career professional. Together the career professional and the individual decide how many of the seven career tools will initially be assigned. When working with groups, the career professional evaluates which sections are most appropriate to open up, given the nature of the group process and the volume of participants.

Upon entering the website, the individual will see the relevant sections highlighted. Assigned career tools can be explored in any order. In "Position" the individual is asked to describe the present context for career/life decision-making and to evaluate likes and dislikes in past career and life roles. "Destination" invites the person to reflect upon their goals for eight areas of life: career, learning, relationships, home, body and health, leisure, financial goals and spiritual growth. "Interests" prompts the individual to remember the complex array of topics she/he knows something about, based on career/life experiences. "Skills" asks the person to identify four types of transferable skills: social, practical, information and creative. "Values" helps the individual define her/his most important values and evaluate how they are realised in present circumstances. "Style" helps the individual find adjectives that describe her/his customary approach to life. The seventh step in the process is "Compare". Before moving to this section, it is recommended that the person should research presenting career opportunities. In Compare, she/he can evaluate the most viable career options against personally meaningful criteria, as described in the six other career tools.

Each of the seven options offers a new perspective on an individual's career and life. More is not always better, and thus completing one step can be as powerful as completing all seven. However, when all seven steps are completed, it is easier to imagine the range of potential career moves and to embed those choices into the context of the total life-space.

After their first visit to the website, individuals can easily return. Results are saved page-by-page, which allows the individual to sign in and out of the system any number of times. Although it is possible to work through all sections of CareerStorm Navigator in four hours, each person is encouraged to use as much time as it takes. Individuals approach self-reflection in many different ways, and some end up spending 2–3 times the recommended time. The interactivity of the web-based process engages them in a dialogue that is meaningful and this is reflected in their use of time. Completing the entire career tool over several days may result in a deeper learning experience than trying to complete everything in one sitting.

Debriefing the results occurs when the individual has completed the assigned sections of the career tool. This dialogue can take place one-to-one or in a group setting. It can occur face-to-face or on the telephone (including teleconference with a group). In addition, there may be only one opportunity to discuss the results or many, depending on the total process provided.

CareerStorm Navigator is globally available on the internet in multiple language versions. Development was originally funded by companies offering online recruitment services (e.g. Monster.com and Helsingin Sanomat) and offered to the public free of charge (from 1998 to 2003). Access now is available only to organisations and career professionals who can work with individuals in its use. Everyone authorised to access the career tools can do so easily from any computer connected to the internet. No installation or special technical skills are required. Upon arriving at the secure website, each person signs in with an email address and password and is taken to their personal view of the system.

CareerStorm Navigator is used in a variety of settings, including corporations, educational institutions, career service organisations and private practices. Within corporations, it can support talent and leadership management, internal mobility, development discussions, team building, recruitment or outplacement. University career advisers use the career tool with undergraduate, graduate, postgraduate and alumni students. Private practitioners are helping individuals of all ages make meaningful transitions in their careers and lives. Satisfaction of career professionals using CareerStorm Navigator is not dependent on their work setting, but more on the degree of alignment of their thinking with its constructivist approach.

Surveys done in co-operation with Monster.com with participants from 80 countries indicated that CareerStorm career tools were valuable for a wide selection of individuals (with little deviation in age ranging from 16 to 60, educational background or country of origin). Feedback from career professionals using the present version of CareerStorm Navigator suggests that adults who are educated or have extensive work experience seem to benefit from the career tools more than others. They are more likely to experience a "eureka moment" during the web-based process, and need less support from the career professional. If we choose one criterion of success only, it is the individual's interest and ability to reflect upon his or her career and life.

Career professionals can reach CareerStorm on the website www.careerstorm.com. Free teleclasses are offered to career professionals from around the world. A training course is provided to all who want to apply the career tool. When participants cannot be reached face-to-face, a blended learning approach is utilised: e-learning, teleconferences and practicum using the career tools with individuals.

CareerStorm Navigator: constructivism in action

One of the greatest impediments to the spread of constructivist approaches is the lack of career tools specifically grounded in this approach. Many career professionals support a view of the individual as a dynamic creator of meaning and recognise the complex influences on career decision making. Paradox-ically, the best-known career tools available to professionals today were designed several decades ago and are founded on trait-and-factor approaches. Most computer-assisted guidance systems are also rooted in this tradition, and their goal is frequently to perform "matching" between personal traits and occupational descriptions. In contrast, constructivist theory has been the major inspiration in developing CareerStorm Navigator. The chief aim is to enable the individual to deliberate more clearly, more fully and more effectively in the continuous process of life decision making.

A major inspiration in developing CareerStorm Navigator was Vance Peavy's work (1998, 2004, see Chapter 11 of this book). His life work was to develop a constructivist or SocioDynamic approach to counselling, and he carried out pioneering work to devise practical counselling methods and tools that honour the individual as an expert in his/her own life. In this regard, CareerStorm intentionally avoids the use of "client" with its connotations of power imbalance in the counselling relationship. Further, individuals and career professionals are construed as negotiating partners whereby power rests with each.

A parallel can be drawn between Peavy's life-space mapping and the CareerStorm Map and Compass. Following Peavy's ideas, CareerStorm was designed as a process that is much more like a dialogue in and of itself. It is a dialogue that is not only about the self, but encourages individuals to reflect upon other people and contexts in which their life experiences are embedded. Technically, the nature of the web – interactivity, hypertext links and graphic interface – supports the type of process created in CareerStorm. It is easier to simulate a dialogue on the web than it is on pen and paper. There are some elements of surprise hidden in the interactivity. The process is more intelligent, and responds to some extent to what choices the user makes. Web-design is not an art but a craft. When something looks and feels easy, this is evidence of a lot of background work into its design.

In our aim to generate qualitatively sensitive tools, we are concerned with shifts in individual perspective and circumstances across time. CareerStorm Navigator is best used as a life-long career development tool. It is useful to update one's "map and compass" at least once a year, so that new life experiences can be integrated. The aim of the web-based process itself is to empower individuals to systematically reflect upon their work and life experiences as they change. The process supports individuals in giving continuing attention to the unique solutions they can and want to provide at different times in their life.

In practice

CareerStorm Navigator can be integrated into practice in many different ways. Corporations, universities or private practitioners use it with individuals and groups. When career professionals work with individuals, they cannot widen access to career development services, but they still benefit from the unique benefits of integrating a web-based tool into their practice.

Feedback from career professionals indicates that when CareerStorm Navigator is used with individuals, more progress is achieved in less time than in the traditional counselling/coaching process, the interactive nature of the process facilitates effective learning experiences and "eureka" moments, and a counselling/coaching process which may be conducted entirely from a distance via phone and email is greatly enhanced. When CareerStorm Navigator is used with groups, some additional benefits are gained. For example, a larger number of individuals are able to receive guidance, individuals are able to learn with and from one another thereby reducing pressure on the facilitator to "provide" answers and our work is more time and cost effective. Utilising web-based career tools in combination with guided group-based activities is one way for career professionals to widen access to career development services. A sample process will demonstrate what is possible.

Sample group process

CareerStorm offered a three-step process to a professional association who wanted to offer career development support to its members. The three steps were: (1) an initial group meeting, (2) individuals' access to web-based career tools, and (3) a final group meeting.

Before the process could begin, the event was well marketed by the association through their magazine and their web-pages. Participants had to commit to two three-hour sessions and web-based homework. In the initial meeting, the 30 participants engaged in small group activities and listened to the facilitator speak of career/life navigation. Towards the end, participants received instructions on how to sign in to CareerStorm Navigator and had an opportunity to ask questions about their homework task.

During a two-week period, participants completed the required homework (*Skills* and *Interests*), and some took advantage of the option to complete more sections. Only one participant required support to get into the system (she had tried a wrong web-address). An email was sent to the participants five days before the second meeting to remind them of the required homework task and to prepare them for the second meeting.

The final group meeting involved a group-based debriefing activity during which time participants turned their interests and skills into a list of viable career paths. During the final activity, participants engaged in action planning.

Feedback was positive, overall rating of 4.1 on a scale of 1 to 5. In the final dialogue with the group, one participant noted that although the process had been challenging and had required more time than she had expected, it helped her develop a better understanding of how she could direct her career in the future. Another participant told the group that when she completed the homework nothing happened, but the next day, as she was walking on the street, she knew what her next step would be and she immediately wrote her ideas up in a proposal.

The only drawback in a group setting is that participants are always at different stages of readiness. Some have a clearer idea of what their strengths are than others. Some are used to reflecting upon themselves and others are not. However, the very same diversity makes the group process so valuable.

This process of moving 30 participants through a rather in-depth self-assessment and career action planning process required about eight hours of the facilitator's time. One-on-one dialogues would have involved considerably more time. It is useful to consider the contribution of the web-based career tool. Could the group processes have been as effective with pen and paper based homework? Perhaps, yes. But, the total process would have been different. The obvious difference is that the web is interactive. Interacting with a career tool on the web, that uses the input you submit to formulate new questions to you, is more like a dialogue with another person, while writing something down on paper is more like a monologue.

In addition, CareerStorm's experiences indicate that there is something different about sending a group of people to the same web-address. The website becomes an additional space that participants together inhabit during their group process. It is a space where their responses are saved and some may return to re-evaluate their circumstance later on. The web generates a sense of continuity and community unlike pen and paper homework.

Conclusion

Career development specialists have an opportunity to play an increasingly important role in shaping lives of individuals and organisations in the twenty-first century. By utilising web-based career tools in combination with group-based activities, career professionals can offer support to many more individuals than we do today. The internet can host resources that are easily accessible to individuals on an ongoing basis through a life-time of important career and life decisions. Access to internet-based career development services is already possible. It is waiting for us to manage the change process of helping individuals to benefit from the best of the web-based career resources. Some support for effective integration and presentation of internet-based materials can be found from the constructivist theoretical perspective. Using the CareerStorm Navigator provides an example of what future web-based career development work might look like. The challenge is to engage in investigation into the effectiveness of such processes in meeting career guidance outcomes for a wide and diverse array of individuals.

References

Arthur, M. B., Inkson, K. and Pringle, J. K. (1999) *The New Careers: Individual Action and Economic Change*. London: Sage Publications.

Gati, I., Kleiman, T., Saka, N. and Zakai, A. (2003) 'Perceived benefits of using an internet-based interactive career planning system'. *Journal of Vocational Behavior*, 62, 272–86.

Grubb, W. N. (2002) *Who Am I: The Inadequacy of Career Information in the Information Age*. Paper prepared for the OECD Career Guidance Policy Review. Retrieved 23 January 2004, from http://www.oecd.org/dataoecd/32/35/1954678.pdf.

Guridi, J. R., Amodarain, J., Corral, J. A. and Bengoetxea, J. (2003, October) *Demand Led Financing of Lifelong Learning*. Paper presented at the Organisation for Economic Cooperation and Development Conference, Bonn, Germany.

Harris-Bowlsbey, J. (2003) 'A rich past and a future vision'. *The Career Development Quarterly*, 52, 18–25.

Herr, E. L. (1997) 'Career counselling: a process in process'. *British Journal of Guidance and Counselling*, 25, 81–93.

Ibarra, H. (2003) *Working Identity: Unconventional Strategies for Reinventing Your Career*. Boston, MA: Harvard Business School Press.

Jarvis, P. (2002) *Career Management Paradigm Shift: Prosperity for Citizens, Windfall for Governments*. Retrieved 23 January 2004, from http://www.lifework.ca/papers.htm.

Manuele-Adkins, C. (1992) 'Career counseling is personal counseling'. *The Career Development Quarterly*, 40, 313–21.

McMahon, M. and Patton, W. (2002) 'Assessment: a continuum of practice and a new location in career counselling'. *International Careers Journal*, 3(4), (The Global Careers-Work Cafe). Available: http://www.careers-cafe.com.

McMahon, M., Patton, W. and Tatham, P. (2003) *Managing Life, Learning and Work in the Twenty-first Century: Issues Informing the Design of an Australian Blueprint for Career Development*. Subiaco, WA: Miles Morgan.

O'Halloran,T., Fahr, A. and Keller, J. (2002) 'Career counseling and the information highway: heeding the road signs'. *The Career Development Quarterly*, 50, 371–6.

Onnismaa, J. (2003) Epävarmuuden paluu. Ohjauksen ja ohjausasiantuntijuuden muutos. Ph.D. dissertation, University of Joensuu.

Organisation for Economic Cooperation and Development (2004) *Career Guidance and Public Policy: Bridging the Gap*. Paris: OECD.

Patton, W. and McMahon, M. (1999) *Career Development and Systems Theory: A New Relationship*. Pacific Grove, CA: Brooks/Cole.

Peavy, R. V. (1995) *Constructivist Career Counseling*. ERIC Document Reproduction Service No. ED401504.

Peavy, R. V. (1998) *SocioDynamic Counseling: A Constructivist Perspective*. Victoria, Canada: Trafford.

Peavy, R. V. (2004) *SocioDynamic Counselling: A Practical Approach to Meaning Making*. Chagrin Falls, Ohio: Taos Institute.

Poehnell, G. and Amundson, N. (2002) 'CareerCraft: engaging with, energizing, and empowering career creativity', in M. Peiperl, M. Arthur and N. Anand (eds), *Career Creativity: Explorations in the Remaking of Work* (pp. 105–22). New York: Oxford University Press.

Richardson, M. S. (1993) 'Work in people's lives: a location for counseling psychology'. *Journal of Counseling Psychology*, 40, 425–33.

Richardson, M. S. (1996) 'From career counseling to counseling/psychotherapy and work, jobs, and career', in M. L. Savickas and W. B. Walsh (eds), *Handbook of Career Counseling Theory and Practice* (pp. 347–60). Palo Alto, CA: Davies-Black.

Sampson, J. P. (2002) 'Quality and ethics in internet based guidance'. *International Journal for Educational and Vocational Guidance*, 2(3), 157–71.

Savickas, M. L. (1992) 'New directions in career assessment', in D. H. Montross and C. J. Shinkman (eds), *Career Development: Theory and Practice* (pp. 336–55). Springfield, IL: Charles C. Thomas.

Savickas, M. L. (1993) 'Career counseling in the postmodern era'. *Journal of Cognitive Psychotherapy: An International Quarterly*, 7, 205–15.

Subich, L. M. (1993) 'How personal is career counseling?' [Special section]. *The Career Development Quarterly*, 42, 129-131.

Watts, A. G. (2002) 'The role of information and communication technologies in integrated career information and guidance systems: a policy perspective'. *International Journal for Educational and Vocational Guidance*, 2(3), 139–55.

Watts, A. G. and Fretwell, D. H. (2004) *Public Policies for Career Development*. Retrieved 21 July 2004, from http://www.trainingvillage.gr/etu/up/oad/Projects-Networks/Guidance/Policy_review_survey/Synthesis_reports/World_Bank_discussion_paper.pdf.

Index

ability 33, 59, 95
absolute truth, impossibility of 4, 46
academic achievement 78
achievement profiling 91–2
action 32, 33–4; plans 91
active engagement 85–92, 94, 178
Adams, M. 154
Adler, Alfred 71
African community experience 73–6
age 33, 59, 70, 72
agency 8, 52, 103, 164–5, 168, 177; as
    basic assumption of constructivism
    47; social necessity of 179
Akhurst, J. and Mkhize, N.J. 51
Albert, S. W. 16
Alcoholics Anonymous 113
Amundson, N.E. 16, 17, 85, 86–7, 94,
    178; on 'backswing' 88–9; and
    creativity 150, 153; Pattern
    Identification Exercise 89–90; and
    Rogers' conditions for counselling
    22, 98; and sort cards 177
Amundson, N.E. and Poehnell, G. 87,
    92; the wheel 88(fig. 7.1)
Amundson, N.E., Harris-Bowlsbey, J.
    and Niles, S.G. 87
Amundson, N.E., Parker, P. and Arthur,
    M.B. 102
Anderson, H. and Goolishian, H. 127
Antaki, C. 111
apartheid 77
Arbona, C. 165
Arthur, M. B. and Rousseau, D.M. 177
Arthur, M. B., Claman, P. H. and De
    Fillippi, R.J. 179
Arthur, M.B., Inkson, K. and Pringle,
    J.K. 188
Arthur, N. 61, 62
Arthur, N. and Collins, S. 57, 59, 60

Arthur, N. and McMahon, M. 58, 60,
    62, 97, 107
Arthur, N., Brodhead, M., Magnusson,
    K. and Redekopp, D. 61
assessment see career assessment
Athanasou, J.A. 176
autobiographies 9, 31; see also
    narratives/stories
autonomy 50; see also agency
awareness: self-awareness 179, 180;
    tacet levels of 5

Bakhtin, M. 139
Barresi, J. and Juckes, T.J. 70
Baumeister, R.F. and Vohs, K.D. 116
Beck, U. 139
Becvar, D.S. and Becvar, R.J. 70
behaviour change 34
behaviour rehearsal 8
beliefs 33, 70, 77–8
Berg, I.K. 123
Besley, A.C. 37
biographies 31, 117; see also
    narratives/stories
Blumer, H. 124
Blustein, D.L., Schultheiss, D.E. and
    Flum, H. 61
Borgen, F.H. 164
Bourdieu, P. 142
Bradley, R.W. 166
Bronson, P. 117
Brookfield, S. 178
Brott, P.E. 17, 73, 76, 111, 118; and
    assessment 166, 167; and card sorts
    181
Brown, D. 47, 58
Brown, D. and Brooks, L. 124, 163
Brown, S.D. and Ryan Krane, N.E.
    115, 116

Bujold, C. 17, 182, 184
Butler, C. 177

Campbell, C. and Ungar, M. 17, 111, 112, 114, 116, 117; on effects of counselling 118
Campbell, J., Moyers, B. and Flowers, B.S. 110
card sorts 9, 89, 134, 164, 168, 176–9; case study 181–4; identifying themes through 114; Intelligent Career Card Sort (ICCS) 179–84
career assessment 9–10, 47–8, 50–2, 134, 144–6; advantages of qualitative assessment 166–7; creative processes in 154–5; criticisms of qualitative assessment 167; history of 163–5; practical applications of qualitative assessment 170–2; processes of qualitative assessment 167–9; progress-scaling 129–32; psychometric 168; quantitive 163, 164, 165–6; self-assessment 129–32, 164–5; tools 47–8, 134, 176–84, 194–9; worldviews and 163, 164, 167
career choice 32, 188, 190
career counsellors see counsellors
career development 6–7, 47–8, 51, 165, 177, 187; CareerStorm Navigator as tool for 194–9; chance and 97; content and process 95, 96 fig 8.1; contextual influences 61–2, 165, 166, 192–3; helping strategies (Chen) 72–3; holistic nature 101, 139, 165; subjective and objective 179; theories 58–9, 66, 94, 97; worldviews and 59, 94, 165 see also multiculturalism
Career Development Quarterly 165
career management/decision-making 31, 46, 50, 85, 177, 188–9; life navigation and 191; skills 190; see also solution-building counselling
career maturity 47, 50–1
career narratives see narratives/stories
CareerStorm Navigator 194–9
career theory: American dominance in 49–50; constructivist 6–7, 47–52, 94; criticisms 70–1; as guide to counselling 45; learning recognised by 100; and the mix of career and

life 139, 194; worldviews 3–4, 94, 163, 164, 165, 167; see also career development, theories
Carson, D.K. 151, 152, 153, 155
change: and stability 4
Chen, C.P. 6, 9, 71; career development strategies 72–3
Christensen, T.K. and Johnston, J.A. 18, 111, 181
class status 32, 35, 72
Cochran, L. 9, 17, 70, 94, 101, 103; and narrative approach 181; on purpose of career counselling 118
cognitive approaches to counselling 33–4
cognitive science 4
Cohen, L., Duberley, J. and Mallon, M. 46
Coles, R. 112
collaboration 23; see also counselling relationship
collage 79, 151, 154
collectivism 50, 51
Collin, A. 35
Collin, A. and Young, R.A. 3, 6, 30, 31; see also Young, R.A. and Collin, A.
Collins, S. and Arthur, N. 62, 63
Combs, G. and Freedman, J. 88
community 51; African community experience 73–6
connectedness 100–2
Constantine, M.G. and Erickson, C.D. 58, 59
constructivism 4, 164; assessment tools and 176–84, 194–9; career theory and 6–7, 47–52, 94; core assumptions 47, 48, 52–3; culture and 8, 48–52, 58; developmental context 46; developments in approaches to career counselling 6–7, 30–1, 37–8; epistemology 3–4, 6, 178; as influence on active engagement 85–92; and the nature of the counselling process 7–8; philosophical shift towards 45; in psychology 4–6, 47; quality of internet career guidance and 191–9; underpinning worldview 3–4, 10–13, 95, 124, 163, 165, 167
contextual action theory 94
contextualist worldview 3–4
Cook, E.P., O'Brien, K.M. and Heppner, M.J. 58, 62

Cornford, I., Athanasou, J. and Pithers, R. 100
counselling process: action plans 91; assessment *see* career assessment; connectedness 100–2; consolidation 90; constructivism and nature of 7–8, 140; decision making 90–1; defining client's concerns 87–8, 126, 128; emotion's role in 8, 23, 77; exploring the problem 88–90; feedback 132–3, 140, 169; language's role in 8–9, 70, 76; learning 103, 141; meaning-making 102–3, *see also* meaning-making; narrative as backbone to 118–19, *see also* narratives/stories; negotiation 8, 87; outcomes 140; progress-scaling 129–32; questioning 125–32; referrals 88; reflection 102; in SocioDynamic counselling *see* SocioDynamic counselling; in solution-building session, *see* solution-building counselling; STF and 100–3; techniques 86–7, 91–2, 118–19, 127; using CareerStorm Navigator 195–6
counselling relationship: assessment and 9–10; connectedness 101–2; constructivist nature of 7, 23, 66 *see also* meaning-making; and counselling strategies in a diverse setting 76–9, 86; cultural influence on 60–1; empowerment through 61–2, 168, 179, 184; establishment of 86–7; mattering climate of 86, 98, 178; necessary conditions for counselling (Rogers) 98, 152; reality-checking's dependence on 32
counsellor education 10–13, 24, 35, 38–40, 91, 101; assessment guidance 170–2; creativity in 153–5; narrative and 119; in use of SocioDynamic tools 146
counsellors: aims 6–7, 126; as change-agents 178; as co-authors of life stories 8–9, 17–18, 21–4, 102–3, 112, 118; cognitive complexity and 63, 72; creative arts used by 155; cultural infusion 57–61, 72, 77 *see also* cultural auditing; learning and practice 24–5, 38–40, 72; listening skills 31, 126, 141; narrative skills 113–14; as negotiating partners 7–8, 190; as non-judgemental audience 114; personal qualities 152–3; as providers 7–8; questioning skills 126–9; shift from expert to facilitator 7, 190, 193; in social action and advocacy roles 62; social justice and culture awareness 61–2; speaking skills 126; system models used by 132, 133(fig. 10.2); three main tasks (Peavy) 100
creative art therapy 154
creativity 85–6, 150–6, 159, 169, 179; creative arts and 151, 155–6; guided reflection on 157–8; *see also* meaning-making
crime 79
cultural auditing 62–3, 64–5
cultural contexts 33, 46, 48–55; of African communities 73–6, 77–8; career development theories and 58–9, 139; counsellors and cultural infusion 57–61, *see also* cultural auditing; cultural tools 5, 139; diversity in 10, 70–3, 76–9, 115–16, 166; multiculturalism 58, 59–60; social justice and 61–2, 115–16
Curtis, S. 39

Dagley, J.C. and Salter, S.K. 165
Davidson, S.L. 69
decision making 90–1
deconstruction 47, 48, 49, 58–9; of meaning in stories 113; and reconstruction 52–5, 59, 73
de Jong, P. and Berg, I.K. 123, 128
Denzin, N.K. and Lincoln, Y.S. 76
De Shazer, S. 89, 123
developmental psychology 3
Dewey, J. and Bentley, A. 8
dialogical listening 141, 142–4
dialogue 7, 17–18, 23, 168
disability 33
discourse theory 37, 61
discrimination 61; *see also* equal opportunities
divergent thinking 152
diversity, cultural 10, 70–3, 76–9, 115–16, 166
Dolan, Y. 124
drawing 79, 86, 89
Durrant, M. 125
dysfunction 34–5

education 74, 79; counsellor *see*
counsellor education; *see also*
academic achievement
Ellen, R. 177
Emmett, J. 178
emotion: evoked by creative art
therapy 154; role in counselling
process 8, 23, 77
empathy 23, 98, 118, 152
empty chair technique 8, 129
environmental interaction 3, 4, 5, 13,
46, 124; models of occupational
matching and 58–9, 164; systemic
barriers of 61–2, 66, 78–9; *see also*
recursiveness
epistemology 3–4, 6, 178
equal opportunities 59, 115; cultural
constraints of 61; giving voice
through narrative 115–16
Erickson, Milton 123
ethnicity 58, 70, 72
ethnopsychology 71
Evans, K.M. and Larrabee, M.J. 71
expertise 9, 192; shift of counsellor
from expert to facilitator 7, 190, 193

family 51, 73, 75–6, 78–9, 86, 165;
card sorts and 182–3; influence in
adolescence and middle age 96
family therapy 94, 152, 155
feedback 5, 132–3, 140, 169
Fitzgerald, L.F. and Betz, N.E. 59, 61
Flores, L.Y., Wang, Y., Yakushko, O.,
McCloskey, C.M., Spencer, K.G. *et
al.* 165
Ford, M. and Ford, D. 5–6
Fouad, N.A. and Bingham, R.P. 49, 58,
60
Foucault, Michel 37
Frankl, Victor 71
Freedman, J. and Combs, G. 21
Frey, D.H. 151
Fried, J. 178
Friedman, S. and Fanger, M.T. 125

games 75, 77, 79, 89, 168
Gati, I., Kleiman, T., Saka, N. and
Zakai, A. 190
gender 33, 58, 59, 72, 74, 95;
stereotyped sex roles 78
genograms 9, 154, 164, 168
George, E., Iveson, C. and Ratner, H.
128

Gergen, K.J. 32
gestalt therapy 8, 129
Giddens, A. 138
Gladding, S.T. 151, 154, 155
Gladding, S.T. and Henderson, D.A.
150, 151
Gladwell, M. 89
Glavin, K. 51–2
goals, vocational 33, 34, 71, 87, 90;
solution-building counselling and
125–6, 128–32, 134; solution-
focused counselling and 124
Goldman, L. 9, 70, 166, 167, 168,
176
Gottfredson, L. S. 3
Granvold, D.K. 5, 6, 7, 9
Grubb, W.N. 188, 190, 191
guided imagery 8, 119, 154
Guridi, J.R., Amodarain, J., Corral,
J.A. and Bengoetxea, J. 192
Gysbers, N.C., Heppner, M.J. and
Johnston, J.A. 52, 59, 114, 178

Hage, J. and Powers, C.H. 138, 139
Hansen, L.S. 178
Hargrove, B.K., Creagh, M.G. and
Kelly, D.B. 60
Harris-Bowlsbey, J. 190
Hartung, P.J. 58
Hartzell, N.K. 117
health 72, 165
Henderson, D.A. and Gladding, S.T.
155
Heppner, M.J., O'Brien, K.M.,
Hinkelman, J.M. and Humphrey,
C.F. 119, 153, 154
hermeneutics 6
Heron, J. 178
Herr, E.L. 76, 188
Herr, E.L. and Niles, S.G. 62
Hickson, J. and Christie, G. 71, 72
Hickson, J., Christie, G. and Shmukler,
D. 71
Ho, D.Y. F. 59
Holland, J.L. 58, 110, 112, 113
Holmes, A. 103
Hoskins, M. and Leseho, J. 21
Hotchkiss, L. and Borow, H. 58
Hudson, F.M. 59
humanism 37
humour 78
Hurt, F. 150
hypnosis 124

Ibarra, H. 193
ICCS (intelligent Career Card Sort) 179–84
individualism 50, 58
industrial economies 138
Inkson, K. and Amundson, N.E. 21, 88
integrated models 35, 60–1
Intelligent Career Card Sort (ICCS) 179–84
internet 89, 187, 191, 199; CareerStorm Navigator 194–9; and self-service approach to career information 188–90
Ivey, A.E., Ivey, M.B. and Simek-Morgan, L. 52, 54

Jansen, S.E. 69
Jarvis, P. 188, 192
Joffe, S.E. 70
Jones, L.K. 164
Journal of Vocational Behaviour 4, 46

Kelly, G. 129
Kidd, J.M. 77, 178
Kierkegaard, S. 138
kinaesthetic learning style 166, 177
Knowdell, R. and Chapman, E.N. 176
knowledge: constructivist understanding of human knowing 7, 23, 70; economy 179–80, 192; as interactive process 5; life narratives and 8; objective 3–4; systems theory approach to 6; tacet levels of awareness 5; ways of knowing 180, 182–3; *see also* epistemology
Krumboltz, J.D. 7, 9, 69, 94

Langer, E.J. and Moldoveanu, M. 179
language: fundamental to meaning and knowledge 7, 8; role in counselling process 8–9, 76, 125–6; as a social phenomenon 70
Larsen, D.J. 147
Launikari, M. and Puukari, S. 60–1
Law, B. 21, 31
learning processes 5, 100, 103, 141, 184; life-long 192–3; for new counsellors 10–13; tools for 31
learning styles 166, 177
Lee, F.K. and Johnston, J.A. 178
Lengnick-Hall, M.L. and Lengnick-Hall, C.A. 151
Leong, F.T.L. and Hartung, P.J. 59, 60

Leung, S.A. 59, 60
Lewin, K. 141
Lewis, T.F. and Osborn, C.J. 124
lifelines 9
life-maps 9, 134, 139, 142, 154, 197; life-space mapping in SocioDynamic counselling 144–6
life narratives *see* narratives/stories
life roles 51
life-space 101, 141–2, 144–6, 168, 197; maps *see* life-maps
listening skills 31, 126, 141
Living Systems Framework (LSF) 5–6
logical-positivist worldview 10–13, 45, 71, 94, 95, 153; assessment and 163, 164, 165, 167; 'test and tell' counselling and 21; *see also* positivism
Longworth, N. and Davies, W.K. 103
Luniewski, M., Reigle, J. and White, B. 177
Luzzo, D.A. and MacGregor, M.W. 165
Lyddon, W.J. 3
Lyddon, W.J., and Alford, D.J. 167
Lyddon, W.J., Clay, A.L. and Sparks, C.L. 21
Lynch, G. 8

McDaniels, C. 164, 165
McLeod, J. 111–12, 113, 115, 118
McMahon, M. 25, 97, 98, 100, 107; practical session on working with storytellers 24–6
McMahon, M., Adams, A. and Lim, R. 10, 11, 94
McMahon, M. and Patton, W. 9, 10, 16, 22, 70, 124; and creativity 150, 154, 155; criticisms of positivist assessment 192; and group situations 181; and qualitative assessment 166, 167, 168–72; STF 95, 97, 168 *see also* Systems Theory Framework; *see also* Patton, W. and McMahon, M.
McMahon, M., Patton, W. and Tatham, P. 100, 188
McMahon, M., Patton, W. and Watson, M. 97, 104, 107, 167, 183; My System of Career Influences (MSCI) 168
McMahon, M., Watson, M. and Patton, W. 97, 107, 167
Mahoney, M.J. 47

Mahoney, M.J. and Lyddon, W.J. 4
Mahoney, M.J. and Patterson, K.M. 4
Mair, M. 115, 119
Mandela, Nelson 51
Manuele-Adkins, C. 94, 194
Maree, J.G. and Beck, G. 79
marital status 70, 72
meaning-making 4, 7–9, 17, 30–1;
    assessment and 167, 168;
    consciousness-raising and 62; of
    counsellors 60–1; holistic approach
    to 178; negotiated 17–18, 66,
    102–3, 168; and postmodern
    identity 30–1, 69–70; social
    interaction and 124; SocioDynamic
    counselling and 138; solution-
    focused counselling and 124; see
    also constructivism; creativity
mechanistic worldview 3
Merttens, R. 38
metanarratives 113
metaphors: for career counselling
    21–4, 25, 27; in counselling process
    88, 89, 118; in counsellor education
    24, 154
Mignot, P. 23
Miller, Gale 124, 125
Miller, J.H. 94, 124, 132, 133
Millington, M.J. and Reed, C.A. 177
Milwaukee Brief Family Therapy
    Centre 123
mindfulness 179
mind-mapping 89
Mirvis, P. and Hall, D. 178
Missouri, University of 119; career
    development course for 121–2
Mohlala, S.C. 77, 78, 79
Monk, G. 21–2
Monk, G., Winslade, J., Crocket, K.
    and Epston, D. 103
Morgan, A. 20–1, 102–3
motivation 34
motivational interviewing 124
motor theory 5
multiculturalism 58, 59–60; see also
    diversity, cultural; ethnopsychology
Murray, P.E. and Rotter, J.C. 151–2,
    155

narratives/stories: behaviour change
    and 34, 114; card sorts and 180–4;
    context of approach through 36–7;
    counselling use in African context
73–6; in counsellor training 38–40;
deconstruction 113; definitions
111; holistic context 17; human
lives as multi-storied 17, 18–21, 98,
192; identifying themes across 9,
113–14, 117; key ideas 111–12;
life-long importance of 110;
meaning-making and 8–9, 17–18,
30–1, 61–2, 168; media of storytelling 36, 79, 114–15; and
metanarratives 113; mindfulness
and 179; postmodern perspective
on 69–70, 79; practical session on
working with storytellers
(McMahon) 24–6; 'problem' and
'solution' stories 113; rationales for
use in cross-cultural counselling
70–2; reading 117–18; and reality-
checking 32–3; re-authoring 9, 16,
20–1, 112; self-esteem and 36; in
Systems Theory Framework 97–8,
101–3; truth and 112–13; universal
quality of 115–16; University of
Missouri's use of 121–2; writing
116–18, 121–2
narrative therapy 37, 116, 124; role
and qualities of therapist 21–2
neuro-linguistic programming 124
Niemeyer, G.J. and Niemeyer, R.A.
    167

objectivism see positivism
O'Brien, K.M. 165
observation records 10, 12 fig 1.1
O'Connell, B. 33, 124, 125
OECD (Organisation for Economic
    Co-operation and Development)
    188, 189, 192
O'Halloran, T., Fahr, A. and Keller, J.
    189
O'Hanlon, W.H. and Beadle, S. 124
O'Hanlon, W.H. and Weiner-Davis, M.
    89
Okocha, A.A.G. 166, 167
Onnismaa, J. 190
organismic worldview 3
Osipow, S.H. 94
Oxenford, C. 176, 178, 179

Parker, H.L. . 177
Parker, P. 169, 180
Parker, P., Arthur, M.B. and Inkson, K.
    180

Parsons, Frank 147, 163–5
passions 77; *see also* emotion
Patsula, P. 87
Pattern Identification Exercise
(Amundson) 89–90
Patton, W. 61
Patton, W. and McMahon, M. 16, 17,
45, 48, 50, 58; and the changing
world 188; and individual response
to information 191; shift of
counsellor from expert to facilitator
193; STF 60, 94, 95, 97, 132 *see
also* Systems Theory Framework;
and systemic influence on
experience 70; the therapeutic
system 99(fig. 8.2); *see also*
McMahon, M. and Patton, W.
Patton, W., McMahon, M. and Watson,
M. 97, 107; *see also* McMahon, M.,
Patton, W. and Watson, M.
Peavy, R.V. 6, 17, 167, 176, 177;
CareerStorm Navigator and 197; on
creativity 150, 153–4; and cultural
tools 5; and dimensions of
constructivist counselling 7–8, 100,
178; and life-space 101, 141–2,
144–6; and mindfulness 179;
SocioDynamic model 21, 33, 94,
137–42, 144–7, 176; three main
tasks of a counsellor 100; and views
of self 192; working with
storytellers 9, 16, 20, 102, 103
Pedersen, P. 59
Pedersen, P. and Ivey, A. 63
Peiperl, M., Arthur, M. and Anand, N.
150
Pelsma, D. and Arnett, R. 178
personality 95; *see also* self-identity
person-centred therapy 124
Plant, Peter 189
Poehnell, G. and Amundson, N. 85,
188
Pope, M. and Minor, C.W. 79, 154
Pope, M. and Sveinsdottir, M. 163
positivism 3–4; and approaches to
counselling 7; *see also* logical-
positivist world view
poststructuralism 37
poverty 79
proactive cognition 5, 6
psychodrama 8
psychology: career (vocational) 3, 6,
49, 164; constructivism in 4–6, 47;

cultural-historical school 139;
developmental 3; indigenous 71; as
part of personal life 178;
worldviews and 71–2

qualitative assessment *see* career
assessment
Quinn, J.B. 179

race 72; *see also* ethnicity
reality: constructivist view of 4;
language and 7, 8; realist view of 4;
stories and 32–3; *see also* truth
recursiveness 95–6, 98, 99(fig. 8.2),
100, 101
reflection 100, 102
Reid, H.L. 37, 38
religious beliefs 33, 70
resources 36, 114, 129, 165; expertise
and 192, 193; inner 124, 127;
internet 189–91, 194–9; joint
(counsellor/client) 140
respect 23, 126
résumés 116–17, 118–19
Richardson, J.T.E. 167
Richardson, M. S. 6, 8, 9, 147, 194
Rifkin, J. 138
Roberts, K. 32
Rogers, C.R. 37, 71; necessary
conditions for counselling 22, 98,
152
role play 8

Sampson, J.P. 189
Savickas, M.L. 6, 8, 9, 17, 30; on
career behaviour 51; and career
theories 46, 50, 59, 111; on
exploration of the past 32; on
immediate action 34; and narrative
approach 35, 36, 52, 100, 102, 117;
and personal nature of career
193–4; and reflection on childhood
heros 117; and reform of
counselling discipline 166; shift of
counsellor from actuary to
biographer 21, 193; and supportive
relationships 101
Schlossberg, N.K., Lynch, A.Q. and
Chickering, A.W. 86, 98, 178
Schwartz, C.E., Chung-Kang, P., Lester,
N., Daltroy, L.H. and Goldberger,
A.L. 177
self-awareness 179, 180

self-development 47, 139
self-esteem 36
self-identity 17, 20, 51, 178, 192;
    constructivist view of the person 4,
    47; counsellors and 53; culturally
    appropriate 36, 50; in
    SocioDynamic counselling 139;
    systems theory and 6, 47
sex roles 74, 78
Sexton, T.L., Whiston, S.C., Bleuer,
    J.C. and Walz, G.R. 134
sexual orientation 33, 59, 70, 72, 95
Sharf, R.S. 46
Sherwood, N.E., Story, M. and
    Neumark-Sztainer, D. 177
singing 75
Skovholt, T.M., Morgan, J.I., and
    Negron-Cunningham, H. 119
Slaney, R.B. and MacKinnon-Slaney, F.
    176
Smith, D. 119
social constructionism 4–5, 61, 70; see
    also constructivism
social justice 61–2, 115–16
social systems 47, 51, 53, 61–2
social theories 138, 139
SocioDynamic counselling 6, 21, 33,
    94; concept of the self in 139;
    contribution to 'third birth' of
    career counselling 147; creativity
    and 153–4; dialogical listening 141,
    142–4; life-space mapping 141–2,
    144–6; origin 137–8; strategies
    140–2; tools 139, 146; underlying
    philosophical ideas 138–40; see also
    Peavy, R.V., SocioDynamic
    model
socioeconomic status 33, 58
solution-building counselling:
    characteristics of 133–4; envisioning
    preferred future 128–9; feedback
    132–3; goal clarification 134;
    progress-scaling 129–32; prompts
    127; questioning techniques
    126–32; solution-focused
    counselling principles of 125–6; use
    of systems theory framework 132,
    133(fig. 10.2)
solution-focused counselling: applied
    to solution-building career
    counselling 125–6; constructivist
    nature of 124
solution-focused therapy 123–4

Spangar, T. 147; see also previous name
    Vähämöttönen, T.T.E.
Spangar, T. and Arnkil, R. 147
Spokane, A.R. and Glickman, I.T. 165
Stead, G.B. 46, 48, 49, 50, 57, 61; on
    cultural nature of counselling 63,
    70; and multiple realities 58, 60
Stebbins, R.A. 179
Steenbarger, B. 3, 4
Sternberg, R.J. and Lubart, T.I. 151
STF see Systems Theory Framework
    (STF)
stories see narratives/stories
Subich, L.M. 94, 166, 168, 178, 194
Subich, L.M. and Simonson, K. 163
Sue, D.W., Allen, E.I. and Pederson,
    P.B. 33
Super, D.E. 3, 100, 101, 110
Swanson, J.L. 58
systems theory 5–6, 9, 124
Systems Theory Framework (STF) 60,
    94–5, 168; and the counselling
    process 100–3; as a map for career
    counsellors 97–9; template for
    practical applications 104–6;
    theoretical overview 95–7

Takai, R. and Holland, J.L. 176
Te Ruru 124
therapeutic counselling 34–5
therapeutic system (Patton and
    McMahon) 99(fig. 8.2), 100
Thornhill, A. and Saunders, M.N.K.
    177
timelines 134, 154
Tlali, M.T. 70
Townsend, K.C. and McWhirter, B.T.
    100
truth: constructivist view of 4, 31, 46,
    58; narrative versus historical
    112–13; objective 4; see also
    reality

unemployment 69, 79
UNESCO (United Nations Educational,
    Scientific and Cultural
    Organisation) 97
Usher, R. and Edwards, R. 37

Vähämöttönen, T.T.E. (later Timo
    Spangar) 138, 140, 146
Vähämöttönen, T.T.E., Keskinen, P.A.
    and Parrila, R.K. 137

Valach, L. and Young, R.A. 31, 34; *see also* Young, R.A. and Valach, L.
vocational psychology 3, 6, 49, 164
Vocations Bureau, Boston 163, 164
Vondracek, F.W., Lerner, R.M. and Schulenberg, J.E. 3
Vygotsky, L. 139

walking the problem 86, 89
Watson, M.B. 49, 52
Watson, M.B. and Stead, G.B. 49
Watson, M.B., Duarte, M.E. and Glavin, K. 50
Watts, A.G. 189
Watts, A.G. and Fretwell, D.H. 193
Weick, K.E. 179
West, L. 31, 36
Whiston, S.C. 70
Whiston, S.C. and Brecheisen, B.K. 165
White, M. and Epston, D. 9, 35, 37
Williams, B. 59
Willis, C.J. 154
work: African ethos 75; centrality of 51, 58; life roles and 51

worldviews 3–4, 10–13, 59; career assessment and 163, 164, 167; career development and 59, 94, 165 *see also* multiculturalism; of clients 33; counselling and 16–17, 21, 71, 94, 97–8; effects on psychology 71–2
writing: journal 115, 179, 182; résumés of career narratives 116–17, 118–19; as therapeutic act 114–15

Yaxk'in, A.J. 22–3
Young, R.A. and Borgen, W.A. 6
Young, R.A. and Chen, C.P. 165
Young, R.A. and Collin, A. 4–5, 6, 57; *see also* Collin, A. and Young, R.A.
Young, R.A. and Valach, L. 8, 32, 94; *see also* Valach, L. and Young, R.A.

Zinker, J. 129
Zunker, V.G. and Norris, D.S. 168
Zytowski, D.G. and Swanson, J.L. 164, 165